JEWISH ENCOUNTERS

Jonathan Rosen, General Editor

Jewish Encounters is a collaboration between Schocken and
Nextbook, a project devoted to the promotion of Jewish literature, culture, and ideas.

>nextbook

PUBLISHED

FORTHCOMING

THE WORLDS OF SHOLOM ALEICHEM · Jeremy Dauber

ABRAHAM · Alan M. Dershowitz

MOSES · Stephen J. Dubner

BIROBIJAN · Masha Gessen

JUDAH MACCABEE · Jeffrey Goldberg

SACRED TRASH · Adina Hoffman and Peter Cole

THE DAIRY RESTAURANT · Ben Katchor

JOB · Rabbi Harold S. Kushner

ABRAHAM CAHAN · Seth Lipsky

THE EICHMANN TRIAL · Deborah E. Lipstadt

SHOW OF SHOWS · David Margolick

JEWS AND MONEY · Daphne Merkin

DAVID BEN-GURION · Shimon Peres and David Landau

WHEN GRANT EXPELLED THE JEWS · Jonathan Sarna

MESSIANISM · Leon Wieseltier

Burnt Books

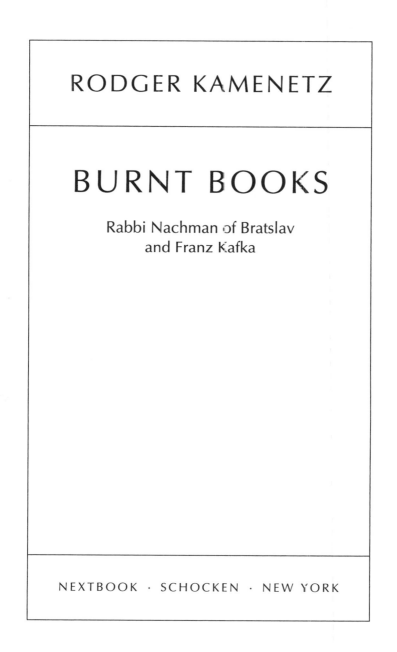

RODGER KAMENETZ

BURNT BOOKS

Rabbi Nachman of Bratslav
and Franz Kafka

NEXTBOOK · SCHOCKEN · NEW YORK

Copyright © 2010 by Metaphor, Inc.

All rights reserved. Published in the United States by
Schocken Books, a division of Random House, Inc., New York,
and in Canada by Random House of Canada Limited, Toronto.

Schocken Books and colophon are registered trademarks of
Random House, Inc.

Library of Congress Cataloging-in-Publication Data
Kamenetz, Rodger, [date]
   Burnt books : Rabbi Nachman of Bratslav and Franz
Kafka / Rodger Kamenetz.
       p. cm.
   Includes bibliographical references.
   ISBN 978-0-8052-4257-7
   1. Nahman, of Bratslav, 1772–1811. 2. Kafka, Franz,
1883–1924. 3. Kamenetz, Rodger, [date]—Travel.
4. Cabala—History. 5. Hasidism. 6. Hasidim—Legends.
I. Title.
   BM755.N25K35 2010
   296.8'332092—dc22
   [B]   2010010120

www.schocken.com
Printed in the United States of America
First Edition
2 4 6 8 9 7 5 3 1

For Anna Lisa Crone, my sister-in-law

MAY HER MEMORY BE A BLESSING

CONTENTS

Contents

Part III
Journeys

Burnt Books

INTRODUCTION

Parallel Lives

Rabbi Nachman of Bratslav and Franz Kafka. A nineteenth-century rebbe. A twentieth-century literary master. Two Jewish souls. When I hear the voice of one, I can't help but hear the other. Kafka is thoroughly secular and Rabbi Nachman is deeply religious. Kafka is a master of irony and Rabbi Nachman is a master of faith. Yet I feel a secret conversation between them and want to know how this can be.

I find a clue in something the scholar Gershom Scholem once said. To understand kabbalah in our time, first we would have to read Franz Kafka.

Now this is puzzling, considering what we know of Kafka's life. If Kafka is a kabbalist, he's the first with no deep working knowledge of Hebrew and no actual Jewish religious practice. But Gershom Scholem's words carry weight. He was the foremost academic authority on Jewish mysticism in modern times.

Perhaps in a certain sly way, Scholem meant to change not our evaluation of Kafka, but what we mean by kabbalah in our time. The puzzle of Kafka the kabbalist makes more sense when you read him alongside Rabbi Nachman. A descendant of the Baal Shem Tov, Rabbi Nachman is the one great rebbe of the past who speaks most powerfully to our own skepticism and doubt. He is an acknowledged master of kabbalah.

The comparison grows more intriguing because in the last four years of his life Rabbi Nachman also became a master of fiction. He told a series of fantastic tales that brought something very new into Jewish literature. So here we have Kafka the teller of original tales and Rabbi Nachman the original teller of tales, Kafka the kabbalist and Rabbi Nachman the kabbalist.

As I engaged with the lives and writings of these two masters, the journey asked more of me than an intellectual puzzle. Kabbalah challenges us to read with more depth. It asks: What if all of our reading is secretly a sacred journey in which learning to read deeper deepens the reader?

The Zohar, the great medieval masterwork of kabbalah, proposes this mystical theory of reading. To the kabbalist, reading takes us through four levels of depth. At the deepest level, one arrives at a contemplation of an otherwise entirely hidden God.

Rabbi Nachman's tales take us on this journey in reading. If Professor Scholem was correct, so do Kafka's fictions. Below the plain meaning, one finds allusion to Jewish texts, original interpretations or midrash, and new portraits of God.

There's another way to read their fictions—as autobiography of the soul.

Too often, Franz Kafka's work is read as simple autobiography, but I read in his fiction the struggle of a Jewish soul with modernity. Rabbi Nachman is always the secret hero of his tales, though in no simple sense. The soul he believes himself to be has had many lives and is so unaccountable, so distant from our ordinary conceptions, that it is exceedingly difficult to portray him. No one ever did, in the sense that we have no drawing, no portrait, no likeness. Usually he's represented by an empty chair. So trying to see him in any sense is difficult.

That's true for Kafka as well, though for a very different reason. Rabbi Nachman left us no face, and Franz Kafka left us too many. Sometimes it seems there are as many Franz Kafkas as there are readers. Finding real portraits of these men—their soul portraits—requires a journey deep into their writing.

Their stories reveal the struggles of an intensely lived life, in which every moment and every gesture aches with meaning. This is how they lived and how they wrote, as if living out an intense story, or a deep dream.

As for outward circumstances, Rabbi Nachman lived a hundred years before Franz Kafka, and a thousand kilometers to the east. I see two men reaching for each other across space and time. But they don't quite touch. That near miss intrigues me.

Rabbi Nachman was a Hasidic rebbe concerned for the spiritual fate of the secular Jew, and Kafka a secular Jew who nourished himself with the tales of Hasidic rebbes. They lived on either end of the *haskalah*,* the historic shift in Jewish life from religion to secularism, the Jewish Enlightenment. Rabbi Nachman feared the *haskalah* would bury the Jewish soul alive; Kafka lived the last third of his life seeking to uncover his.

Haskalah means "enlightenment," from *sekhel* (intelligence). The enlightened are known as the *maskilim*.

One goal of the *haskalah* was full political emancipation for Jews. Rabbi Nachman witnessed the incipient Jewish secularism that came in the wake of Napoleon's conquest of Europe. Kafka lived at the bleak end of the process when the high hopes of Jewish assimilation collapsed in the face of persistent hatred. Each man explored, in his own way, three elemental configurations of modern Jewish identity: religion, secularism, and Zionism.

Rabbi Nachman was a religious Jew responsive to the challenge of Jewish secularism; Kafka, a thoroughly secular Jew who loved the paradoxical parables of Hasidism. Rabbi Nachman journeyed to the land of Israel, and Kafka dreamed of journeying there to the end of his days. Their stories and their lives reflect deeply on one another.

Each was physically thin and each cycled psychologically from low to high, from extreme self-doubt to outrageous ecstasy. Each had a quarrel with fathers. Both starved themselves of food and distanced themselves from the pleasures of sex. Both died of tuberculosis, tragically young.

And each, at the very end, asked a close friend to burn his books.

This book will follow the journeys of Rabbi Nachman and Kafka. It is also a journey of my own.

In the Prague Summer Program over the past ten years, I created a course on Kafka and the kabbalah. My classroom at Charles University overlooked the crowded Prague Jewish cemetery, and I lived in the Jewish quarter two blocks from where Kafka was born. Like many tourists, I spent hours on the cobblestone streets of Prague following Kafka's peregrinations, for he lived all over the popular Old Town Square and beyond. In today's Prague his face is ubiquitous, on posters, on T-shirts, on sugar packets, and in tourist shops. I bought many odd Kafka souvenirs, including a certain coffee mug that will play a part in what follows.

Rabbi Nachman's face is much harder to see. To come closer to this fiery soul, I made a pilgrimage in 2008 to Ukraine with the tens of thousands of Jews who visit his grave in Uman each Rosh Hashanah. On the way I also visited Kamenetz, my eponymous hometown, which was the destination of a signally important journey for Rabbi Nachman. So my journeys became part of the story as well.

When I saw the narrow bridge leading to the fortress of Kamenetz, I remembered the setting for my favorite tale of Rabbi Nachman's, "The Humble King."* The plot closely tracks Kafka's great unfinished novel, *The Trial*. In both stories, the hero confronts a legal system that seems entirely corrupt. Both stories make a midrash on the book of Job; both stories ask the deepest religious questions—about the seeming absence of divine justice.

Other tales ask to be read together. Kafka's breakthrough story "The Judgment" and Rabbi Nachman's "The Rabbi's Son" both explore the anguished rupture between a father and a son. In other works, both men remake the same Jewish parable of the king's messenger to explore the problem of the sophisticate who yearns for simple faith. Kafka's "The Metamorphosis" and Nachman's "The Turkey Prince" both speak to the modern meaning of the old doctrine of transmigration of souls.

Is it possible that Rabbi Nachman somehow influenced

---

*This tale is sometimes called "The Wise Man and the King," but "The Humble King" is the title in the first edition of Rabbi Nachman's tales.

Franz Kafka? We know Kafka read Martin Buber's German rendition of the tales. Perhaps some literary detective could follow this trail. But my experience in reading felt more uncanny. Often I found that a Franz Kafka story asked a question that a Rabbi Nachman tale answered.

Since kabbalah presents an expansive theory of the universe far beyond time and space, mere literary influence feels too pedestrian. A more intriguing proposition is that Franz Kafka actually influenced Rabbi Nachman. This is, in a very exact sense, preposterous.[1] But as there are many journeys in this book, one might think of it as another tale told along the way.

PART I

Burnt Books

1

The Joke

Once a tale was told by Rabbi Nachman about a wise man who journeyed to find a portrait of a humble king. This king was said as well to be mighty and good. Yet the land he ruled was full of deceit. In the end, the wise man overcomes all the obstacles to make a portrait of this very paradoxical king.

The people who first heard this tale might have been ancestors of mine. They lived in Podolia in the western Ukraine; the traditional capital of Podolia is called Kamenetz-Podolsk.* Not knowing for certain, I consider that town the homeland of my name.

Kamenetz was never welcoming to Jews. In 1757, the Bishop of Kamenetz forced traditional rabbis to debate Jewish followers of the false Messiah, Jacob Frank. The rabbis lost and the bishop ordered the Talmud burned in the public square. And that is not the most sorrowful event that ever took place there.

On my way to Uman I visited this beautiful town, look

---

*The Ukrainians transliterate the town today as Kamianets-Podilskyi. But I like the old name, which it bore under Russian rule in the time of Rabbi Nachman.

ing for some connection to my family history, but few traces of Jewish life remain there today. Once upon a time, Rabbi Nachman of Bratslav also journeyed to Kamenetz. But exactly "what he did there," all his biographer and amanuensis Rabbi Nathan could say, "is a complete mystery which no one on earth will understand until the coming of the *Mashiach*, speedily in our days, Amen."[1]

It was easy for me to enter the town. Although the wise man is warned that the land of the humble king could be entered only on a narrow bridge defended by cannon, he also enters with ease. But I found no visible traces of my past. The wise man faced a nearly impossible task fetching a portrait of the humble king.

For one thing, no one in the land had ever seen his face. He kept himself hidden behind a curtain, removed from his subjects. So once the wise man entered the land he went on an intelligence mission.

"The wise man made up his mind that he had to know the essence of the country. And how could he know the essence of the country? By the country's jokes."

The essence of a country is its jokes. That's an unexpected note in a folktale. But Rabbi Nachman was no simple folk artist. He told tales as he made up tunes and as he danced—because he was a personal spiritual leader and a holy man, a rebbe and a tzaddik. He might seem to us a nearly mythical creature, because two hundred years after his death, especially after the Holocaust, rebbes are an endangered species.

His full name is Nachman ben Simcha, Nachman the son of Rabbi Simcha. His father is a bit of a mystery. But his father's father was Rabbi Nachman of Horodenka, a well-known follower of the Baal Shem Tov who resettled in the land of Israel; his paternal uncles were also important rebbes. His mother's Jewish lineage (*yichus*) was even more prestigious. She was the granddaughter of the Baal Shem Tov, the founder of Hasidism, who lived and was buried in the small Ukrainian town of Medzhibozh. Rabbi Nachman grew up in his great-grandfather's house. As a child he fed on the stories told by visitors to the Baal Shem Tov's grave, where he also spent long hours communing with his great-grandfather's soul.

He was born to be a rebbe, that was clear from childhood on. But as he matured, he came to understand a greater destiny. The Hasidim believed that in each generation one tzaddik could be—might be—the Messiah himself, if only people received him in repentance.

Rabbi Nachman hinted broadly that he was *the* tzaddik of his generation, the *tzaddik ha-dor*. In particular, he grouped himself as the fifth and last of a series of tzaddikim: Moses, Rabbi Simeon Bar Yohai, Rabbi Isaac Luria, and his great-grandfather, the Baal Shem Tov, all charismatic leaders who served the great task of redemption. And all men who either wrote books or whose words were recorded by their disciples.[2]

In his time, many Hasidim might have been puzzled by Rabbi Nachman's claims. He always had a very small following. He fought with other rebbes, and they drove him from town to town. How could such a man claim to be *tzaddik ha-dor*?

The question of who Rabbi Nachman is, and who he

claimed to be, challenges any would-be biographer. Few today have ever met anyone like him. He was a Jewish shaman who could bind his soul to the living and the dead, who knew the lower and higher wisdom of kabbalah; he was a healer, a wonder-worker, whose every gesture and word teemed with significance. Is he best understood as a man or as a soul?

Some have tried to make a clinical case of him. One prominent scholar concluded from his tales that he was insane. More recent readings have strongly implied he was a manic-depressive. When you read about some of the stranger episodes in his life, this is plausible, but I believe Rabbi Nachman is best understood by disregarding clinical categories, for his own vocabulary of the soul is more profound and nuanced than that of modern psychology or contemporary cognitive science. The terms he lived on deserve respect.

A soul is hard to portray, and, though Rabbi Nachman lived at the edge of modernity, his situation is remote to our sensibility. In small Jewish villages, shtetls, in Ukraine, lands and commerce were often managed by Jewish middlemen under the protection of Polish landlords. Woods and farmlands were within a short walk, and as a child he frequently prayed in fields, in meadows, and in forests. Sometimes he prayed while riding on horseback. Mud, snow, and ice made travel in Ukraine difficult in winter, and at all times horse and carriage was slow. It took a whole day's journey to traverse fifty miles.

His personal life could baffle us. Married soon after his bar mitzvah, he frequently abandoned his wife and daughters and took mysterious journeys with one of his close male followers at a moment's notice. He was in his own way a hunger artist, for he fasted for days at a time, and sometimes from Sabbath to Sabbath. He tried to kill all desire for sex and food. After his first wife, Sashia, died, he married his second wife on condition that they have no sexual relations. There's no record of her name, but she once said plaintively, "I imagine you. I call you, but I never knew you."

His presence was everything to his followers, men who would leave their own families behind and travel difficult distances just to see his face. But they left no portrait or description. We can see the intricately carved wooden chair he sat in and the tuft of the white woven yarmulke he wore, the beaten silver kiddush cup that he used. We know that a window of his house faced the Breslov marketplace. I glimpse him in the details scattered in the voluminous works of his first and most important biographer, Rabbi Nathan, who is the main source for any biographer.[3] The fateful morning he abandoned Breslov for Uman, he prayed, drank a cup of coffee, and climbed into a wagon. I almost see him for a moment there, but he slips away. Rabbi Nathan's main concern is to portray his master's soul.

So while Kafka's face is a familiar icon, we have no drawing or portrait of Rabbi Nachman. His Hasidim today say he was thin, with red hair, a deep voice, and beautiful eyes.[4] But could any depiction really explain his inner spirit?

The wise man has a challenge in fetching a portrait of the humble king; my humbler task as I journeyed to Kamenetz and then Uman was to fetch a portrait of a rebbe.

I was not alone in my desire to see him. Two hundred years after his death, tens of thousands still answer his call. On his own last journey from Bratslav to Uman, he said,

"My fire will burn until the coming of the Messiah." What is that fire, and where in a human being does it burn?

I feel that fire in his tales. To his Hasidim, they are holy scripture. They still attract the serious attention of scholars and offer spiritual guidance to those on the path. Judged strictly as literature, they can seem rough. They aren't highly polished like Kafka's fictions. But they begin something new in Jewish literature. Rabbi Nachman is the father of the modern Yiddish tale.

For all their modernity, they also touch an ancient depth, for they stand in a unique place—at the border between kabbalah and literature.

In Rabbi Nachman's tales we can read all four levels of depth that the Zohar alludes to. First, they can be read in the plain sense as simple stories. And as in biblical stories, simplicity hides depth. (This plain level is called *peshat.*) Next, they are studded with hints and allusions to biblical and Talmudic texts. (This is *remez,* or hint.) At a third level, they make midrash, original interpretations of Scripture. (This is known as *derash.*) Indeed, these stories carry so many biblical allusions and kabbalistic references that fully interpreting them would be—and is for some—a life project. Since the composition of the Zohar, at the end of the thirteenth century, no work of mystical Jewish storytelling has been as complex and imaginative and intricate.

At level four, the deepest secret level (*sod*), the tales recast the cosmic myth of the Lurianic kabbalah into a very urgent story. They allude, sometimes quite subtly, to an overall myth first taught by the greatest master of the kabbalah, Rabbi Isaac Luria, who is also known as the Ari, which means "the lion."

This lion lived in sixteenth-century Tsfat, where he reworked the kabbalah of the Zohar. He uncovered hidden references in the Torah to events before the beginning in Genesis, to all human history, and to the final end of time, which would come with the Messiah who would redeem all.

The very first tale, "The Loss of the Princess," illustrates how Rabbi Nachman embedded the Lurianic myth into his seemingly simple fairy tales. The plot is relatively simple. A king has six sons and a daughter. One day, in a fit of anger, he lets slip a curse: "May the Evil One take you away."* The daughter leaves, descending to the world as we know it. Then the king regrets his anger and sends his viceroy to retrieve her. But retrieving her is not easy. Every time the viceroy is about to save her, he makes an error that prolongs his mission. He falls asleep.

The viceroy pursues the princess through various landscapes and encounters strange figures, including talking birds and giants. At the very end of the tale, when he is about to enter the city where she lives, the story is suspended. But we are told that in the end he does save her. Even in outline, "The Loss of the Princess" resonates with the longing for redemption, a vital longing that punctuates the rhythm of Jewish history.

How does the kabbalah of Isaac Luria appear in this tale?

---

*Literally he says, "The no-good should take you." At the midrashic level—and every tale is a brilliant midrash—this refers to the ten sayings of Creation in the beginning of Genesis, which is followed by an eleventh saying, in the negative: "It is no good for man to be alone" (Genesis 2:18), a statement that begins the story of male and female. At a kabbalistic level, it refers to the shattering of the vessels where the *sefirah* of *Malkhut* falls to a lower level.

Luria described three phases of reality: the withdrawal (*tzimtzum*), the shattering of the vessels (*shevirat ha-kelim*), and the repair of the world (*tikkun olam*). In simplified form: originally there was nothing but God. The Creation process begins with the contraction of God (or concentration) to make an empty space. Into that created void are emanated light and also vessels to hold this light. But some of the vessels are too weak, and they shatter. Fragments of the shattered vessels and some of the light fall out of their proper place into lower worlds. This initial catastrophe is called "the shattering of the vessels"—it is the source for all the evils of the world. But there is a third phase, the repair of the world, or *tikkun olam*. In this phase human beings have a part to play: by doing *mitzvot*, we have the opportunity to lift the fallen sparks to higher places. The ultimate redemption comes when the Messiah appears to lift the final sparks and complete the repair. In simplified form, Luria's myth of time and history encompasses the vast scope of human experience; within its framework, human events partake in a universal cosmic drama.

Luria describes these three phases in terms of the primordial events of Creation, but insofar as they "occur" before the creation of time and space, they are actually perpetual and archetypal. They put their stamp on all events in time.*

Tzimtzum explains the seeming absence of God, and the shattering explains the evils of the world, including the exile of the Jewish people and their expulsion from Spain. The

---

*A modern-day analogy is the Nobel Prize–winning discovery by Arno Penzias and Robert Wilson of the cosmic microwave background radiation evidence of the big bang, which we are still able to "hear." In that sense, the big bang is still ongoing and reverberating.

repair of the world encompasses all the efforts to make the world better, from individual acts of kindness to the final redemption, in which exiles will return to the land of Israel and the shatterings of history will be healed.

The Ari saw these three phases of reality hidden in the deepest readings of the Torah, and he encoded them in abstruse kabbalistic language. But Rabbi Nachman recast them as story, enabling those not well versed in kabbalah to experience the power of Luria's thinking with direct emotion.

"The Loss of the Princess" begins with an allusion to *tzimtzum*, for after banishing his daughter and sending the viceroy on his mission, the king withdraws completely from the story. Several tales follow this same pattern. A king sets the plot in motion and then drops out of the story. The king's withdrawal allows the story space to exist and narrative time to unfold.

The second phase, the shattering of the vessels, is far more prominent in the tales. This is, after all, the mess we live in. One tale speaks of a great storm, another of separation between bride and groom. In "The Loss of the Princess" it is the rupture between father and daughter. All of these disruptions represent the primordial shattering of the vessels (*shevirat ha-kelim*) which occurs when "light" from the infinite divine proves too powerful for the vessels designed to hold it. In "The Loss of the Princess," the shattering comes when the king's initial burst of anger sends his daughter down into the world.

This cosmic catastrophe—a crack in the foundation of Creation—is the origin and template of all the divisions, evils, and exiles that follow in human history.

But no shattering is permanent, because the process of

redemption is also ongoing. This applies in our personal lives, as Rabbi Nachman tells us beautifully: "If you believe that you can damage, then believe that you can repair." Our very capacity to hurt others also holds the promise that we can fix that hurt.

Rabbi Nachman's tales carry the grander hope of a final redemption, which is the third phase of the Lurianic myth. At some point, the redeemer will come and repair all the damages of history, just as in "The Loss of the Princess," at some point the viceroy will recover the princess and return her to the king.

The redemption is still in the future when the story abruptly ends. But the promise is there. "How he saved her, Rav Nachman did not say, but he did save her."

Rabbi Nachman's tales build a bridge between the most esoteric Jewish wisdom and modernity. Yet paradoxically, many do not mention Jews. We hear instead of kings and princesses and viceroys and emperors, giants and dark forests with singing trees and a morning light that laughs out loud. A hero drinks from a spring of red wine and falls asleep for seventy years. Or a hero acquires a magical instrument that translates the speech of animals. Rabbi Nachman's tales share the spirit of his contemporaries, the Brothers Grimm. His achievement is unique in Jewish literature: kabbalah clothed in a fairy tale.

Rabbi Nachman originally told his tales in Yiddish, the language of his heart and of the people. Several seem prompted by a casual incident. A cantor has a torn caftan. A Hasid arrives with news of a Napoleonic battle. But this rebbe sees depth everywhere. The grandest and most elaborate tale, the seven-part "Seven Beggars," is a quadruple frame tale, a tale within a tale within a tale within a tale. Rabbi Nachman told it over a span of ten days. But it all began because someone presented him with a snuffbox.*

Given their overall complexity and depth, their initial performance as improvisations must have astonished the first listeners. Rabbi Nachman's followers gathered around him in the *shtetls* of Breslov† and Medvedevka, usually at Sabbath meals and certain holidays. While other rebbes also told stories and tales, Rabbi Nachman's are unique for their imaginative elaboration and their depth. Nothing like them has been told before or since. He knew their significance and carefully instructed his secretary and editor, Rabbi Nathan, to assemble them after his death, and he specified that the book be published in both Yiddish and Hebrew.

Rabbi Nachman had no successors and established no dynasty. Other Hasidim mocked his followers and called them the "dead Hasidim." In a real sense, his writings have become his successors. Today more than half a dozen groups, or *havurot*, claim to be Hasidim of Rabbi Nachman, cherishing the tales as a precious legacy. He instructed his followers to read and study them and thought them appropriate for synagogue.

In time, Rabbi Nachman's tales moved beyond his immediate followers to a larger Hasidic world. One hundred years after the first tale was told, Martin Buber brought out a Ger-

---

*The storytelling began on a Friday night, March 30, 1810, continued the next Wednesday, Friday, and Sunday, and was completed on Tuesday, April 10.
†Bratslav is the name of the town in Ukraine, but his followers call it "Breslov."

man version that introduced them to modern readers. The tales popularized Hasidic wisdom among alienated younger Jews. Among the readers was Franz Kafka.

Rabbi Nachman's stories still speak to contemporary readers because they acknowledge the temptation of materialism and sophistication, and the yearning for simplicity and soul. His tales call to the secular imagination from a place beyond it and wrestle openly with questions of doubt and atheism. If we listen carefully to them, we can get a deeper sense of the mystical realm where Rabbi Nachman lived and breathed every day. And we can hear the answers he would have given to today's atheists.

In recent years, atheism has become fashionable literature. Believers are flailed as credulous readers of antiquated books, and prayer to God is likened to talking to an imaginary friend. Overall, the new atheists rely heavily on mockery, and here they join the mockers and jokers in Rabbi Nachman's tale of the humble king.

Rabbi Nachman recognizes the paradox: mockery carries a certain truth. Jokes convey the essence of the land, exposing its deceit and lies, including the lies of organized religion. In that sense atheism is cleansing. But do these jokes tell all we need to know about the king? That question remains for the wise. It only gets answered—and in a surprising way—at the very end of Rabbi Nachman's tale.*

Hearing of the land of deceit and jokes, the first listeners, two hundred years ago, might have thought first of their own Podolia. Living in oppressive circumstances,

*See Chapter 38, "The Big Joker."

squeezed between their Polish overlords and Ukrainian natives, Rabbi Nachman's Hasidim had reason to doubt the reality of God's justice, and must have grappled privately with the heretical thought that "there is neither judgment nor judge."

Ukraine means "frontier," and Podolia in western Ukraine is the frontier of the frontier, a province torn for centuries by war, attacked by foreign armies from all directions, and ravaged by bands of brigands. Rule changed hands from Lithuanians to Poles to Turks, then back to Poles, then, in Rabbi Nachman's time, to the Russians. Each ruler brought a different flag and different worship. As Rabbi Nachman told his tale, Napoleon's forces were remaking the map once more. Who ruled the land was constantly up for grabs, and for this reason Podolia was riven with religious controversies between Christian and Christian, Christian and Turk, Jew and Christian, and Jew and Jew.

Two major Jewish heresies raged there in the seventeenth and eighteenth centuries. The scars they left behind were still remembered in Rabbi Nachman's day. His Hasidim believed that the Baal Shem Tov had died while combating the false Messiah Jacob Frank, an itinerant merchant born in Podolia who led many Jews to convert with him to Catholicism. The struggle with him, the Baal Shem Tov said, left two holes in his heart.

Frank viewed himself as a reincarnation, a *gilgul*, of an earlier false Messiah, Sabbatai Zevi, a Turkish Jew who captured a significant following in Europe, and especially Podolia, in the seventeenth century.

Some argue that Podolia was fertile ground for Jewish heresy because of all the Jewish blood mixed in the soil.

More than fifteen thousand Jews were massacred between 1648 and 1649, in the uprising led by the Cossack leader, Bogdan Chmielnicki. Today Ukraine remembers Chmielnicki everywhere. His statue oversees a main square in Kiev, and again in Kamenetz near the fortress. He's a feared Cossack astride his horse, swinging a club studded with spikes, the *bulava*. His long mustaches are on the five-hryvnia note. The one unifying national hero of a divided country is a notorious and relentless Jew-killer.

For whatever reason, Podolia became a homeland of Jewish heresy. Hasidism, which arose in Podolia, was also viewed at first by more traditional Jews as yet another heretical movement. These Jews, centered in Lithuania, became known as the opponents, or *mitnagdim*. (The day of Rabbi Nachman's *bris*, a ban against the Hasidim was promulgated by the greatest *mitnaged*, the Gaon of Vilna.)

Gershom Scholem argued that Hasidism first arose in Podolia as a dialectical response to the Sabbatians. The new movement shifted emphasis away from the dangerous messianism to more individualized religion. The substitute goal of each Hasid became nearness to God (*devekut*). The Messiah was put on hold, though not forgotten.

To his followers, the rebbe served as a local Messiah. He was an intermediary with the higher realms, in matters of business, marriage, childbirth, sickness, and death. They came to him with their written requests (*kvitlach*) and their payments (*pidyonim*). In return he gave them his prayers, his tales, his tunes, his dancing, and his Torah.

But with Rabbi Nachman we see a turn back toward the Messianic impulse. He presented himself as a very special rebbe with a unique capacity to descend to the lowest spiritual places, to personally face the emptiness and meaning-lessness there and lift the fallen sparks back to their proper heights. He is the hero who rescues the lost princess and uplifts the souls of the living and the dead.

At the same time he was uniquely frank and open about his own spiritual struggles, and likewise demanded frank and open confession from his followers,* which was a unique practice among Hasidim. These new elements make him seem the most existential Hasidic master, the most psychological, the most relevant to our spiritual struggles today,[†] for the yearning for connection, for community, and for an inspiring religious leader has not completely died out in our time.

Our secular Jewish sensibility has its historical roots in Rabbi Nachman's time, and as he told the tale of "The Humble King," he was looking far ahead to a new challenge. The *haskalah* or Jewish enlightenment had already spread from its original centers in late-eighteenth-century Germany into Ukraine. Many educated and well-to-do Ukrainan Jews, physicians, merchants, and bankers became *maskilim*, "enlightened ones." The *maskil* emphasized Jewish culture and secular learning over Jewish religion. What began as an intellectual trend became a civil war within European Jewry, dividing families and disrupting long-

---

*A confession is a *vidui* and for a time the Breslovers were known as *viduiniks*—confessing Hasidim.
[†]A very different book could be written about Rabbi Nachman and Freud.

settled patterns. *Maskilim* were active in the town of Uman in 1802 when Rabbi Nachman briefly sojourned there on his way east from Medvedevka to settle in Breslov. Three prominent *maskilim* walked in while he was speaking on a Friday night. The Rebbe "turned the focus of the lesson to a geometrical problem found in the Talmud," and the *maskilim* were impressed enough to return the next day to discuss it with him. The Rebbe declared later that he would return someday to Uman, to do more work with them.

In general, the *maskilim* of his time were more drawn to secular learning than Torah, and often mocked the Hasidim and their pious ways. They were the jokers and mockers in Rabbi Nachman's tale of the humble king.

Yet instead of dismissing the *maskilim* completely, Rabbi Nachman felt a special duty to face their questions. He once told a follower, "I am a *'know-what-to-answer-an-atheist,'*"[5] that is, he was a living embodiment of a rabbinic obligation to personally refute all heretics he encounters. But first he had to answer the voice of the heretic he heard in his own heart.

As an expert on heresy, Rabbi Nachman was careful to distinguish two types of atheism. The first type of atheist is influenced by science or philosophy. To this atheism, he had an answer. Due to the primordial disaster of the shattering of the vessels, sparks of spiritual energy are scattered in every realm of thought, glints and gleams of divine truth. By seizing on these sparks held in common, the Rebbe could argue the ideological atheist back to the complete truth.

But a second type of atheism cannot be answered by an argument. It is rooted in a profound feeling of emptiness. Franz Kafka defined this feeling for the whole world, for he lived with it every day, as he wrote in his diary: "I am divided from all things by a hollow space."

It so happens that "hollow space" (in Hebrew, *halal hapanui*) is how the kabbalah of the Ari describes the emptiness left by the divine withdrawal, the *tzimtzum*.

Hasidic masters like Rabbi Nachman understood this primordial event as ongoing and archetypal. We detect the *tzimtzum* in our own lives. Depression, for instance, is a personal manifestation of *tzimtzum*. And if we go deep enough into our own hollow places, we can feel that the root of all our despair is the total absence of God.

This is the atheism of the hollow space. It is a place of nothingness Rabbi Nachman knew personally and deliberately faced into again and again.

Rabbi Nachman said that this second kind of atheism cannot be answered with an argument.

It can only be answered with a song.

The question raised by the tale of the humble king, about "who rules" the land of deceit, was urgent to Rabbi Nachman's Hasidim in Podolia. With rule of their land switching from a Polish king to a Russian czar, and with Napoleon's armies marching from the west, they needed a fresh portrait of a God who too often felt completely hidden from view. How could a king who is mighty, and a man of truth, be said to rule a land where history is a bitter joke?

The same question echoes on the streets of Kamenetz today. The pretty town is under reconstruction, designed to attract tourists to the "pearl of Podilla," with its pastel buildings newly painted and its picturesque cobblestone streets. It is painful to imagine these same streets in the summer of 1941—where more than twenty thousand Ukrainian and Hungarian Jews were penned up in a makeshift ghetto before being marched to the edge of town. These men were forced to dig a huge mass grave. Women were lined up naked, holding their babies. And all were shot and killed.

In the town square today, no markers remember these horrific events, no mention is made in the official tourist brochure where the town is dubbed "a flower in stone." But Kamenetz is an historical site of a certain awful kind. Here, the Nazis brazenly committed their first open mass murder. Tens of thousands of Jews were killed for being Jews, and no king, hidden or revealed, mighty or good or humble, said a word.

Suppose we were reliving today the story of the humble king; suppose as wise men or women, or those who hoped to be wise, we journeyed into the strange country of our own contemporary sensibility. If we were to seek the joke that defined the "essence of the country," we could do much worse than the following parable, which is called "Before the Law."

Before the Law stands a doorkeeper. A man from the country comes to this doorkeeper and requests admittance to the Law. But the doorkeeper says that he can't grant him admittance now. The man thinks it over and then asks if he'll be allowed to enter later. "It's possible," says the doorkeeper, "but not now."

Since the gate to the Law stands open as always, and the doorkeeper steps aside, the man bends down to look through the gate into the interior. When the doorkeeper sees this he laughs and says: "If you're so drawn to it, go ahead and try to enter, even though I've forbidden it. But bear this in mind: I'm powerful. And I'm only the lowest doorkeeper. From hall to hall, however, stand doorkeepers, each more powerful than the one before. The mere sight of the third is more than even I can bear."[6]

The poor man from the country! He does not know how to gain admittance to the Law. He tries bribery, pleading, "curses his bad luck," grows old and childish, grumbles to himself, begs the fleas on the doorkeeper's collar to help him change the doorkeeper's mind.

Finally his eyes grow dim and he no longer knows whether it's really getting darker around him or if his eyes are merely deceiving him. And yet in the darkness he now sees a radiance that streams forth inextinguishably from the door of the Law. He doesn't have much longer to live now. Before he dies, everything he has experienced over the years coalesces in his mind into a single question he has never asked the doorkeeper. He motions to him since he can no longer straighten his stiffening body. The doorkeeper has to bend down to him, for the difference in size between them has altered greatly to the man's disadvantage. "What do you want to know now?" asks the doorkeeper; "you're insatiable." "Everyone strives to reach the Law," says the man. "How does it happen, then, that in all these many years no one but me has requested admittance?" The doorkeeper sees that the man is nearing his end, and in order to reach his failing hearing, he roars at him: "No one else could gain admission here, because this entrance was meant solely for you. I'm going to go and shut it now."[7]

Were I a wise man looking for the essential joke of modern times, I would choose this parable, written in December 1914 by Franz Kafka. It has the sharp flavor of modernity—a bitter ironic essence we call the Kafkaesque.

For what could be more Kafkaesque than to spend one's whole life standing before the Law with its spiritual light gleaming just to learn, when it is too late, that the gate you have come to was designed to shut on you?

Whatever the "Law" represents—the truth, the Torah, God, or one's own highest aspiration—the spiritual journey of the man from the country ends with an abrupt joke. For some this joke seems too bitter to offer spiritual nourishment. Instead it represents the absolute futility of the quest. For them, "Before the Law" is a parable for nihilists.

Others detect traces of redemption. To Gershom Scholem the parable points to the borderland between faith and doubt. In giving us a glimpse of the inextinguishable light streaming from the Law, the parable condenses the five-thousand-year yearning of the Jewish soul.

Which country does Kafka's "joke" describe? A dark land of nihilism, or the hope of the gleaming light? The futility of the spiritual quest, or the inextinguishable yearning of the soul?

Does it make any sense to insert Kafka's parable into

Rabbi Nachman's tale as if they belong to the same story? And if we did, what portrait of the king, if any, does Kafka lead us to? What would we learn for our own journey toward what is good and what is true, what is possible to believe and what is most real in our time?

2

The Coffee Mug

Someone must have betrayed Franz Kafka, for without having done anything particularly wrong, he woke up one fine morning as a coffee mug.

I had just been reading a book of Kafka aphorisms, written when his diagnosis of tuberculosis weighed heavily on him. I reached for my souvenir Kafka mug, which has a nice sketch of him in silhouette, in a bowler hat, standing at the far end of a cobblestone street in Prague.

"It isn't necessary that you leave home . . ." I read. That's a laugh I thought, you tried all your life to leave home . . .

Sit at your desk and listen. Don't even listen, just wait. Don't wait, be still and alone. The whole world will offer itself to you to be unmasked, it can do no other, it will writhe before you in ecstasy.

I was taking Kafka's advice to heart, not listening, not waiting, just being still and alone, when I heard something rattle. It was the coffee mug on my desk. Kafka was making long strides down the cobblestone street. With each step the cup trembled, and he became less sketchy, more photographic. When he reached the surface of the mug, he popped off headlong into space, a full-size apparition.

We were breathing together, I and Kafka, Kafka and I. Beneath the hat brim I saw his eyes looking back at me. It was Kafka near the end, fall 1923, when he lived in Berlin with that young Hasidic beauty, Dora Diamant, when he'd finally escaped the dense gravity of mother Prague and of his baleful father, when he'd finally found it "necessary" to "leave home."

The year, he'd told Dora, he'd finally escaped his "ghosts."

I saw a man of forty, still boy-like and handsome, his nocturnal eyes, his large angel-wing ears. A slight drawing in around the lips was the only indication of his illness. He looked from me to the black coffee mug, inscribed FRANZ KAFKA in white letters, and seemed taken aback. He'd imagined a bug with human consciousness; a mole constructing its burrow, and at the very end, a singing mouse named Josephine. Strange incarnations.

But a coffee mug?

He turned away to study the top row of my bookshelf. He was taller and lankier than I'd imagined, maybe six feet. He read the first spine quizzically. Kafka? I was thrilled to hear him say his name out loud. He read all the spines: *Kafka. Kafka. Franz Kafka. How could there be so many books?* The Trial. The Castle. Amerika? *Hadn't he asked Brod . . .*

I wanted to explain, but he was already tugging at a thin volume that had caught his eye. It was a Schocken paperback and he took in the cover: a very large letter K. *"I find the letter K offensive, almost disgusting and yet I use it; it must be very characteristic of me."* Framed within the lower legs of the K, the beefy stolid face of his father, Hermann. Framed in the upper arms was himself in a ridiculous outfit, his hair slicked down and parted in the middle; a high, tight formal collar and cravat. He looked like a boy caught shoplifting. *Letter to His Father*, he read. *This too?* He looked back at me. Strangely he spoke perfect English, with no accent.

You're an industry, I said and immediately regretted my flippancy. But he was already on to a thick red volume. *F.B.*, he whispered, not even wishing to pronounce her name. His long fingers trembled.

F.B. Felice Bauer, the plain Jewish woman from Berlin who'd had the misfortune to be his ex-fiancée twice. He'd tormented her for years with his philosophical indecisions about marriage. The relationship was primarily epistolary, as many of his relationships were, even with himself. *"I am made of literature,"* he'd written her, *"I am nothing else, and cannot be anything else."* "Made of literature" meant he lived much more as writing than as flesh. Cherishing his memory, she'd been reluctant to part with those letters. Now they filled six hundred pages for the world to read. (Her letters to him he had dutifully burned.) Kafka pushed *Letters to Felice* back into place with his long fingers.

I have never been here before, he said, *my breath comes differently . . .*²

That aphorism came from the book I'd been reading. He was already turning back into literature. He seemed dizzy and I gestured to my couch, which I keep in my study for daydreaming purposes.

—I imagined ghosts, he said, as he lay down his wonderful head. *I imagined demons*. He looked again at the mug. *But not this*.

He shuddered once and vanished between the cushions.

Kafka, a trained lawyer, left no will. His literary legacy was defined by two notes to his best friend. They proved to be a conundrum. They asked Max Brod to burn all his work. Yet the day before he died, Kafka corrected page proofs for a new collection of stories, *A Hunger Artist*. Did he want to publish or not? His actual feelings about his books were maddeningly ambivalent.

Some hints about his feelings as an author in his later years can be found in "A Hunger Artist," one of several late Kafka parables about the writer's life. The "hunger artist" had once been highly celebrated, touring the European capitals, performing extended feats of self-starvation. But his art has fallen out of favor, and he's been relegated to the circus. Not even the big top, he's been shunted to a side-show cage, near a menagerie. Still exceedingly proud of his lonely art, he undertakes the longest fast ever attempted.

One irony is that no one notices his feat. For weeks the crowds have rushed past his cage on their way to other attractions. Even the sign recording the number of days without meals has gone untended.

Another irony comes as he dies. With his last breath, the hunger artist admits that fasting for him is actually no great accomplishment "because I have never been able to find the kind of nourishment I like."[3] Choosing art over life was easy for him, because he didn't care all that much for life. The same was true for Kafka, too—even on his next-to-last day in the Kierling sanitarium outside Vienna. Tuberculosis had spread to his larynx, his voice was gone. But when the page proofs arrived, he wrote on a slip of paper, "Now I want to read it," and on another slip, "It will excite me too much, perhaps, and yet I must experience it all over again."

His dear friend Robert Klopstock watched him working on the page proofs. Kafka was propped up in a chair and "tears rolled down his cheeks for a long time." Here was the last irony. As he reviewed *A Hunger Artist*, Kafka weighed no more than ninety pounds himself.

Kafka always felt his writing usurped his life. He feared the survival of his literary work would condemn him to a painful afterlife. He was right to fear it. We readers have never allowed Kafka properly to die; he hovers in his work like a ghost.

Though Literary Theory 101 states that we must not confuse an author with his narrator, few Kafka readers can resist the temptation. For us, K., Joseph K., Gregor Samsa are all Kafka. The man fused long ago with his stories; and that monstrous half word/half man, "Kafka," has become for us a sensibility, a critique, a torment, an atmosphere, and that strange humor we call the Kafkaesque.

In 1941, the poet W. H. Auden raised Kafka to a high level of literary fame. He saw him "bearing the same kind of relation to our age as Dante, Shakespeare and Goethe bore to theirs."* It's a provocative assertion, given that the other writers left behind monumental works: Kafka left us fragments and parables, and unfinished novels.

But Auden's wartime evaluation of Kafka's importance would be revised further upward by postwar history. As the world absorbed the immense tragedy of the Shoah, Kafka moved up from "writer of his generation" to prophet. The haunted victimage of Joseph K. in *The Trial*, the torture in the Penal Colony, all the worst nightmares of his fiction had

---

*"The Wandering Jew," *New Republic*, February 10, 1941, 185f. Auden wrote, "Had one to name the author who comes nearest to bearing the same kind of relation to our age as Dante, Shakespeare and Goethe bore to theirs, Kafka is the first one would think of."

become actualities. His status as a twentieth-century classic is unassailable, but we don't know yet what the twenty-first century will do to him.

For the time being, the Kafkaesque remains a byword for every bureaucratic travesty or cruel irony of fate on the planet. Seventy times a day—per Google—his name is in the news. A financial newspaper derides "the Kafkaesque nature of . . . a hybrid luxury SUV"; a social critic rails against the "Kafkaesque nightmare" of the New York food stamp system; in Madrid, a sportswriter laments the "Kafka-esque sacking" of a soccer coach; others decry "Kafkaesque airline security measures," while a lawyer in provincial Canada complains a teacher was led into a "Kafkaesque zoo"; over in Islamabad, Pakistan, the political situation is "Kafkaesque"; in San Diego immigration officials are charged with documenting an immigrant's pain "with Kafkaesque efficiency." An Egyptian intellectual writes in Cairo, "When I say I've been castrated, I mean in the Kafkaesque sense." Meanwhile in Algiers that same day, an OPEC official says that "fixing oil output levels has become " 'a kafkaesque situation.' " From the Cadillac Escalade to castration, the Kafkaesque still rules the world with an uneven, wavering hand.

If fifty years ago Kafka defined the modern age, post-modernity has repaid the favor with cheap perversity. Con-sider the career of the cockroach.

Most everyone thinks Kafka wrote a story about a cock-roach. He's famous for it. But he used no such word in any story. Once he did write "cockroaches" in a letter to his lover Milena Jesenská. With deadpan irony, he describes "luxuriating in the anti-Jewishness" of a Czech nationalist mob in November 1920, who ransacked the old Jewish Town Hall in Prague and burned Torah scrolls snatched from the storied Alt-Neu Synagogue. "To stay on here regardless would be no more heroic than cockroaches are when they can't be driven out from the bathroom."

But there's no "cockroach" in "The Metamorphosis." Instead the story begins, "Gregor Samsa woke from uneasy dreams one morning to find himself changed into a giant *ungezeifer*."* The German word means "vermin."

Kurt Wolff published several volumes of Kafka works. When he hired a theatrical illustrator to do the cover art for "The Metamorphosis," Kafka wrote back in fear. "It struck me that the illustrator might want to draw the insect itself. Not that, please, not that! I do not want to restrict him, but only to make this plea out of my deeper knowledge of the story. The insect itself cannot be illustrated. It cannot even be shown from a distance."[4] No such delicacy prevails today.

Like the scarab beetle of an Egyptian mummy, our trashy age has designated the cockroach as Kafka's eternal companion in the literary afterlife. A cockroach crawls on the cover of the otherwise authoritative *Franz Kafka Encyclopedia*. A cockroach crawls at the base of Prague's first official monument to Kafka (on Holy Spirit Street). Such are the infested laurels for the Dante of Auden's "age of anxiety."

The career of the cockroach illustrates a general depreciation of the Kafkaesque. Tourist shops in Prague remember

---

*Kafka's *ungezeifer* appears in a story written in 1914 but retrospective reading is irresistible; the Nazis called the Jews in concentration camps *"ungezeifer."* They were pests, who carried disease; and they were exterminated using a pesticide, Zyklon B.

this careful, precise, deeply inward-directed artist as Kafka the key chain, Kafka the mouse pad, Kafka the coffee mug. He may have avoided anti-Semitic mobs in Prague, but the cockroach caught up with him in the afterlife. Now mobs of readers pursue him around the world.

Kafka's fame is relentless and global. Kafka is now read in every language you can think of, from Turkish to Icelandic. He's well-known in Japan and is a bigger success in Korea. He's read all through Latin America. Germany, the United States, France, and Great Britain are all centers for important Kafka scholarship. Generations of young people have found in Kafka an icon of the absurd. There are many explanations for his ubiquity, but one that appeals to me is simply that there are so many Kafkas to go around. Faced with enigmatic texts that gleefully evade definitive interpretation, every reader invents a new Kafka.

In the beginning was Max Brod's Kafka. As his first biographer, close friend, and literary champion, Brod influenced all other readings. He had strong Jewish interests and presented his friend as a Jewish religious seeker, as Kafka the Jewish saint.

But after World War II, the hipper and cooler French surrealist and existentialist Kafkas took over. They blend into the absurd, haunted Kafka probably best known to readers. He is brother to Kafka the prophet of the Holocaust and Kafka the scathing critic of all bureaucracies, and cousin to the Marxist Kafka, social critic and champion of the working class, who arose despite decades-long Stalinist aversion to his work.

Then there are all the nationalist and ethnic Kafkas. Quite properly, Kafka has been studied as a German, and as a Czech writer. (I am trying to imagine for myself the Korean Kafka. . . .) There are the formal Kafkas such as Kafka the dramatist, Kafka the satirist, Kafka the fantasist, and Kafka the novelist. There's a Freudian Kafka and a Jungian Kafka and all the other psychological Kafkas; there's the Kafka of fathers and sons, the Kafka of sisters and brothels—he frequented such establishments. Kafka also pursued Czech shopgirls, and very young women. So there's the Kafka of women, the Kafka of dead brothers, and a queer Kafka, too. There are Kafkas of economics, of sociology, of politics and history; there are Kafkas of political geography, Kafka the citizen of the Austro-Hungarian empire, Kafka the citizen of Prague. None of these Kafka ghosts are wholly implausible, but their sheer proliferation tends to be overwhelming. One can make a rough estimate from the massive authoritative bibliography[5]—all thousand pages of it—that a new book about Kafka is published somewhere on the planet every ten days.[6]

Are all these Kafkas real, or can a ghost acquire any face it needs? What can any reader do, except scare up another ghostly face to haunt Kafka's literary remains, guided by personal obsessions and projections?

Mine, anyway, is the old-fashioned Jewish Kafka. I brought him to Uman—as a coffee mug.

It would not be easy to carry a cheap coffee mug six thousand miles on a Jewish pilgrimage.

I made an aliyah, not to the promised land, but to the old country, flying from New Orleans to Frankfurt, from Frankfurt to Kyiv going east, going deeper and deeper into the past, to my nominal ancestral past—for Ukraine is the land of Kamenetz—and to my spiritual past.

But I didn't travel alone. I brought Kafka with me. More than fifteen thousand Jews would arrive for Rosh Hashanah 5769—and while I was away stock markets crashed all over the world—but I was hoping to renew my spiritual currency by performing a *shidduch*, a match. These two dead Jews must meet, for their spirits still haunt the world.

The time of year was just right. For religious Jews, Rosh Hashanah is the birthday of the world, when God renews the promise of Creation and accepts the role of king for another year. Rosh Hashanah begins the days of awe, when each soul is judged and that judgment is sealed.

For me, Rabbi Nachman is Rosh Hashanah and Franz Kafka is Yom Kippur.

Rabbi Nachman loves Rosh Hashanah. He believed himself to have a special new insight into the Jewish New Year. He once proclaimed, "My whole mission is Rosh Hashanah," and also "The entire world depends on my Rosh Hashanah."[7] He is a master of beginning. He is always beginning anew, taking off in new directions and on sudden journeys. Such was his journey to Kamenetz, to the land of Israel, and at the end to Uman. Franz Kafka is all about Yom Kippur, the day of judgment: the last chance, the knifing in the quarry, the gate closing on the last gleam of light. He dates his real beginning in writing to the night after Yom Kippur, 1912, when he wrote "The Judgment" and discovered his great subject—guilt and punishment.

These two men are also united by fire. At the very beginning of his real life in writing, on the night after Yom Kippur Kafka discovered within him a "great fire" and he never forgot it. At the end of his life, as Rabbi Nachman was leaving Breslov for Uman where he knew he would soon die, he told his closest followers, "My fire will burn until the coming of the Messiah."

Fire, but also water. We know that Franz Kafka would sometimes drift in a little boat under the seven bridges of Prague on the charming Vltava River. Once a friend crossing the Charles Bridge happened to glance down. He saw Kafka, lying on his back, eyes closed, daydreaming, as if in an opened coffin. What did that look like? he was asked. "Like the day of judgment."

As a young man Rabbi Nachman also liked to venture out in a little boat "in the very middle of the river . . . far from shore." "The boat would rock violently in the heavy current and seem ready to sink. The Rebbe had no idea how to remedy the situation and he would lift his hands and cry out to God with true devotion," whirling, nearly capsizing, deepening his faith by risking his life.[8] So let's bring them ashore, my rebbe and my Kafka, two Jews drifting in troubled waters.

3

The Waiting Room

Thursday, September 25,
Four Days Before Erev Rosh Hashanah, 2008

I was in a large waiting room in the Frankfurt airport. And I was waiting. The boarding desk for my flight to Kyiv had not yet opened. In a crowd of international travelers, I saw a man in his thirties, with a black beard, in a long black coat, a large black hat, with strings hanging from his shirt. I approached him.

You are going to Uman for Rebbe Nachman.

He smiled. He told me he has been before. He lives in Savannah, so we are both technically southerners. He was carrying several large Rebbe Nachman *sforim*—holy books, the "Collected Teachings" that were published in the Rebbe's lifetime. I love the Jews who lug books.

I wondered if he was lonely as a Nachman Hasid in Savannah. I doubt there is any group of Breslovers there. Because Rabbi Nachman left no successor, today there is no single Rabbi Nachman organization, as there is with Chabad or Satmar or other Hasidic groups that can trace their lineage back to a single rebbe. Instead, various Breslover *havurot* have their own leaders. There are important centers and communities in Jerusalem, Bnei Brak, and Tzfat in Israel; in Williamsburg in Brooklyn, in Monsey, New York, and Lakewood, New Jersey, as well as smaller minyanim and study groups in Los Angeles, Chicago, Boston, and Baltimore. There's also an energetic spin-off group known colloquially as Na Nachs, mostly Israeli. A more scholarly group, the Breslov Research Institute, or BRI for short, is based in Monsey and Jerusalem and has translated and published in English most of the Rabbi Nachman canon. BRI would be my hosts in Uman.

Yaakov and I talked and then, when the ticket counter finally opened up, we got in line together and talked some more. After a while I suggested we ask to sit together on the flight.

His wife called on the cell phone. It was four days before Rosh Hashanah, a very important time for Jewish families to gather together. Many Breslover wives complain about their husbands leaving home at Rosh Hashanah, and many men I later met in Uman sounded sheepish and made feeble jokes about the same situation. It's troubling to contemplate, for Jewish life, as I was raised, was more about the family gathering than the praying. But rebbes coming between husbands and wives is not new. In Rabbi Nachman's day, at major Jewish holidays Hasidic courts were all male and men left their families behind to journey to be with their rebbes.

As we were both doing today, flying off to Uman.

Uman is completely unknown, of course, an obscure town in an obscure land, but in Ukraine it is "famous" for the beautiful Sofiyivka Park.

Count Potowski built the park in 1802 to honor his Greek wife, Sofiyah. Its lavish gardens, fountains, waterfalls, and ponds illustrate scenes from the *Iliad* and the *Odyssey*. A Russian traveler in the year Rabbi Nachman died, 1810, wrote, "If you want to have a true concept of the Elysian Fields, or the paradise on the earth, come to see 'Sofiyivka' and be amazed at a genius of creation."[1] (Even Rabbi Nachman once said about the park, "To be in Uman, and not go there? . . ."[2]

Sofiyivka Park was recently voted the number one tourist attraction in Ukraine. Rabbi Nachman did not make that same list, yet every year nearly twenty thousand mostly foreign visitors, mostly Jewish men, come to Uman, about three hours by car south of Kyiv.

Yaakov told me about the appeal of the Rosh Hashanah gathering, the *kibutz* at Uman. "People are glowing. They don't have anything but they have faith and you can feel their happiness. I've read Rebbe Nachman and thought I understood. But until I came to Uman, I didn't understand."

He has come six times. He feels there's something deeper and more profound about Rabbi Nachman than any other rebbe. That's why non-Hasidim study Rebbe Nachman, he said, and also many Sephardim, that is, Jews from the Middle East and North Africa.

"Rabbi Nachman," he said, "is a teacher for our time. He is our *Moshe rabbeinu*, the tzaddik for our time."

Moshe rabbeinu . . . that means "our rabbi, Moses." It's how the rabbis talk about Moses, retroactively incorporating the first Jewish teacher into their club. Tzaddik literally means "a righteous one" and many a rebbe is called a tzaddik, but "the tzaddik for our time" sounds like the larger claim Rabbi Nachman made for himself that so outraged his fellow rebbes in Ukraine: that of all the rebbes of his time, he was the special rebbe of rebbes, the "tzaddik ha-dor" or "tzaddik of his generation."

But that was two hundred years ago. So how is it that

Yaakov of Savannah says that this Rabbi Nachman, who died in Uman in 1810, could be a tzaddik for *our* time? Is the Rebbe in some sense still alive for him? But I didn't ask these questions. I asked: Are there Jews like me there?

"All kinds of Jews come to Uman," Yaakov said. He told me of an acquaintance with a farm in Europe. "I don't know if he's observant at all, but he calls out to God in the fields as Rebbe Nachman taught. One year he didn't come because a horse of his died and he had to attend to it. Otherwise every year he's there."

After we got our tickets and checked our bags, we went upstairs to the boarding area. It was seven or so in the morning. Yaakov wanted to daven with tefillin, that is, to do his obligatory morning prayers, wearing leather prayer amulets. Deuteronomy tells us that these "signs" should be between our eyes and on our hearts. One black leather cube is wrapped with leather straps around his right arm, the other strapped between his eyes against his forehead. It's a pretty common sight in the Jewish world, but rarer in Frankfurt, Germany.

The departure lounge hadn't opened. Later the ticket taker would arrive, and you would have to pass by him and show your ticket to sit in this same area. But for now we just walked in with other early birds. Yaakov went to a sunlit window to pray; I sat with him, conscious of affiliating with him, Jew and Jew, Kafka Jew and Nachman Jew, feeling oddly protective.

I didn't know why I was caretaking him. Maybe because Yaakov looked so much the Jew. I was incognito, another attenuated heir to the Enlightenment that swept Europe in Rabbi Nachman's time, and, just as the Rebbe foresaw, became the greatest threat of all to Jewish spiritual survival. Jews like me, Jews like Kafka, were the problem Rabbi Nachman tried to repair. To be with Jews like me or Kafka was one reason he abruptly departed Breslov and spent his last days in Uman in the homes of secular atheists.

But he chose to die in Uman for more mysterious reasons. Yaakov put on his tefillin and prayed facing the sunny window. The ticket taker arrived. By now several passengers had roosted in the departure lounge and he had to patiently uproot them, to begin the boarding process. Passengers got up; he walked over to another group and told them; more got up. As the departure lounge emptied, I was more and more conscious it was only Yaakov and I left. I didn't want to leave him alone. I was also concerned that he wouldn't be able to finish his prayers. I waited and waited, torn between being a good obedient international air traveler and a good brother Jew. Now the early birds who'd been shooed out of the lounge were waiting in line to get back in. They were waiting for Yaakov to finish praying.

I noticed that Yaakov seemed completely oblivious to all my little cautions. I carried the full neurotic load for both of us. Eventually I got up and left. And then I was standing in line. But the line didn't move, because instinctively the Ukrainian airline gatekeeper waited for Yaakov to finish his prayers.

Finally, Yaakov kissed his book, wrapped his tefillin, and put them in their pouch. He walked out and went to the end of the line. No one said a thing or gave him a glance.

After we reentered the waiting room, Yaakov asked me what I write about, and I told him a little. I mentioned my interest in kabbalah.

Yaakov let me know that only those who practice the Torah life can be vessels for that holy energy. Otherwise, he added, what is the point of just talking about it?

Point well taken.

I replied that my writing spreads the word to other secular Jews, even further away from any concept of Judaism as a spiritual practice. I am a bridge out there. (Unless I'm a bridge to nowhere.)

It was something I'd been thinking about anyway. Scholem says Kafka was a kabbalist. But what does this mean? How could Kafka be a kabbalist if he didn't live the "Torah life"?

Which he surely didn't. Kabbalah is fun to talk about, and Madonna proved it may be fun to dance to, but to Yaakov kabbalah is much more serious. You would have to acquire a certain level of refinement through the daily practices of Judaism in order for kabbalah to be more than just theoretical. A commitment: keeping kosher, putting on tefillin, and praying every morning, even in an airport.

Otherwise you are just spinning out ideas, and for what purpose? So he told me.

4

Kafka the Kabbalist

When Gershom Scholem left Berlin in August 1923, the last year of Kafka's life, he was also lugging books. A lifelong bibliophile, he was a major collector of kabbalistic texts, but he also treasured all the slim Kafka books available then. He was making the aliyah to Palestine that Kafka had daydreamed about for more than a decade.

Fifty years and much sorrowful history later, Gershom Scholem returned to his native country to receive a German literary award. In Munich, he informed the Bavarian Academy of Arts that when he first came to Palestine he read and reread "with true attentiveness, with an open heart and with spiritual tension" only three works: the Hebrew Bible, the Zohar, and the collected works of Franz Kafka, "three collections on which over the course of three thousand years were impressed that spirit customarily referred to as the spirit of Judaism."[1] Scholem had returned to Germany to reclaim Kafka for the Jews.

Kafka's complete writings, he said, had acquired "the halo" of Hebrew canonicity. But this is a very strange idea. Kafka wrote in German, and struggled much of his adult life to learn Hebrew. Anyway, how could secular writing be part of a sacred canon? Should we add Kafka to the back of the Bible or read him as haftarah in shul? It's as if at the beginning of the twentieth century, Kafka had brought down a strange new torah, with moles, dogs, jackals, a talking ape, a dying bug, a circus freak, and futility.

At the end of the first century CE, the rabbinic sages essentially fixed the original sacred canon of divinely inspired works. Scholem reopened the question by suggesting that even a secular literary work could be canonical, provided it were "subject to infinite interpretation." He added that such writing often "constitutes a work of interpretation" in itself, that is, it is a midrash. With his redefinition of the canonical, Scholem lifted Kafka right out of German literature to the higher shelf of holy Jewish scripture.

Scholem's definition rests on the rabbinic thesis that every word of the Torah has "seventy faces." That is, Scholem says, "the word of God carries infinite meaning . . . far-reaching, all-embracing, and unlike a human word, cannot be applied to a specific context of meaning: God's word is infinitely interpretable, indeed it is the object of interpretation par excellence."[2]

When Auden spoke of Dante, Shakespeare, Goethe, and Kafka as representative of their age, he placed them at the high end of the literary scale. But Scholem pushes that scale through the clouds. Literary work rises to the canonical if it is somehow "infinitely interpretable."

Next to the Torah, Scholem placed on his canonical bookshelf the Zohar or Book of Splendor, a hybrid work of commentary and fiction. The Zohar presents a mystical midrash chapter and verse on the Torah, and so "constitutes a work of interpretation." As fiction, it tells a picaresque narrative of wandering Jewish mystics discoursing in fields and inns, who discover a hidden saint in a donkey driver and a child genius expounding supernal Torah.

The Hasidim do not consider the Zohar fiction, but believe the author is a second-century Talmudic sage, Rabbi Simeon bar Yohai. In his first great feat of scholarship, Scholem demonstrated that the Zohar actually belongs to the age of Dante and was authored by the Spanish kabbalist Moses de Leon, before 1300. Like the *Commedia*, the Zohar offers a comprehensive tour of heavenly and purgatorial realms, a metaphysical reality map, the kabbalah of the *sefirot*. The *sefirot* are attributes of the divine, like wisdom, kindness, understanding, strength. They bridge the huge gap between an infinite divine being, the *Ein Sof*, and the all too finite human mind.

The Zohar's storytelling and mystical content strongly link the book to Rabbi Nachman's tales, and his followers believed something like this, too, for they believe their rebbe is a reincarnation (*gilgul*) of Rabbi Simeon bar Yohai. The Zohar also offers, as previously mentioned, an important mystical theory of reading. Torah is read at four levels: plain (*peshat*), allusion (*remez*), allegory (*derash*), and secret (*sod*). Using the first letters of the Hebrew terms spells out "prds" or *pardes*, paradise. To the mystic, reading Torah is a journey to paradise. This concept of four levels of depth applies as well to the holy tales of Rabbi Nachman and, if Scholem is right, presumably to the secular writings of Franz Kafka.

But what is Kafka doing on a sacred bookshelf? The many Kafka ghosts, and the thousands of pages of critical bibliography, suggest multiple, if not infinite, interpretation. As for being "itself a work of interpretation," Scholem saw *The*

Trial as the most profound modern-day midrash on the most profound biblical story, the book of Job.

Reading Kafka as a midrash on Job is important for Scholem because he contends that "absolute greatness" in literature comes only when the writing "shed[s] light upon the theological contents of experience." The greatest literature illuminates the greatest questions: why we are here, the meaning of our life, and the meaning of our suffering and our death. Specifically, Scholem saw Kafka's parable "Before the Law" as "a kind of summary of Jewish theology, which . . . radiates a powerful inner melancholy. Here the true Talmudic thinking breaks its light into a rainbow of colors."[3]

But Scholem also sees kabbalah in Kafka. In "Before the Law," Kafka leads the reader to "those mystical theses that lie on the narrow boundary between religion and nihilism." Scholem refers to the kabbalah's speculation about the ultimate nature of God. He means the "portrait of the king" no one has ever seen, who is the humble king in Rabbi Nachman's tale.

But how is it possible to consider Kafka as a kabbalist, given his lack of traditional Jewish education? Wouldn't a kabbalist be someone with a wrinkled forehead steeped in difficult esoteric texts? When people talk about kabbalah casually, they usually mean the Zohar's system of the *sefirot*, often depicted in charts showing circles connected by lines or channels, what one friend called the "wiring diagrams."

Or they may know something about the light and the vessels that Yaakov alluded to, which refers to the later kabbalah of Rabbi Isaac Luria, the Ari. It's quite likely that Franz Kafka knew something of these things, for he studied kabbalah a bit with some of his friends, and read voraciously.[4] But specific knowledge of abstruse arcana is not at all what Scholem meant by Kafka the kabbalist.

There are many reasons one might call Kafka a kabbalist, not the least of which is that he himself mentioned it in his diary during a period of intense self-scrutiny and nervous breakdown in January 1922, two years before he died.[*] Then there are his stories, which seem to evoke a magical world where people wake up in insect bodies and dogs and apes can talk—here Kafka refreshes the doctrine of *gilgul* or reincarnation. There's also Kafka's feeling that his writing was trafficking with ghosts and embracing demons in the netherworld.

But the most important point for Scholem is how intensely Kafka experienced guilt. For Kafka every day is Yom Kippur. He feels constantly judged and acts as if an "invisible tribunal" were monitoring his every move. The kabbalist feels this, too: the world is being judged at all times, and no event is without meaning. Every moment can bring a blessing or a curse, a reward or a punishment. Kafka lives in "intense and unremitting anxiety," a sense of "chronic threat" characteristic of medieval Jewish life.[*5] Or as Scholem says, Kafka provides "a secularized description for a contemporary person of the feeling of the kabbalistic world."[6]

Kafka has the feeling of that world, but not the promise of redemption. He feels judged but has no way to see the judge. His daily feeling about the world is pure medieval, but his language and sensibility are utterly modern. So he opens a bridge between us, in our ironic postmodern sensi-

---

*Cf. chapter 29, "A New Kabbalah."

bility, and the faith-based medieval kabbalah. So powerful is this feeling of "chronic threat" in Kafka that Scholem insisted that "one would have to read the works of Franz Kafka"—particularly *The Trial*—"before one could understand the Kabbalah today."[7]

But if Yaakov is right, a Jew like me, or a Jew like Kafka, had no truck with kabbalah. As assimilated secular Jews we had no vessels of Jewish practice to contain the holy light.

Some would also say kabbalah can make you crazy. Certainly in the past there was a concern that those who studied kabbalah be well grounded in Jewish practice, for fear that its insights might blow their minds.

But in an age of quantum mechanics, and that four-letter alphabet of creation that writes the human genome, is kabbalah as mind-blowing as it once was? Thanks in part to Scholem's success as a scholar, its teachings have spread far and wide, drifting out of academia into the mass market, to Web sites and kabbalah-made-easy courses.

The esoteric just isn't esoteric anymore; the secrets of kabbalah are a click away. But for that very reason the actual significance of kabbalah—the real sensibility behind it—may be further removed from us than ever.

To really understand Kafka the kabbalist, I would have to bring him to Uman.

As we flew over Germany, Yaakov mentioned that he helps a certain Rabbi Gabbai, who restores Jewish graves and cleans forgotten Jewish cemeteries all over the world. It is quite possible some of my Kamenetz ancestors are buried in Ukraine, though I can't be sure, for my grandfather actually emigrated from a small border town further north, between Latvia and Lithuania. During this trip I planned to visit Kamenetz-Podolsk to see if I could detect any faint ancestral vibes. The name Kamenetz had to come from somewhere.

Most of the passengers were Ukrainian. I was very nervous about visiting Ukraine because of "the history" I know a little of, a history of pogroms and Cossacks on horseback, and Jewish blood and murder and victimage. I knew one reason Rabbi Nachman chose Uman for his final resting place was for the sake of the souls of thousands of Jewish martyrs buried there, victims of a massacre of 1768 at the hands of rebel Cossacks known as Haidamaks. A rebbe's work is never done: even dead, Rabbi Nachman continues his holy work, lifting these souls.

In this world, the Ukrainian passengers didn't pay us much mind. Vodka for breakfast: they were real cowboys. As the plane descended, one stood up and opened the overhead. The old Ukrainian Airlines craft shook and the stewardess shook her finger, but she was too sensible to get out of her seat. The cowboy ignored her.

As we taxied in, this same stewardess passed out immigration cards, faded print on flimsy paper. I imagined a pesky overhang of Soviet-style paranoid bureaucracy. So I read the instructions carefully:

"This card must be presented together with the passport to Ukrainian border authorities. When crossing the state border of and is kept for the whole period of stay in Ukraine."

It all seemed very official and the English was only mildly cryptic. I filled out the form until I came to this line: "Name and address of receiving company (person)." I was stumped

Who in Ukraine was receiving me? Yaakov made a suggestion, and so I wrote in block letters:

RABBI NACHMAN OF UMAN

Who receives us and how will we be received? I did wonder how Rabbi Nachman would receive me. In my favor, at least I was bringing along Franz Kafka. But which Kafka was I really bringing? On any given day in Prague he could be Czech or German or Austro-Hungarian, and even as a Jew he faced a multiple-choice test: secularist or Zionist, Yiddishist or Hebraist, atheist or mystic. One day Kafka devoted himself with great intensity to the history of Hebrew literature, or wrote his own midrash on the Talmud. On many days, with several teachers, he studied Hebrew grammar and wrote Hebrew sentences in his notebooks with the names of agricultural implements. He took great interest in Eastern European Jewish refugees and their welfare and made several plans to emigrate to Palestine in the company of different young Jewish women. He campaigned publicly for the Yiddish language and fell in love with Yiddish actors and the Yiddish theater. But at an odd moment, maybe between Hebrew lessons, he could write in his diary, "What do I have in common with the Jews? I hardly have anything in common with myself."

Still I was pretty sure Franz Kafka would be the kind of pilgrim the Rebbe would most wish to receive. In his last days in Uman, the Rebbe lived in the homes of atheistic Jews and played chess with them. He was reengaging with the *maskilim* he'd encountered during his brief sojourn eight years earlier. His puzzled Hasidim had followed him from Breslov, no easy journey. He told them fiercely he preferred keeping company with the chess players. "You would shake me off like feathers on your coat." Rabbi Nachman was not an easy master to follow.

He wanted to save the souls of Jews who soon enough would be ruined by the values of the European Enlightenment. This is one reason why in the last four years of his life, he began clothing his deepest teachings in fairy tales. He wanted to reach skeptical ears.

His strategy worked and is still working; his tales still attract secular Jews and now they had brought me and Kafka to Uman to see the Rebbe. It was not Kafka's first rebbe and not mine either. But the last rebbe Kafka had appealed to had turned him down flat, and I hoped this time he'd get a better response.

I was doing it because, reading their work, I can't shake the idea that somehow, in some realm, they had met before.

There are numerous similarities in their lives, and there's a strange compatibility in their fiction, down to the details: each writes about a father who causes his son's death, both have stories with talking animals. In *The Trial* and "The Humble King," both men write a midrash on Job, using the metaphor of a cosmically unjust legal system.

Both men wrote unfinished stories. *The Trial* ends, but was never finished—for Kafka wrote the ending before the middle. Nor will we ever know how Land Surveyor K.'s quest for *The Castle* ends, or what the Great Wall of China might have promised had Kafka not abandoned it.

Two of Rabbi Nachman's best-known tales also don't quite end, but in his case, despair is ultimately only an illusion and futility but a postponement. However much his tales deal in the shattering of the vessels and the withdrawal of the divine, they always carry the promise of *tikkun olam*, the general repair of the world. Built into his incomplete stories is the promise of completion in his listeners, if only they would play their part in redemption. Boiled down, the urgent message of every Nachman tale recalls the last line of Rilke's celebrated sonnet: "you must change your life."*

What really brings these writers together is their attitude toward writing. Writing was more important to Kafka than life. For Rabbi Nachman, writing was also a life-and-death matter. When you read about how carefully he supervised the publication of his works in his lifetime, how he sent one of his followers to keep watch as the books were bound, we get a hint of what writing books meant to him. Each left behind a disciple who devoted himself for decades to preserving his writing after his death.

So it's strange to contemplate one more coincidence in their lives. Each at the end asked a very close friend to burn his books.

---

*"Archaic Torso of Apollo." Rilke was born in Prague eight years before Kafka. They published together in *Hyperion* in 1908, and Rilke may have attended a reading Kafka gave of "The Metamorphosis" in 1917.

5

Last Request

DEAREST MAX, my last request: Everything I leave behind me (in my bookcase, linen-cupboard, and my desk both at home and in the office, or anywhere else where anything may have got to and meets your eye), in the way of diaries, manuscripts, letters (my own and others'), sketches, and so on, to be burned unread; also all writings and sketches which you or others may possess; and ask those others for them in my name. Letters which they do not want to hand over to you, they should at least promise faithfully to burn themselves.

Yours,

FRANZ KAFKA[1]

This is the ink version of Kafka's last testament. Rummaging in his friend's room, Brod also found a second note in pencil, which reads in part, "Of all my writings, the only books that can stand are these: 'The Judgment,' The Stoker, Metamorphosis, Penal Colony, Country Doctor and the short story: Hunger-Artist."*

*Hans Politzer, *Franz Kafka: Parable and Paradox* (Ithaca, N.Y.: Cornell University Press, 1966), p. 295. According to Politzer, the "reference to

The total legacy of work that "can stand" makes a 236-page book.*

Both notes request the total destruction of his writing, were it possible: "When I say that those five books and the short story can stand I do not mean that I wish them to be reprinted and handed down to posterity. On the contrary, should they disappear altogether that would please me best. Only, since they do exist I do not wish to hinder anyone who may want to, from keeping them.

"But everything else of mine which is extant . . . everything without exception" is "to be burned."

Everything else . . . without exception. Both notes emphasize burning all the letters and notebooks. But "everything else" also includes *The Trial* and *The Castle*. If Kafka truly intended them for the fire, why did he leave the manuscripts with Brod (and others) that he might well have burned himself?

Brod had no easy task interpreting his friend's last requests and in a note published in the 1925 edition of *The Trial*, explains why he ignored them.

---

the desk in his office indicates that it [the note in ink] was written sometime after the fall of 1920 when he had returned once more to work for a short time, and certainly before July 1922, when he retired from the Workers' Accident Insurance Institute for good.

*Kafka did not spare his first slim book, *Meditation*, that today would be called "short-shorts." *Meditation* is, however, quite interesting. These intense one- or two-page pieces hover on the border between fiction and nonfiction and show Kafka anticipating the literary minimalism of Nathalie Sarraute and today's "short short stories."

When in 1921 I embarked on a new profession, I told Kafka that I had made my will in which I had asked him to destroy this and that. . . . Kafka thereupon showed me the outside of the note written in ink which was later found in his desk and said, "My last testament will be quite simple—a request to you to burn everything." I can still remember the exact wording of the answer I gave him: "If you seriously think me capable of such a thing, let me tell you here and now that I shall not carry out your wishes."[2]

And he did not. Because, as Brod said, Kafka's work is a "treasure."

But why did Kafka ask that his books burn in the first place? A hasty answer is: he'd been burning his work all along.

The scholar Reiner Stach[3] estimates that "thousands of manuscript pages that were written over the course of fifteen years disappeared in his living-room stove. These were the fruits of the entire first half of his life as a writer." Brod notes, "Kafka performed the function of his own executor on part of his literary estate. In his lodgings I found ten large quarto notebooks—only the covers remained; their contents had been completely destroyed."

Kafka burned his work at the beginning; he burned it to the very end. Altogether, he burned thiry-four hundred pages, or about 90 percent of everything he ever wrote. Living in Berlin with Dora Diamant in the autumn of 1923, he had a short happy period where he produced "a considerable volume of work," at least ten notebooks' full. It burned.

One clear motive was literary perfectionism. "Kafka felt

unsure of most things in life," his final companion, Dora Diamant, said, "but when it was a matter of literature, he was unapproachable and knew no compromise."[4] Kafka could be blunt in criticizing others and toward his own work, she said, he had "inexorable severity."*

One Kafka biographer, Frederick Karl, blames this perfectionism on pride, while Scholem thought it was shame. But Kafka spoke of personal liberation.

"I have been reproached for having burnt some of what Kafka wrote," Dora Diamant said, looking back twenty years later. The works she burned include a play, and a story about the Beilis ritual murder trial. We also lost the last page of "The Burrow" ("Die Bau"). "I was so young then"—she was nineteen—"and young people live in the present and perhaps in the future too. After all, for him all that [burning] had been nothing but self-liberation."

He often read to me what he had written. He never analyzed, never explained. Sometimes it sounded humorous to me, with a sort of self-mockery. Time and again he said: "Well, I wonder if I've escaped the ghosts?"

That was the name with which he summarized everything that had tormented him before he came to Berlin. He was as though possessed by this idea; it was a kind of sullen obstinacy.

He wanted to burn everything that he had writ-

---

*Even his most perfect short story. "Great antipathy to 'Metamorphosis,' " he wrote in his diary. "Unreadable ending. Imperfect almost to its very marrow" (Franz Kafka, *Diaries*, trans. J. Kresh and M. Greenberg [New York: Schocken Books, 1976], p. 253, January 19, 1914).

ten in order to free his soul from these "ghosts." I respected his wish and when he lay ill, I burnt things of his before his eyes.[5]

"Ghosts" suggest that he was haunted by the "tyranny of the past," and "tyranny" describes the hold on his imagination of Prague, his past, and especially his father, Hermann.

His feelings about his father underlie his 1912 breakthrough story, "The Judgment," about a father who orders his son's suicide. The content is significant, but more relevant to the issue of burning is how Kafka felt about the writing process itself. Kafka felt that the night he wrote "The Judgment" he had discovered the one true way for him to write. He took time the morning after to memorialize the event in his diary:

This story, "The Judgment," I wrote at one sitting during the night of the 22nd–23rd, from ten o'clock at night to six o'clock in the morning. I was hardly able to pull my legs out from under the desk, they had got so stiff from sitting. The fearful strain and joy, how the story developed before me, as if I were advancing over water. Several times during this night I heaved my own weight on my back. How everything can be said, how for everything, for the strangest fancies, there waits a great fire in which they perish and rise up again.[6]

Kafka thinks in metaphors, beginning with water and ending with fire.

Kafka loved swimming, and now as a writer he was also "advancing over water" with fearful strain and joy. Elsewhere, he speaks of his "immersion" into dreamlike states. He was going deeper. Depth psychology was in the air and Kafka's "immersion" into waking fantasy closely parallels the waking descents Jung began experimenting with a few months after "The Judgment," that led to his formulation of the archetypes.

There's no evidence Kafka knew of Jung, but the great fire also evokes Jung's alchemical process. The element of fire is destructive and transformative. Kafka's obsessive fantasies of guilt and pain, which he calls "strange fancies," pass through a "great fire," and lose their impurities. The merely personal elements—the ghosts—burn away. They "perish" and "rise" because they have now become lighter than memory. In the fiction-writing process, memories and feelings are rearranged and transmuted into new gold, into an indubitable story.

Kafka quickly devoted himself to the new process, for he now viewed his old piecemeal way of writing as "the shameful lowlands." "I realized that everything written down bit by bit rather than all at once in the course of the larger part (or even the whole) of one night is inferior."[7] This had severe practical implications for his life, for Kafka was relentless and "inexorable" in pursuing this new way of writing.

After attaining a law degree, Kafka worked for a workman's accident insurance company. He was one of only two Jewish employees. If he wanted to remain independent and eventually leave his father's house, he had to keep his job, for Kafka knew that his writing was experimental and that he would not make a living from it. Yet he might have worked this out, for the job ended at two p.m., leaving afternoons and evenings for his writing. Kafka insisted, however, that he had to write only late at night. He described the demands of his new schedule in a letter to a friend:

> From 8 to 2 or 2:30 in the office, lunch until 3 or 3:30 from then on sleeping in bed . . . until 8:30 then 10 minutes of exercise, naked at an open window, then one hour of walking alone or with Max or another friend, then supper with my family . . . then at 10:30 (but often even at 11:30) sitting down to write and remaining at it according to my strength, desire, and luck until 1, 2, 3 o'clock, once even until 6 a.m.

The discovery of the great fire seemed to lead to insoluble problems. But initially Kafka was in an exalted mood. He rushed to his sisters' room to read them "The Judgment" and read it again later to his friends. He himself pronounced the work "indubitable." Brod records in his diary, "Kafka in ecstasy . . . writing through the nights . . . Kafka in incredible ecstasy."[8]

Kafka had reached a new emotional height. The complete devotion to his ritual of writing that followed has a religious intensity and I would say that for Kafka the act of writing—when it led to the great fire—was a religious experience. This otherworldly concept of writing brings him close to the views of Rabbi Nachman.

6

Miraculous Event

Like Kafka, Rabbi Nachman directed others to burn his writing. He also burned his own writings quite often. One time, to make a point, he even burned his writing before his Hasidim, including Rabbi Nathan, who tells the story:

> Several people once came to see the Rebbe. He took a piece of paper and wrote on it. He then held the paper in his hand. He said, "How many lessons are written on this paper! Many worlds are nourished through the smoke of these lessons."
>
> The Rebbe then took the paper and burned it with the flame of the lamp. He then said, "There are many lessons that have never been put into writing. To write them alone and draw the Torah into written letters is in itself a unique experience."

Rabbi Nathan added his own interpretation of these words: "The world is not yet ready for these teachings. But even to put them into written letters is a very unique merit."

The gesture suggests that the act of writing in itself is profoundly important even if no one ever reads it, a prospect most writers today would find difficult.

So I asked my friend and teacher, a longtime Hasid of Rabbi Nachman, Rabbi Ozer Bergman, to explain further. We had been corresponding for years, ever since he wrote me about one of my books, wondering why I was interested in Rabbi Nachman. One year he invited me to come to Uman, and that also became a theme in our correspondence, though I doubted it would ever be real.

Now we communicated via Skype from Jerusalem to New Orleans. Since he is also an author and an editor for the Breslov Research Institute, I thought he would have a special insight into my problem with a writer burning his work.

What did Rabbi Nachman mean by saying the mere act of writing was a "wondrous event" *(chiddush nifla)*?

He told me, "When I was early in my connection to Breslov in the *Life of Rabbi Nachman (Sefer Chayey Moharan)*, the old Hebrew edition starts off with a history: this lesson was given on such and such a time, on such a place. This happened, during, before, after in this place and date. Who cares? I thought, big deal. I have the lesson. What do I care when it was? Then I thought, July Fourth is an important day. When the Magna Carta was signed is an important date. It makes a difference when it happened; it's very important. A *chiddush nifla*, even though there are historical events that are famous in public, there are historical events we don't know about that are just as critical."

Writing is a "miraculous event." Certainly many young writers would agree, though not precisely in Rabbi Nachman's sense. But wondrous yes, or why write at all—joyful, pleasurable, satisfying, an emotional release. Most young writers feel this, and Kafka felt it, too. Musing in his daybook, he speaks of "the calm consciousness of having entirely filled this word with oneself"; that "every word would be linked to my life, which I would draw to my heart and which would transport me out of myself."

So Kafka felt it primarily as an emotional escape: "I live only here and there in a small word in whose vowel I lose my useless head for a moment." "I have had now, and have had since this afternoon, a great yearning to write all my anxiety entirely out of me."[1]

But when he drew down Torah, Rabbi Nachman wasn't writing to relieve anxiety. He was writing to be a channel, a connection between one world and another. He was certain his teachings came not from within himself but from a higher source. They are revelations "drawn into letters" and are known reverently in Breslover lingo as *torot*, the Rebbe's torah.

By writing words and then burning the page, Rabbi Nachman made dramatically clear the "unique merit" of his writing in and of itself. For not every tzaddik was capable of holding back his revelations. Rabbi Nachman spoke of lower-level tzaddikim who "immediately reveal what they see." Their more constricted consciousness causes their visions simply to spill out of them as soon as they are brought down. They are tell-all rebbes, they blab. But "other Tzaddikim have souls from a higher level. They are from a spacious realm and have room to keep their vision to themselves."[2] Such a tzaddik was Rabbi Nachman.

This sounds immodest but when Rabbi Nachman referenced his gifts as a rebbe, he was showing respect for the sources he felt he was drawing on. Modesty was no virtue when it came to discussing the upper worlds.

Writing reflected a movement of the tzaddik's soul, a journey in which higher worlds were brought down, which is to say that the tzaddik's soul ascended. The writing was evidence of a movement of the soul, and a movement of worlds. That is why it was a *chiddush nifla*, a wondrous event. And it had consequences for the world, so he believed.

Translated into secular terms a *chiddush nifla*, a wondrous event, does sound like a good description of Kafka's feelings of ecstasy after writing "The Judgment." Unfortunately, they were not feelings Kafka could long sustain.

7

Wavering at the Heights

Just two weeks after "The Judgment" Kafka went into a tailspin because his father demanded his time for managing a family asbestos business. This disrupted his already complex schedule and threatened his newly established nocturnal writing schedule. But Kafka could not face his father directly. Instead he wrote Max Brod for help in a letter that plays with a suicidal fantasy:

> I stood at the window for a long time and pressed against the pane, and it would have suited me at many moments to startle the toll collector on the bridge by my fall. But the whole time I felt too firm to let the decision to smash myself on the pavement penetrate to the necessary depths. It also seemed to me that staying alive interrupts my writing . . . less than death would . . . 10/7–8/1912.[1]

The letter worked. Brod became sufficiently alarmed to intervene with Kafka's mother, Julie, who then intervened with Hermann Kafka and gave Franz the reprieve from the asbestos factory that he sought. Instead of facing his father directly, Kafka chose this roundabout means to get his way. There is no doubt the letter was a clever manipulation.

Kafka never actually tried to kill himself, despite telling Brod once that "every day I wish myself off the face of the earth."[2] But Kafka frequently rehearsed in his diary the suicidal fantasy of jumping out the window evoked in his letter to Brod. "To run against the window and, weak after exerting all one's strength, to step over the window sill through the splintered wood and glass" (1911). He fancies other modes of self-destruction: "In despair. Today in the half-asleep during the afternoon: in the end the pain will really burst my head. And at the temples. What I saw when I pictured this to myself was really a gunshot wound, but around the hole the jagged edges were bent straight back, as in the case of a tin can violently torn open."[3] In fantasy, he is constantly playing around the edges of his own wound.

In his fiction, the same impulse led him to closely contemplate the death of the protagonists. As Gregor Samsa or Joseph K. expire, Kafka must have felt a weird release. On the same day that he wrote the parable "Before the Law," he boasted to Brod about his newfound powers as a writer:[4] "On the way home . . . told Max that I shall lie very contentedly on my deathbed, provided the pain isn't too great. I forgot . . . to add that the best things I have written have their basis in this capacity of mine to meet death with contentment."

He manipulates the reader with "fine and convincing passages [that] always deal with the fact that someone is dying.

"But for me, who believe that I shall be able to lie contentedly on my deathbed, such scenes are secretly a game; indeed, in the death enacted I rejoice in my own death, hence calculatingly exploit the attention that the reader concentrates on death." The same could be said of his suicide note to Brod, and his final notes as well.

Kafka greatly admired Tolstoy's long story "The Death of Ivan Ilyich," which describes the death of the protagonist and events just after. This is the plot of "The Judgment" and the significant works that followed in this first period, "The Metamorphosis" and *The Trial.* Two stories at the end repeat the pattern: "A Hunger Artist" and his very last work, "Josephine the Mouse Singer."

In his diaries, Kafka muses on operas where a tenor sings his heart out as he expires,* adding that such "dying-singing" is what we do throughout our lives.

He was equally fascinated by the events just after death: the stream of "unending" indifferent traffic over the bridge after Georg Bendemann jumps off it, the indifferent sweep of the broom of the charwoman in "The Metamorphosis" that consigns Gregor Samsa's insect corpse to the trash, the brusque order of the overseer after the dying words of the hunger artist: " 'Now then, clear things up!' said the overseer, and they buried the fasting-artist, straw and all."

There's the final execution scene of *The Trial:*

> But the hands of one of the partners were already at K's throat, while the other thrust the knife deep into his heart and turned it there twice. With failing eyes K. could still see the two of them immediately before him, cheek leaning against cheek, watching the final act. "Like a dog!" he said; it was as if the shame of it must outlive him.[5]

*The aria *"O bel alma inamorata"* in *Lucia di Lamermoor,* for instance.

Judgment and punishment, and the shame that outlives death, are themes in Kafka's fiction and a preoccupation in his fantasies. He calmly imagines them, as he brags to Brod, but his bravado covers up considerable unease. He may have felt that he was being calculating in manipulating the reader, but especially after his own diagnosis of tuberculosis, he revised his view. His "capacity" to view his death calmly looked more like a compulsion.

Despite his "ecstasy" in this first period, Kafka had severe misgivings about writing and was not sentimental about creativity as such. While some speak today of tapping the unconscious—like a beer keg?—Kafka came to a much darker view. He was aware of a compulsive quality to his writing. Though he was no suicide, in a very real sense he understood that his life was at stake in his writing. His nights were usurping his days. How could the carefully arranged schedule he required accommodate a wife or child? In the early period of his engagement, he fends off a hopeful notion put forth by Felice's father, that her fiancé is merely a man "with literary interests." The case is far more dire, he warns Felice. "I have no literary interests, but am made of literature. I am nothing else, and cannot be anything else."

He retells a story about a cleric with a beautiful singing voice. "One day a priest heard the sweetness of these sounds and said: 'This is not the voice of a man, but of the devil.' By exorcism, he drove the demon out, 'whereupon the corpse (for this body had been animated by the devil instead of a soul) disintegrated and stank.' The relationship between me and literature is similar, very similar to that."

The letter to Brod invokes suicide by falling from a height; Kafka uses the same metaphor of ascent and descent two years later to describe his writing process. In this short period he produced works that guaranteed his literary immortality: "The Judgment," "The Metamorphosis," "In the Penal Colony," and *The Trial*. But the intensity of his writing and the late hours were exhausting him. He became depressed about sustaining it all:

> What will be my fate as a writer is very simple. My talent for portraying my dreamlike inner life has thrust all other matters into the background; my life has dwindled dreadfully, nor will it cease to dwindle. Nothing else will ever satisfy me. But the strength I can muster for that portrayal is not to be counted upon: perhaps it has already vanished forever, perhaps it will come back to me again, although the circumstances of my life don't favor its return. Thus I waver, continually—fly to the summit of the mountain, but then fall back in a moment. Others waver too, but in lower regions, with greater strength; if they are in danger of falling, they are caught up by the kinsman who walks beside them for that very person. But I waver on the heights; it is not death, alas, but the eternal torments of dying.[6]

This language of rising and falling, ascent and descent, would have been familiar in spiritual terms to Rabbi Nachman. The Baal Shem Tov speaks of aliyah and *yeridah*, ascent and descent, as an inevitable spiritual cycle. For the Hasid, the ascent brought nearness to God, or *devekut*. It is impossible to always be at the heights. Inevitably one must fall away.

But Kafka thought in images, not spiritual concepts, and his reflections on his fate as a writer left him with painful images to contemplate. He was "wavering on the heights," which meant his writing was now a high-flying agony. Like the hunger artist, his art stole its nourishment from his life, which was "dwindling dreadfully." Instead of ecstasy, there were now images of "the eternal torments of dying."

Hasidic masters also speak of dying to self—*bittul ha-yesh*, the annihilation of self in the pursuit of spiritual heights. Rabbi Nachman practiced fasting and sought to destroy his urge for sexual contact. He claimed to do so for the sake of reaching higher spiritual levels, higher rungs. Kafka, too, denied himself the normal patterns of life, of marriage, for the sake of his art. But he could not sustain these efforts and he also came to doubt their ultimate value.

Kafka's real life was in his nocturnal writing. But between flights there were long layovers. After the miraculous works of 1912 to 1914, Franz Kafka had two more strong periods: 1916 to 1918, which brought many of the stories and fables collected in *A Country Doctor*, and 1922 to 1924, when he wrote *The Castle* and "A Hunger Artist." He could never give up writing completely, nor could he shake his misgivings about it. Ten years after first boasting to Brod of his "unique" ability to calmly face his death, he complained more darkly to his friend of being possessed. "Last night as I lay sleepless and let everything continually veer back and forth between my aching temples, what I had almost forgotten during the last relatively quiet time became clear to me:

namely, on what frail ground or rather altogether nonexistent ground I live, over a darkness from which the dark power emerges when it wills, and, heedless of my stammering, destroys my life."

One solution to this pain would be to give up writing, but Kafka told Brod that to be a "non-writing writer" would be madness. Yet the alternative was no better:

"Writing is a sweet and wonderful reward, but for what? In the night it became clear to me, as clear as a child's lesson book, that it is the reward for serving the devil."[7] This late letter was written after his final notes to Brod. Did it reflect the whole truth? In ignoring Kafka's last request, Brod chalked up such thoughts to despair. "Certain unhappy experiences," Brod wrote, "had driven him in the direction of a kind of self-sabotage and therefore also toward nihilism as far as his own work was concerned." Maybe, but Kafka's images tell a different story:

> This descent to the dark powers, this unshackling of spirits bound by nature, these dubious embraces and whatever else may take place in the nether parts which the higher parts no longer know, when one writes one's stories in the sunshine. Perhaps there are other forms of writing, but I know only this kind; at night, when fear keeps me from sleeping, I know only this kind. And the diabolic element in it seems very clear to me. It is vanity and sensuality which continually buzz about one's own or even another's form- and feast on him. The movement multiplies itself—it is a regular solar system of vanity.

The language would not be unfamiliar to a medieval kabbalist. For Rabbi Nachman, demons were quite real. For

Kafka, too, writing about his own death was no longer "secretly a game." Now he feared that being "made of literature" meant he'd never properly lived, and could never properly die. Any posthumous appreciation of his work could only make matters worse, spawning new planets in a solar system of vanity.

In the outer bands can be found the orbit of the cockroach and the coffee mug.

8

Burnt Books

On the evening of the last day of his life, Rabbi Nachman gave his disciples the key to a chest. "As soon as I
am dead," he told them, "while my body is still lying
here on the floor, you are to take all the writings you
find in the chest and burn them. And be sure to fulfill
my request."

Rabbi Nachman was thirty-eight years old. He addressed
his final request to a person he knew would surely carry it
out, his first disciple, Rabbi Simeon. Their connection dated
back twenty-five years.

They first met on Rabbi Nachman's wedding day, which
by Hasidic custom came not long after his bar mitzvah. He
used the occasion to test his friends. From childhood on,
Rabbi Nachman had adopted a strategy of concealing his
spiritual attainments. Here he pretended to be a joker. We
don't know precisely what he said—he may have joked
about marriage or mocked the ceremonies. Some of his
friends fell for the bait and showed themselves unworthy of
his company. But Simeon, who was already a grown man,
"stood there astonished and did not answer, for he wanted
no part of such things. Our master said to him, 'Aren't you

human? Don't you want worldly things?' Simeon answered him, 'I am a simple man and I seek simplicity.' Then our master replied. 'It seems that you and I will be getting to know each other.'" He had attracted his first and most deeply loyal Hasid, a strong, simple man of God who would accompany him on his most difficult journeys.[1]

On his deathbed, Rabbi Nachman relied on this "simple man" to carry out his orders to burn his manuscripts. He knew he could count on him because Rabbi Simeon had already burned work for him, two years earlier, in 1808.

The two men were in Lemberg*—today's Lviv—where the Rebbe had gone to seek medical treatment. This in itself was a desperate resort, for Rabbi Nachman often railed against *"doctorei"* who were frequently *maskilim*. But the Rebbe knew he had the same illness that had taken his wife and infant son, tuberculosis.

That did not mean he believed in medicine. The illness of a rebbe had a metaphysical cause: it was a punishment from the upper world—for writing a book.

> He called for R. Simeon and with tears running down his cheeks. He sighed and said, "There is no one to ask for advice." The Rebbe told Simeon he had a book in his house for the sake of which he had lost his wife and children. For this book they had died and he himself had sacrificed himself greatly. Now he did not know what to do. He saw that he would be forced to die there in Lemberg. Only if this book were to be burned could he survive.[2]

*At that time under Austrian rule.

According to Rabbi Nathan, who was not present but wrote the account, "the Rebbe was uncertain and did not know what to decide. It caused him great anguish to think of burning this awesome and holy book for which he had sacrificed himself so heavily. There is no way of communicating the exaltedness of this book. If it had survived, everyone would have seen the greatness of the Rebbe eye to eye."

After much anguish and much weeping, Rabbi Simeon replied passionately as a friend, "If there are any grounds for supposing that your life depends on this, there is no doubt it would be better to burn the book so that you should remain alive." After more anguish, crying, and consultation with his doctor, at last Rabbi Nachman said, "If that is the case here is the key to my drawer. Go quickly. Hurry! Don't delay! Hire a carriage and travel to Breslov. Don't get held up by the rain and the snow. Go as fast as you can to Breslov, and when you get there take two books. One of them is lying in the drawer, the second is in my daughter Udil's chest. Take them and burn them."

Rabbi Nathan comments: "These two books were one because one of them was a copy of the other. I myself had made the copy."

We can feel a contrast between his two most important Hasidim: Rabbi Simeon the simple, wholehearted man and Rabbi Nathan the sophisticated intellectual; Rabbi Simeon the book burner and Rabbi Nathan the author and editor. Both men represented a different side of the Rebbe. But Rabbi Simeon retreated and became a solitary mystic in the land of Israel after the Rebbe's death. Rabbi Nathan carried on the practical leadership of the movement, though he never took the title "rebbe."

Rabbi Nathan and the Breslovers endured a great deal of

persecution from rival rebbes after Rabbi Nachman's death. Against strong opposition Rabbi Nathan succeeded in 1815 in publishing the Rebbe's tales. He also wrote the first biography, *The Life of Rabbi Nachman*, and other books chronicling his master's life and teachings. He wrote his own books on *halakhah* and prayer, based on the Rebbe's teachings. He established the first Rosh Hashanah pilgrimage to Uman the year after Rabbi Nachman's death and later helped build a synagogue there, known as The Kloyz.* (Today in its current building, it is the largest synagogue in Europe and can hold three thousand people.) Without Rabbi Nathan's substantial contributions from 1810 to 1844, there would be no Breslover movement today.

Rabbi Nathan was Rabbi Nachman's Max Brod, except the reverence Rabbi Nathan felt for Rabbi Nachman's writing was even more extreme. "I remember," Rabbi Nathan writes, "sitting before him writing out the copy of the book he eventually ordered to be burned. The Rebbe said, 'If only you knew what you are writing.' I felt genuinely humbled and said, 'I really have no idea at all.' The Rebbe said, 'You do not know what it is that you do not know.'"

This book is called by the Breslovers today the *Sefer Ha-Nisraf*, the burnt book. But Rabbi Nathan believed a second book "was on an even higher level than the *Sefer Ha-Nisraf*. This was the *Sefer Ha-Ganuz [The Hidden Book].*" Rabbi Nathan never read this book but the Rebbe told him he "shed his very body" when he wrote it. The Rebbe said it was on the level of "the mysteries of the mysteries." He said the Messiah would explain the meaning of the book.

And yet the hidden book was also burned. We know then

**Kloyz is the Yiddish term Hasidim use for a shul or synagogue.

that by 1806 Rabbi Nachman completed two important esoteric books, which he burned. We can't attribute this burning to self-criticism, literary perfectionism, or Kafka's
"inexorable severity." There is something mysterious and
sacrificial in these acts of burning.

Rabbi Nathan was not in the room when Rabbi Nachman
died. He reports that "the Rebbe died in a state of serenity
and with the utmost composure." But "there was a great
commotion in the room and people began crying loudly. . . .
During that commotion, Rabbi Simeon quickly took the key
the Rebbe had given him" the day before and unlocked the
cabinet with the manuscripts.[3]

Given his great devotion to the writings of his master,
one can imagine how broken Rabbi Nathan felt in that
moment. He followed Rabbi Simeon into the next room,
"weeping bitterly." But it was too late. The "simple man"
was dutifully burning the manuscript in the stove. All
Rabbi Nathan could do, he said, was "inhale the holy
smoke."[4]

9

The Burning Bush and the Thorns

Kafka's initial joy in the great fire contrasts with his feelings about the writing process in the years after his diagnosis of tuberculosis in fall 1917. His speculations grew very dark. Kafka came to believe that his immersions into dreamlike states were entirely diabolical. That may be why, in the last four years of his life, he contemplated destroying his work. Another reason was an unusual moral delicacy. He worried that his fictions might harm others. So he told Gustav Janouch, a young poet introduced to Kafka in 1920 by a colleague at the Worker's Accident Insurance Institute. Janouch idolized Kafka as a writer and as a sage.

Out of huge admiration, Janouch impulsively spent a week's wages binding "The Metamorphosis," "The Judgment," and "The Stoker" in leather. He wrote Kafka's name on the cover with gold letters. Kafka seemed offended and told him, "You overrate me. Your trust oppresses me."

He sat himself at his desk and said, with his hands to this temples: "I am no burning bush. I am not a flame."

I interrupted him, "You shouldn't say that. It's not just. To me, for example, you are fire, warmth and light."

"No, no!" he contradicted me, shaking his head. "You are wrong. My scribbling does not deserve a leather binding. It's only my own personal spectre of horror. It oughtn't to be printed at all. It should be burned and destroyed. It is without meaning . . ."

He took his hands away from his eyes, placed his clenched fists on the table and said in a low, suppressed voice: "One must be silent, if one can't give any help. No one through his own lack of hope should make the condition of the patient worse. For that reason, all my scribbling is to be destroyed. I am no light, I have merely lost my way among my own thorns. I'm a dead end."[1]

Kafka evokes, by negation, the story of the burning bush. Rabbi Nachman used the same story in Exodus to occasion his deepest teaching about burned books.

It was Shabbat Yitro, the Sabbath of the Torah portion Jethro, in Breslov, on February 4, 1809. (Moses was tending the sheep of Jethro, his father-in-law, when he saw the burning bush.) The Rebbe spoke at the third meal of the Sabbath, an intimate gathering at his table as a long Saturday afternoon blended into evening. Scores of men crowded in the room, many who had journeyed a long distance to be with their Rebbe. They would sacrifice to hire a carriage, poorer men would walk for days to be with him. Once, the Rebbe told one of his disciples, "If only I were worthy of seeing the clear, radiant light of the road you travel to be with me."[2]

The closest, most respected Hasidim would sit near the Rebbe, and he would personally hand them scraps of food from his plate. These *shrayim* were considered holy offerings. Other men of lesser status would crowd near the table and sometimes fight for the scraps tossed to them. They would chant the Rebbe's special wordless tunes, his *niggunim*—one well known today is Rebbe Nachman's *devekut*.* It's worth a listen, it is the tune to sing to answer the atheist.

The Hasidim would dance with joy in the room. But at a certain point the Rebbe's attendant would pound the table and ask for silence. Then the Rebbe, speaking softly, would offer a Torah teaching based on the weekly portion. To be in his presence, to see his face, to eat his food, these were all ecstatic moments, but the most exalted experienced was to hear torah from the Rebbe's mouth. The teachings were free improvisations and the Rebbe would emphasize certain points while looking at one Hasid or another: each felt the teaching was meant only for him.

At that third meal, the Rebbe took special note of an important Hasid, Rabbi Yekuziel, the Maggid of Tarhovitze. He was an older man, a student of Dov Ber, the Maggid of Mezritch, and was a leader of over eighty-four small towns and villages. But he'd journeyed the difficult miles to Breslov to be with Rabbi Nachman. He brought a question about revelation and lost books. What happened to all the missing holy books written by the tzaddikim? To the Hasidim, Moses was a tzaddik in a long line of tzaddikim, stretching back to Adam and forward to Rabbi Nachman himself.

With such a long line of tzaddikim of great capacity receiving very high revelations, the Maggid wanted to

*There's a recording of it on Andy Statman's *Between Heaven and Earth*.

know: what happened to their books? Surely they wrote books. Moses brought down the Torah, and Rabbi Simeon bar Yohai, the Hasidim believed, had brought down the Zohar. So where were all the books by all the other tzaddikim?

The Maggid's question was prompted by the dramatic events from a year before in Lemberg, when Rabbi Simeon pleaded with Rabbi Nachman to save his own life and destroy the manuscript we now know as the burnt book. Was the mystery of the burnt book tied in with this greater mystery of all the missing books from the past?

According to Rabbi Nathan's account of that incident, the motivation was to preserve Rabbi Nachman's life. But on this occasion, Rabbi Nachman gave an answer that suggests another reason why he might have burned his books.

Rabbi Nachman's answer deeply impressed the Maggid. After the Sabbath ended, he visited his son-in-law who lived apart from his family. The son-in-law asked his father-in-law about his wife and children, but the Maggid replied,

> Before you ask how they are, ask where I've just come from. I've just come from Breslov. I was there with our Rebbe Rabbi Nachman of Breslov. I asked him something I've already asked many Tzaddikim and they never gave me the right answer. But he gave me the answer clearly and correctly. He revealed a most wonderful teaching about this and as he was speaking I saw flames of fire coming from his mouth."[3]

The fire from the Rebbe's mouth expresses the power of a teaching given orally, immediately, not just the words, but the gestures, the face of the Rebbe, his holy presence, the setting, the intimacy of Hasidim gathered around the table prolonging the sweetness of the Sabbath into extra hours, and the sense of a revelation arising as if casually from the Maggid's question.

"Fire" comes out of the Rebbe's mouth, as from the burning bush. But then the words of the Rebbe needed to be noted down. Rabbi Nathan listened and memorized, for he could only write after the Sabbath ended. He translated doubly, from oral to written, and Yiddish to Hebrew. The lesson, as a "torah" from the Rebbe, had to be written in the holy tongue. The Maggid was also impressed by Rabbi Nathan's prowess in transcription. He "thought it would be quite impossible to put what [the Rebbe] said in writing. Then the next morning that young Rabbi Nathan brought along this lesson, written in ink on paper."[4] And we can still read it today.

The writing is also marvelous, for how can you put fire on paper? Perhaps by a magical reversal, burning a piece of paper could restore the written word to its original holy state of fire, so that Rabbi Nachman can indeed say that "worlds are nourished by this smoke."

10

Fire from the Rebbe's Mouth

I set out to find out for myself what the teaching meant, though with a number of handicaps, including rudimentary Hebrew.* I once again called on Rabbi Ozer Bergman to teach me paragraph by paragraph, line by line, Rabbi Nachman's discourse about burning books.

Rabbi Bergman very patiently explained the background and the many associated texts. I found myself in an unfamiliar world of references. Rabbi Nachman is not a linear thinker. His torah is more like jazz piano improvisation than a classical composition. He jumps from note to note, theme to theme, his ideas link poetically and associatively, pinned together with the magical phrase *behinah*, which means "likeness" or "aspect." A is a *behinah* of B, B is a *behinah* of C. Soon you are pretty far down the alphabet and lost in *behinot*. You don't know quite how you got there. Once Rabbi Nachman himself said, "All my torahs are *behinot*," which is to

---

*For readers who want to explore this in depth, the first stop would be Rabbi Marc Ouakhnine's the burnt book: *Reading the Talmud*, trans. Llewellyn Brown (Princeton, N.J.: Princeton University Press, 1995), which fully opens up both the Talmudic background of the teaching and the philosophical implications.

say, Forget the linear, my torah moves by free association. He once explained to Rabbi Nathan that his "lessons are like entering a palace" of "halls and chambers, anterooms and entrances," all of "awesome beauty, with story upon story." "No sooner do you enter a room and start examining it, wondering at the extraordinary novelty of the design, than you notice an amazing opening leading to another room."[1] This is the mind of the kabbalist, who sees how everything is related to everything else, who understands how this is that, how this is that, how this is that.

Max Brod saw something similar in Franz Kafka. "In a thousand quite easy ways, it seemed he observed interconnections no one had ever noticed . . . minute but accurate perceptions, which gave one a strong desire to build up a whole new system of knowledge."[2]

But free association is not easily assimilated by linear thought. I kept stopping at each point of the lesson, and asked so many branching questions that finally Reb Ozer told me with mild exasperation, "You think like a Litvak." That is, like a Lithuanian. The Lithuanian Jew was known in Rabbi Nachman's time for his hardheaded opposition to Hasidic teachings. From a Hasid, "Litvak" wasn't a compliment.

To give a taste of Rabbi Nachman's teaching on burnt books,[3] I'll confine the discussion to the first two paragraphs. That's plenty, though, because like all of Rabbi Nachman's teachings, they are thick with associations and references.

There are hidden righteous men, the Rebbe begins, *they know faces in the Torah but have to keep their teaching hidden. . . . Even so with him.*

"Him" means Rabbi Nachman. That's how he alludes to his status as a tzaddik. But he is a "hidden tzaddik," which means in part that the world doesn't fully recognize him, and he has teachings that he also deliberately hides.

Sometimes he knows a teaching which has faces, that is to say faces in a teaching, but he must keep it secret and not tell it. Sometimes he does not even write it. At other times he writes it down and then burns it.

As a hidden tzaddik, Rabbi Nachman knows "faces in the Torah"—but for some reason he keeps them hidden. What are "faces in the Torah"? It turns out "faces"—*panim*—carries a huge burden of meaning on its little Hebrew back.

One meaning: to know faces in the Torah means to know interpretations. A tzaddik can derive new meanings from the infinite Torah, can draw them out like water from a well as Rabbi Nachman does all the time, casually in conversation, at Shabbat teachings, in a horse-drawn carriage, endless variations, midrashim from every line of Torah. Once on leaving for a trip he asked Rabbi Nathan, Do you want a blessing or a Torah teaching? Rabbi Nathan said, Torah. You can give me the blessing when you return. He knew that if he didn't receive a "torah" right then and there, it might never be recorded.

This continual flow of interpretation recalls Gershom Scholem's concept of "infinite interpretability," which in turn derives from a rabbinic statement that every word in Torah has "seventy faces." If you do the math, every sentence conceals a huge number of possible meanings.*

---

*Just for fun I did the math. A ten-word sentence in which each word has 70 meanings, would give theoretically 2,824,752,490,000,000,000

That huge interpretability is a mark of the Torah's divine origin, its holiness. The tzaddik's ability to see "faces" in the Torah means he is a special kind of reader—the book opens to him in a way that for others it doesn't. Kafka, for instance, complained once after a stint of Bible reading that the pages just don't "flutter in my presence." Apparently at that time, Kafka didn't see any faces in the text. For Rabbi Nachman, seeing all those faces, the Torah comes alive.

This leads to another sense of faces, the more intimate, literal, poetic meaning. The hidden tzaddik sees faces in a teaching. Whose faces does he see? There's a clue in another teaching, where Rabbi Nachman says, "In the book of the sage is impressed and portrayed the likeness of the sage."[4]

The hidden tzaddik sees the hidden faces of other tzaddikim, his predecessors. He feels their presence in a teaching. Rabbi Nachman particularly felt a soul connection to Moses, to Rabbi Simeon bar Yohai, to Rabbi Isaac Luria, and to the Baal Shem Tov. In their teachings he can see their faces, he feels their presence—the pages do flutter. Interestingly, all of these tzaddikim either wrote books or had books written from their oral teachings.

But what about Rabbi Nachman's own writing? If it's truly coming from an experience of higher worlds, there's another face to see: his own. The tzaddik sees his own face in a special light, illuminated by the wisdom he derives from the Torah. For when a sage has contact with higher worlds, when he brings down new torah, his face is lit up just as the

---

meanings, or 282,475.2 trillion, assuming each change in meaning is significant.

Torah says that Moses' face was illuminated when he came down from Mount Sinai with the Ten Commandments.*

The ultimate face that the tzaddik can see can be found in the Torah. It is the face of the divine. In the burnt book teaching, Rabbi Nachman alludes to the idea that the spirit of the *Mashiach* or Messiah hovers over the Torah text. Certainly that's the ultimate mystical sense of a "face" in the Torah: it is the face of the divine revealed through the text.

Why would a person who knows such faces in a text keep such knowledge hidden by burning the book after writing it? The Rebbe doesn't answer right away. He speaks instead of publication. It turns out that how a book is read and received is crucially important for him.

> In fact, if this teaching were written it would be a book and the latter would have its place in the world. In these books, there are Names that should be understood in the sense of the Talmudic expression "My Name written in holiness" (Shabbat 116a). However the world destroys that and it is necessary to make it disappear and burn it. But it is good for the world that these teachings and books be hidden and burnt.[5]

Publication means making a "place in the world" for a divine revelation. A teaching has not only "faces" but also "Names," that is, Names of God. The "faces" and the Names are what make the book holy. But the world "destroys" or ruins that. How? Because of heretical misreading.

---

*Exodus 34:30: "When Aaron and all the people of Israel saw Moses, behold, the skin of his face shone; and they were afraid to come closer to him."

When a reader ruins a book, that also damages the Name. Because a holy book is equivalent to a Name of God—a teaching Rabbi Nachman brings in from the Zohar.* And because of that holiness, it's better if the author himself destroys a holy book before the world has a chance to ruin it. The worst desecration is not burning a book but allowing the wrong readers to misread and so pervert the holiness into heresy. For then a book will actually lead people away from God. Therefore, burning a book is better than publishing it if the book is sure to be misread.

Holy books were burning in Ukraine, for fire, as the Rebbe knew all too well, was a constant problem in the shtetls.

There were no fire companies, and no plumbing to supply water. When a fire broke out, everyone had to help carry water in buckets from the wells. In 1806, a fire broke out in Breslov during Yom Kippur while Rabbi Nachman's Hasidim were in prayer. The Ukrainian civil guard invaded the synagogue after the fire was put out and beat up the Hasidim in rage because they hadn't come out from their prayers to fight the fire.

Another fire came during Rabbi Nachman's last Sabbath in Breslov, and just a year after his teaching on burning books. It was a Friday evening, May 4, 1810, and he was sitting with his Hasidim at his Shabbat table in Breslov when there was "a great fire in the street near his house."

---

*Through *gematria* the Hebrew words for *book* and *name* are equivalent; thus a book is in effect a Name of God.

The Rebbe said, "Already, already."

It seems he had a premonition of this fire. People fled as his house burned, but even though it was the Sabbath, some Hasidim rescued the Torah scrolls in the Rebbe's study house.[6] The men waded across the Bug River, holding the scrolls above their heads. The Rebbe joined them and sat up all night in contemplation, watching the smoke rise up from the ruins of his house. Four days later he took off for his final journey to Uman.

Ordinarily it would be forbidden to carry objects out of a house during the Sabbath, but the men who rescued the Rebbe's Torahs were acting in accord with the Talmudic ruling that makes it clear that Torah scrolls and other holy books with divine Names need to be saved from fire, even on the Sabbath. But what about books that contain divine Names but are heretical? Should they be saved? To answer the question today you'd have to think about what makes a book holy and therefore worthy of saving from a fire.

Suppose a book has a kind of holiness to it, even if it's not very pious or Orthodox? Kafka's fiction feels sacred in that way to many readers; certainly to Max Brod. Scholem saw it with reverence, too, when he called Kafka a kabbalist. Should such a book be published or hidden or is it better off burned? In today's Orthodox world, there's a lot of concern about what is a kosher book and what isn't. In our age of freelance spirituality unbound by religion, spiritual books abound, and they talk about God in their own ways. Many Orthodox readers secretly consume such books.

Once I visited a very devout kabbalist in a *haredi* neighborhood in Jerusalem. His walls were lined with traditional "kosher books," those *sforim* with their distinctive thick leather bindings, marked with gold and silver stars and crowns. Then he opened his closet. It was full of books on Buddhism, Hinduism, and the New Age. He read them because they deepened his reflections on kabbalah, but he kept them hidden from view because in the *haredi* world, only kosher books should be read. And a kosher book is pious and is written by an observant Jew. Kafka was neither.

To the rabbis there was no in-between. Heretical books should be burned, divine Names or not. They were passionate about this issue, and when they spoke of books by "heretics," they may have meant Gnostic books or books by early Jewish Christians. Rabbi Tarfon even says, "May I bury my son if I would not burn them [the heretical books] together with their divine Names if they came to my hand." In short, he'd rather see his own son dead than allow such books to live.

But some of the rabbinic sages still had doubts. After all, a divine Name is holy. Can it really be right to burn a book with a holy Name in it? That's where Rabbi Ishmael settles the argument. He points to a priestly ceremony that has roots in the book of Leviticus. It seems to reflect a more primitive patriarchal worldview and in fact the ceremony has been shelved—it has not been performed for two thousand years. The priest writes God's name on a scroll and then dissolves the name in water, which a wife accused of adultery must drink. If she survives the ordeal, she's considered innocent.

Rabbi Ishmael's point is that in the ceremony, God's name is written down and then deliberately destroyed for the sake of preserving a marriage. He argues that "if in order to make peace between man and wife the Torah decreed, Let my Name, written in holiness, be blotted out in water," all the more so, a heretical book with the Name may be destroyed if its existence would cause enmity between "Israel and their Father in Heaven." A heretical book that has holy Names can be destroyed to preserve the "marriage" between God and the Jewish people.[7]

So much for heretical books. But Rabbi Nachman takes Rabbi Ishmael's argument a step further. Just as it might be a good thing under a certain circumstance to burn a holy text with God's Name in it, so it might also be permissible to burn a book by a tzaddik. But why do it? Under what circumstances? When would it be "good for the world" for the book of a tzaddik to be burned? I believe Rabbi Nachman means that a truly holy book could still become heretical if it were read by the wrong person or in the wrong way. The problem is not the tzaddik's book but the heretical reader.

If the world will destroy its "holiness," Rabbi Nachman says, by misreading it, "it is necessary to make [the book] disappear and burn it."

This is how the Rebbe explains why we don't have more books from the tzaddikim. They wrote them and burned them because the world they were living in was simply not ready to receive their secrets. The world—as it was in their time—would "destroy" their holiness and turn good teachings into heresy. And since heresy drives people away from knowing God, it would be "good for the world" not to make such teachings public at the wrong time.

There is much much more to Rabbi Nachman's teaching in the paragraphs that follow: how a holy book is itself a divine Name of God, how the breath of the Messiah hovers over a holy book, how publishing any holy book threatens the cosmic order and unleashes a "jealous spirit." But to pursue his teaching further would lead into depths and difficulties beyond what's needed here.

Though Rabbi Nachman's teaching does not refer directly to the burnt book, I believe it's likely that when the Maggid asked his question, he was thinking about the dramatic events a year earlier in Lemberg.

While Rabbi Nathan's narrative of the incident emphasizes that the reason for burning the book had to do with saving the Rebbe's life, Rabbi Nachman's teaching a year later suggests another motivation. It seems the experience in Lemberg led Rabbi Nachman to a deeper reflection on this mystery of the missing books of tzaddikim.

From the start, all the events surrounding that manuscript were dramatic. Rabbi Nachman wrote and promulgated it in a two-year period beginning at Rosh Hashanah in 1804, when, according to his biographer Arthur Green,[8] his Hasidim were being prepared for an imminent redemption. He told them to recite special midnight prayers. After the birth of his son, Shlomo Ephraim, in May 1805, the preparations accelerated. Rabbi Nachman assigned them private fast days and the special recitation of ten psalms of purification that are still recited at his grave in Uman. (These are known as *Tikkun Ha-Klali*, "The Complete Remedy"). The time of redemption was getting closer.

The manuscript we now call the burnt book was an important part of the preparation, the secrets brought down in it were of immediate consequence, and the act of writing it was certainly a *chiddush nifla* of such high order, and so fraught with implications, that the day Rabbi Nathan copied the manuscript, Rabbi Nachman hurried to the grave of the Baal Shem Tov in Medzhibozh. He lay himself on top of the grave to be as close as possible to his great-grandfather, and immediately prayed for his infant son, Shlomo Ephraim, who had taken ill. He knew in his bones that writing the book was causing his son's illness. He feared that promulgating it—publishing it, in effect—might prove more dire. Nevertheless, though praying for his son, he also sent two of his Hasidim riding from town to town, carrying the manuscript Rabbi Nathan had copied and reading excerpts from the book. That same May, during Shavuos, Rabbi Nachman appeared for the first time among his Hasidim in all white garments, which carries Messianic symbolism.

We don't know exactly what happened, but the whole affair ended badly. The two circuit-riding Hasidim gave up their mission. (Rabbi Nathan later swore that had he been assigned, he would have completed it.) A few weeks after he appeared in white garments, Shlomo Ephraim was dead. After sitting shivah for him, the Rebbe remarked, "The ARI only revealed one secret, and was punished with the loss of his son. But I have revealed many great secrets."[9] Rabbi Nachman believed that just like Rabbi Isaac Luria, he was judged in the higher world for revealing secrets in ours.

The Rebbe's first wife, Sashia, complained in her grief to Rabbi Nathan and another close Hasid, Rabbi Naftali, "that the Rebbe did not take care of himself, that he traveled too much and that he did not intercede to prevent the child's death." They came to the Rebbe with this and he told them, "I suffer inside and outside" and burst into tears. His followers ran away in embarrassment.[10]

We can only speculate about the pain he was feeling. And it underlines his anguish two years later in Lemberg, in the incidents mentioned already, when he asked Rabbi Simeon to burn the manuscript. At that point, with his own life at stake, and with Rabbi Simeon's passionate pleading, he felt he had to burn the book. It seems the judgments and the punishments associated with this one book were never-ending.

Yet it could not have been easy at that point. He had sacrificed his son's life for the sake of the book. That would have made it extremely painful for him to destroy it. He had paid too high a price already.

From the time he first began telling tales, to his crisis in Lemberg, it seems Rabbi Nachman still hoped in some way to redeem that book—and his son's death—by making it possible for the book eventually to be received in a better light. The teaching he gave on burnt books implies this. If new readers could be found—or created—the book could be published. For then it could be received "in holiness."

The teaching also provides a clue about the contents of the burnt book, which Rabbi Nathan, who copied the book, did not himself understand. Secrets were revealed in the book, but the world was not ready to receive it in holiness. "The world would destroy that." What were those secrets? Rabbi Nathan alludes to a teaching about the significance of the mitzvah of hospitality to guests. This is enigmatic but fascinating—who was the mysterious guest who would be arriving? Was it the Messiah?

Biographer Arthur Green surmises from good evidence that the "Burnt Book" indicated that the time of redemption was at hand. This was dangerous stuff in Podolia, where waves of enthusiasm for Sabbatai Zevi and then Jacob Frank had caused so many terrible results. We know that when the circuit-riding Hasidim rode into town, the writing was not received in holiness. Perhaps it was received with hostility and derision. In one town the riders were even accused of being thieves.

Then on top of that, Shlomo Ephraim died. But did that mean the redemption was canceled entirely, or merely postponed?* The Rebbe kept the burnt book from the flames for two more years. That implies he hoped the "faces" in it were still worth revealing. The trick was to change not the book, but the readers. He had to change their consciousness so they could receive the book in holiness. And that required a new tack: storytelling.

A month after Shlomo Ephraim died, in July 1806, Rabbi Nachman announced with seeming simplicity to his followers, "Now I will begin telling tales." Like everything he said or did, it was a statement full of significance.

*Rabbi Nachman later told his followers that the Messiah could have come then, but now would not come for at least another hundred years.

11

Tales of the Seventy Faces

How would telling tales prepare people for the final redemption?[1]

Hasidism had long stressed the spiritual power of telling stories about tzaddikim. As a boy Rabbi Nachman grew up hearing such tales from those old-time Hasidim who came to visit his great-grandfather's grave in Medzhibozh. Jiri Langer, Kafka's friend who became for a time a Belzer Hasid, describes the power of stories as he heard them in their setting.

To relate stories from the lives of the saints (tzaddikim) is one of the most praiseworthy acts a Chassid can do. He will tell them at every opportunity— during a meal, during his studies, on a train journey but especially on the anniversary of a saint's death. He must never forget to add the word "holy" or the phrase, "May his merits protect us!" whenever he mentions the name of a saint. Woe to the listener who protests that he has already heard this or that episode before! Everyone is duty bound to listen patiently to each story even if he has heard it a hundred times already. In this way, over the course of years, everything becomes imprinted on the memory—the heroes' names, their wives' names, the characters connected with them and the place where the various events took place.[2]

Rabbi Nachman teaches, "Know! Telling stories of tzaddikim—i.e., what happened to them—is a very great thing. Through this one's mind is purified."[3] In another teaching, he repeats the same thought and adds, "By means of stories about the tzaddikim the heart is woken and inspired with a great arousal for God, with a very powerful yearning."[4]

Jiri Langer stresses that the tales need not be documentary:

> The Chassidim are aware that by no means everything they relate about their saints actually happened; but that does not matter. If a saint never really worked the miracle they describe it must still have been one such as only he was capable of performing. Rabbi Nachman of Bratslav goes out of his way to point out that "not everything related about the holy Baal Shem, for instance, is true, but even the things which are untrue are holy if told by devout people. The fact is (says Rabbi Nachman) that man is perpetually sunk in a magic sleep throughout his life and is unable to rouse himself except by narrating anecdotes about the saints."[5]

But Rabbi Nachman claims that his tales are far more powerful than the traditional tales of *tzaddikim* he heard as a child and that Jiri Langer heard in his milieu. In explaining their unique power, Rabbi Nachman tells a parable of a prince who is ill. The wise man prepares a concentrated medicine and the prince drinks gallons and gallons. He can keep down very little of it. But some small amount sticks inside him, and this small amount makes him a little better, and then he can take in a little bit more medicine. Eventually, over time, he is cured.

Rabbi Nachman's stories are concentrated medicine, concentrations of story. Most of the teachings packed into them would be misunderstood. But some small drop of the medicine would stick in the belly. And from that healing, more medicine could be taken in, until the person was "cured," that is, brought to repentance (*teshuvah*).

The world had misunderstood Rabbi Nachman's more explicit teaching in the burnt book when he sent it from town to town. And its publication had caused his son's death. The world was not ready for this teaching—which meant each individual had also failed to go deep enough, to change, to do the necessary *teshuvah* that would enable the *tzaddik ha-dor* to reveal himself and bring on the final *tikkun olam*. In a time of growing heresy, represented by the threat of the *maskilim*, the world was too sick to take in his medicine. So the Rebbe had to tell an entirely new kind of story, to change the world, listener by listener, and prepare the groundwork for redemption.

"Now I will begin telling tales." The tale is the concentrated medicine that can lead to *teshuvah* for each listener.

In his letters to Brod and conversations with Janouch, Kafka reveals his fear that his stories were not medicine, but poison. But he also understood the power of story to awaken readers. In an early letter to his friend Oskar Pollak, he proclaimed: "If the book we are reading does not wake us, as with a fist hammering on our skulls, then why do we read it? . . . A book must be the ax for the frozen sea within us."[6] Here Kafka comes closer to Rabbi Nachman, who believed every story could awaken a listener to his or her soul. That's because, again due to the scattering of the sparks, every story contains sparks of divine wisdom.

The ordinary tales of the world Rabbi Nachman called "the tales of the seventy faces"[7] and also tales "amidst the years." We've already seen that seventy is the traditional number of "faces" or interpretations of each word in Torah. But 70 has multiple meanings in the tradition: the seventy years of a person's life, the seventy nations, and the seventy languages of the earth.[8] Tales of the seventy are tales from all nations and languages. They appear merely to refer to everyday life, but secretly they contain scattered sparks of divine wisdom from the primordial shattering of the vessels.

If they could be heard with enough depth, even these scattered sparks could burst into flame and restore people to their souls. They could bring people to *teshuvah*. And we sense this in great literature: that if we listened deeply enough, something in the stories can restore our souls. But seeing that even his Hasidim were more and more captivated by secular philosophy, ordinary stories had lost their capacity to awaken people. People were too deeply asleep. Rabbi Nachman therefore had to tell a new kind of story whose purpose was to spiritually transform his listeners, as is made quite explicit in the opening to the first tale, "The Loss of the Princess": "On my way I told a story, and whoever heard had thoughts of *teshuvah*."

Teshuvah usually is translated as "repentance" but literally means "turning back," "return." (It can also mean "answer.") It is not about feeling bad about the past, but about recovering one's essence. Every one of Rabbi Nachman's stories aims to restore to the listener an immortal part of him or her that has gotten lost.

These tales acquire this special power because they are drawn from a higher source than the "tales of the seventy faces." Rabbi Nachman said they were drawn from the inconceivably highest place of all, the highest wisdom, which in the scheme of *sefirot* is called *Keter* or Crown. This is the first *sefirah*, from which the others emanate. *Keter* is super-subtle, ineffable; other *sefirot* have colors; *Keter* is invisible, it is "nothing." *Keter* is also called "ancient of days." Nachman referred to his new kind of tales as "tales of the ancient years" or, we might say, the days of yore.

That is the lofty kabbalistic theory of his tales as Rabbi Nachman explained it in his teachings. In more contemporary terms, they are also remarkable: myths told at the very edge of modernity. This makes him comparable to his contemporary mythmaker, the English poet and mystic William Blake. Rabbi Nachman smuggles the wisdom of kabbalah across the border to our time.

Myth does not mean *false*. Rabbi Nachman's tales of the ancient of days are true at a much deeper level than surface realism; they have an archetypal quality. Arthur Green, in his discussion of the tales on which mine is based, captures their value beautifully: "A myth is a tale that bespeaks an inner truth portrayed as an ancient truth."[9]

Merely hearing these tales could have magical effects. They could heal the sick, and one tale helped a woman through a difficult childbirth. They could help barren women conceive.

But mainly they were told to bring listeners to *teshuvah*. Since everyone had to make *teshuvah* before the era of redemption could begin, the tales were a necessary first step.

The writing in the burnt book and in the hidden book was presumably discursive—like the multiple volumes of *The Teachings of Rabbi Nachman* (*Likutey Moharan*) that have been translated into English by the Breslov Research Institute. These teachings were published in his lifetime, at the same time the burnt book manuscript was destroyed.

But in "telling tales," Rabbi Nachman was returning to the storytelling core of all Jewish literature. The tales were originally spoken—told in Yiddish—only later written down. (It's not clear to me whether Rabbi Nachman prepared them in writing in any way or simply performed them spontaneously.) In a certain way, they were a return to the origins of Jewish literature itself, which is a remarkable move—a sophisticated teacher like Rabbi Nachman condensing his complex teachings into seemingly simple tales.

In the beginning, at least during the first two years, the tales were told to make it possible to revive the Messianic mission. Rabbi Nachman's teaching on burnt books tells us that a certain kind of reading—and a certain kind of reader—receives a book in a special way that allows it to "have a place" in this world. Rabbi Nachman was fortunate to have such readers, his Hasidim, and especially his most loyal and literate Hasid, Rabbi Nathan.

But Franz Kafka also had a friend who read him like this, who became devoted to him after his death. Through Max Brod, Kafka's writing would also have a place in this world.

12

Kafka's Last Parable

Gershom Scholem's friendship with the literary critic Walter Benjamin has been described as "one of the extraordinary intellectual friendships of the twentieth century."[1] After Scholem left Germany for Palestine, they corresponded intensively, and for seven years, from 1931 to 1938, Kafka was at the center of their correspondence. In an astutely written piece occasioned by the tenth anniversary of Kafka's death, Walter Benjamin observed, "Kafka had a rare capacity to create parables for himself." And one might add, for others. Of all his parables, perhaps the most vexing were his last notes to Brod.

"Given its background," Benjamin writes, "the directive in which Kafka ordered the destruction of his literary remains is just as unfathomable, to be weighed just as carefully as the answers of the doorkeeper before the law. Perhaps Kafka, whose every day on earth brought him up against insoluble behavior problems and undecipherable communications, in death wished to give his contemporaries a taste of their own medicine."[2]

Initially Brod edited and published the unfinished novels: *The Trial* in 1925, *The Castle* in 1925, and *Amerika* in 1927. Then Brod brought out collections of the short fiction. But the elusiveness of the fiction created a huge pressure to publish biographical material. Brod shepherded into print the notebook-diaries, the letters to Brod and other friends, and the *Letter to His Father*. The Kafka oeuvre today includes the aphorisms typed on onion skin paper that I was reading the day he popped off his coffee mug, and slips of paper he wrote on when his voice failed him in his dying days. Kafka's chance remarks, or the reports he wrote in his day job at the Worker's Accident Insurance Institute, have generated waves of articles and books.

Publication of this autobiographical material might seem a particularly perverse outcome. If the great fire transmutes bad memories into the "indubitable," didn't Brod's efforts reverse the alchemy, reduce the fiction back to autobiography, and bring back the ghosts, especially Hermann's? Kafka's personal life is now the proof text for every fable, the solution to every paradox. But did Kafka leave Brod a choice?

Brod knew Kafka was correcting page proofs a day before he died and that his friend frequently pretended to protest when Brod snatched his manuscripts and agented their publication. But then in meticulous correspondence with his publisher, Kafka would be very attentive to every detail regarding covers, typography, layout, and proofreading. Kafka could play the role of the diffident artist because he could count on the enthusiasm of his devoted friend.

So it is plausible that Kafka, knowing Brod's love for his work, anticipated the effect of his final requests. He knew Brod would pass through the gate of this last parable, not languish outside it like the man from the country.

From Brod's side, this was a story of friendship, love, and devotion.

Brod was a year younger than Kafka; they first met when he was eighteen. They were polar opposites. Kafka was tall and introverted; Brod short, humpbacked, but very sociable. Kafka never believed he could make a living as a writer and burned much more than he ever put out; Brod was a prolific professional writer and literary journalist and became well positioned to promote his friend's work.

And Brod adored it. He saw Kafka's fiction in an entirely spiritual light. Brod wrote, "Perhaps there have been men who have had a deeper, that is to say, a less questioning faith than Kafka's—perhaps also there have been men with even more biting skepticism. . . . But what I do know is the unique fact that in Kafka these two contradictory qualities blossomed out into a synthesis of the highest order. Of all believers he was the freest from illusions, and among all those who see the world as it is, without illusions, he was the most unshakable believer."

Walter Benjamin scoffed at Brod's piety, and even wondered how Kafka could have tolerated him as a friend. But Benjamin, who dawdled at many a metaphysical gate, was too severe and perhaps too arrogant. Brod had a direct experience of his friend's spiritual nature, which he sensed "in his personal calm and serenity, in the gentle considered, never hasty character of his being."

Other friends saw his soulful qualities, too, all those truly close to him did. Felice Bauer, who might have had reason to feel otherwise, called him a "saint"; Milena Jesenskà wrote

Brod, "I really think that every one of us, everyone in the world is sick, and that he is the only who is healthy and understands things correctly and feels correctly, and the only pure human being."[3] There's Dora Diamant's sense of his depth: "He not only wanted to penetrate to the bottom of things; he was at the bottom." Robert Klopstock saw his soul in his face at his deathbed in Kierling: "Now we are going there again to Franz. So stiff, so severe, so unapproachable is his face, as his soul was pure and severe. Severe—a king's face from the oldest and noblest stock. The gentleness of his human existence has gone, only his incomparable soul still forms his stiff, dear face. So beautiful is it as an old marble bust."[4]

Those who knew him, who understood his purity and depth, could detect the subtle spiritual light in the writing, too. To Brod, "he who reads Kafka's works with care must again and again catch a glimpse through the dark husk of this kernel that gleams, or rather beams gently through."[5]

In the end, the writing that got sacrificed was not Kafka's but Brod's. Though Max Brod published twenty-four books, including a bestselling novel, a biography of Heine, opera libretti, and plays, he will mostly be remembered as Kafka's friend and literary executor. When he fled the Nazi takeover of Prague in 1939, Brod carried a suitcase full of Kafka manuscripts to Palestine. Some of those papers remain unpublished and are still in dispute, with those who claim Kafka as a purely German writer battling those in Israel who claim Kafka for the Jews.[6] But that is another matter. The reason people are even quarreling over the legacy is because Brod's

*She adds: "I know he isn't resisting *life*, just *this type of life*."

response to the parable of Kafka's last request was to bring his work into the world.

For forty-four years after Kafka's death Brod served as editor, agent, and champion of Kafka's work. He spoke at his friend's funeral oration, and today a commemorative plaque for Brod is set in the wall opposite Kafka's grave, watching over Kafka in death as he did in life.

In his teaching on burnt books, Rabbi Nachman spoke of the world ruining or destroying work because it could not "receive it in holiness." But what of those readers who do? They become the Hasidim of the author, and in that sense, Brod became Kafka's Hasid.

13

Sealed in Flame

From the very beginning, on the night he wrote "The Judgment," Kafka spoke of his best writing emerging as if from another world.

Late at night, his worldly concerns dissolved in a realm of fire. Dora, the only person ever permitted to be around him when he wrote, describes what she saw. One evening in Berlin after supper he "wrote for a very long time, and I fell asleep on the sofa. The electric light was on. All at once he was sitting at my side: I woke up and looked at him. A palpable change was visible in his face. The traces of the spiritual tension were so obvious that they had changed the face utterly."

The great fire was an alchemical realm where the elements of memory and "fancy" are destroyed and reconstituted. In January 1922, in a depressed and retrospective mood, Kafka recast this very experience in Jewish language as akin to the meditations of the kabbalist.

I don't want to make more of the metaphor than Kafka did. Rabbi Nachman said, "My torah is all *behinot*"—aspects, likenesses—linked together freely. So was Kafka's "torah." He thought and felt in images and associations; metaphors flowed as easily for Kafka as water from a tap.

Yet Kafka did come to believe that his lucubrations could have led to a "new secret doctrine, a kabbalah." He did not think he had at all succeeded, only that "there are intimations of this." "It would require genius of an unimaginable kind to strike root again in the old centuries, or create the old centuries anew and not spend itself withal, but only then begin to flower forth."[1]

Did Rabbi Nachman have that genius? His tales did in fact "strike root again in the old centuries"—he even called them "tales of the ancient years." They drew on the tradition of Kabbalah but were entirely new and original. So Rabbi Nachman did not speak of a great fire, but he did understand that when he wrote, he was drawing down from a higher realm. And like the great fire, this realm of consciousness could both annihilate and renew.

In his Torah teachings Rabbi Nachman described his writing process using the schematics of the *sefirot*, which he knew very well. His tales of the ancient years came from the highest of the *sefirot*, *Keter*. But he also described his meditations in story terms, as a journey. So the wise man who wishes to obtain the portrait of the recondite king must travel higher and higher until he reaches the highest place of all, the place where the humble king remains concealed behind a curtain.

Rabbi Nachman's stories then are stories of the journey of the soul to higher realms, and the fire Rabbi Nachman did speak of, and often, was the fire of the individual soul.

Rabbi Dov Baer, the Maggid of Mezritch, once begged heaven to show him a man whose every limb and every fiber was holy. Then they showed him the form of the Baal Shem Tov, and it was all of fire. There was no shred of substance in it. It was nothing but flame.[2]

The soul was Rabbi Nachman's essence and substance, and so on his way to Uman, he swore his fire would "burn until the coming of the Messiah."

To those who loved him, Kafka also emitted a palpable, though quieter flame. Max Brod speaks of "the aura he gave out of extraordinary strength, something I've never encountered elsewhere, even in meetings with great and famous men. The infallible solidity of his insights never tolerated a single lacuna, nor did he ever speak an insignificant word."[3]

Nachman's fire, in fitting his personality and mission, was more intense. "Fire came out of the Rebbe's mouth," said the Maggid of Tarhovitze on hearing the teaching of the burning books. When Rabbi Nathan heard his first teaching from the Rebbe, "he became so enthused that after the Shabbos meal was over he ran out into the open fields crying out, 'A fire is burning in Breslov. Light this fire in my heart!' "[4]

The person touched by the flame of the master becomes his Hasid. He is moved to preserve the flame and pass it on to others. Both Max Brod and Rabbi Nathan felt an ineffable quality in the presence of the master, a quality others who love him less cannot see. And for the sake of this fire, both men devoted the rest of their lives to preserving and disseminating their masters' books.

Whatever Kafka intended by the parable of his last requests to Max Brod, they had one clear effect: Max Brod was bound to him forever. Rabbi Nachman's book burning had the same effect on his faithful secretary, Rabbi Nathan. We can feel it in Rabbi Nathan's reverence for the burnt book, which in all humility he knew he didn't understand. And his reverence for the hidden book, a book he never even read, was even more powerful. By ordering these books burnt, Rabbi Nachman only made more precious the books he left behind. He inflamed his Hasid to do all he could to preserve what remained. For Nathan and Brod, a devotion was sealed in flame.

That is not the only meaning I see in their burning books. That both men could order their works burned indicates how powerful the act of writing in and of itself was to each of them.

I believe the "wondrous event" of bringing down Torah into words was as meaningful to Rabbi Nachman as any publication. And Kafka's devotion to the great fire over ten years must have weaned him from the more obvious satisfactions that writing and publishing can bring. In some sense, both saw writing as the by-product of a movement of the soul.

Of course both men wished to publish, wished to bring books into the world. While he was in Lemberg ordering the destruction of the burnt book manuscript, Rabbi Nachman also edited and saw through the publication of his Torah teachings, which we now know as *Likutey Moharan*. The Rebbe paid very careful attention to the publication of his works in his lifetime. When he had to order the burning of his work, it was with real agony and pain.

Both men, to use Rabbi Nathan's language, wrote books that they "shed their very bodies" to write. Isn't that the meaning of "A Hunger Artist," too? Kafka gave his life to his writing. Rabbi Nachman thought his writing had led to the death of his wife and his son, and to his own fatal illness. So there was an element of pain and despair in the idea of putting these costly books to the flames.

What does *soul* mean in our time? To me it is connected to the riddle of burning books. We feel a special reverence for books and a corresponding sense of desecration when they are burned. Maybe we understand, in some way, that books represent the permanent part of us that can "shed" the body and live on for a time in the new form of words. This is also a *chiddush nifla*, a miraculous event. As we move into the age of the digitized book, will we still feel the same reverence for books that can no longer be burned?

For the time being, we still have the old sense of books as souls on fragile paper. That is why to understand the question of the burnt books more deeply, we have to look at the books by Kafka and Rabbi Nachman that were saved from the fire, for they are like living souls. And through their books, those souls touch other souls.

In Rabbi Nachman's case, the failure of the burnt book to be received in holiness and the death of his son were mingled pain. Yet out of this pain came his new determination—to tell tales. These tales of the ancient years had the power to completely change how people would understand him. They would make his readers his Hasidim.

They still retain that power to move people, drawing me and ten thousand others to Uman.

A hundred years ago, these same tales, retold by Martin Buber, came into Franz Kafka's hands, part of a larger movement toward the Hasidism of Eastern Europe, and the spirituality it represented for a generation of secular Jews who had lost their spiritual roots. So one place for certain that Kafka met Rabbi Nachman was in a book.

This is only a hint, though, of the deeper mysterious communication between them.

They both adapted the same literary form, the Hasidic parable, and made it entirely new. They both wrote stories of a father who causes his son's death, both wrote parables of messengers from a king who cannot deliver their message. Both imagined the pain of a soul reborn into the body of an animal. Then there are all the similarities in their lives. On the way to Kamenetz, I began to imagine that somehow Franz Kafka was a reincarnation, a *gilgul*, of Rabbi Nachman.

PART II

Parables and Paradoxes

14

To Feel at Home

Writing from the rural village of Zürau at the end of September 1917, Franz Kafka thanked Max Brod for sending him recently translated parables of the Hasidic master, the Maggid of Mezritch. They "may not be of the best, but for some reason I don't understand, all these stories are the only Jewish literature in which I immediately and always feel at home."[1]

To feel at home in anything Jewish was no small thing for a personality as homeless as Franz Kafka's. Hugo Bergmann, Kafka's schoolmate, found a Jewish home in Zionism. His friend Jiri Langer left his secular Prague household to be a Hasid of the Belzer rebbe. Kafka flirted with both Zionism and Hasidism but, as a man "made of literature," he found his most significant Jewish home in a literary form.

These young Czech Jews belonged to the first generation of European Jews in a hundred years who sought to be more Jewish than their parents. The emerging forces of Zionism, secularism, and religion played out in a series of generational conflicts between fathers and sons.

In Rabbi Nachman's Ukraine, traditional parents were often troubled when their children became Hasidim. Then as the *haskalah* movement gained influence, families divided again, as Jewish children left the religious fold entirely for the promise of assimilation into the larger society.

But the conflict could be just as tempestuous when young Jews rejected their parents' assimilation. Jiri Langer's parents were horrified by their son's dressing and praying like a Hasid; Kafka's father, Hermann, was angered by Franz's growing Jewish interests.

Franz Kafka was often ambivalent, and late in his life he looked back on his many ventures into Jewishness as no more than "broken radii" of a circle he never completed. But his efforts were actually serious and continual. From 1910 until the end of his life, Kafka attended Zionist meetings, hung out with Yiddish actors, met rebbes, and intensively studied Jewish texts. Through books and live performances he encountered Hasidic masters: the Baal Shem Tov, the Maggid of Mezritch, and Rabbi Nachman.

Kafka read Rabbi Nachman's tales, and both men loved the Hasidic parable. Reading their fictions side by side will clarify how much more they shared.

They did not share the yoke of the Torah. Kafka would never feel at home in traditional Jewish religious practice. Attending a circumcision in December 1911, Kafka observed how dry and secondhand the ceremony felt. "I saw Western European Judaism before me in a transition whose end is clearly unpredictable. It is so indisputable that these religious forms which have reached their final end have merely a historical character."[2] In this, he was his parents' child, for they had broken loose from Orthodox practice as young adults when they left smaller Bohemian towns for cosmopolitan Prague. They belonged to a generation who could take advantage of Austria's emancipation of Jews after 1867.

Julie Lowy, Kafka's mother, had much of the responsibility of raising her younger siblings after her mother died. Her father prospered with a brewery in Podebrady, a spa town on the River Elbe—enough to retire to Prague. Hermann Kafka was the fourth son of a kosher butcher, a position often held by very pious Jews. He came from extremely poor circumstances, from the tiny Bohemian shtetl of Wossek. The marriage was arranged; Julie was twenty-six, close to an old maid at the time, but her father may have felt Hermann's ambition and strength compensated for his poverty and lack of polish.

In Prague, Hermann opened a fashionable "fancy goods" store selling gloves, slippers, parasols, and walking sticks. His shop was on the main square, that Czechs call *Staroměstské náměstí*, Germans the *Altstädter Ring*, and English-speaking tourists the Old Town Square. Eventually he went into the wholesale business.

By around 1900, Czechs were the overwhelming majority in Prague, about 420,000 people. German speakers were a minority of 52,000, half of whom were Jewish. The ethnic German minority were "exclusively upperclass, the owners of lignite mines . . . and arms factories, traders in hops . . . sugar, cloth and paper manufacturers and bank managers. Their social milieu was frequented by teachers, higher officials and government servants. There were practically no members of the proletariat."[3] But rising Czech assertiveness was undermining their power and German-speaking Jews were even more insecure.

In this troubled social landscape, Hermann battled for economic survival. He was a strong man. Julie Kafka regarded her husband, and all his family, as "giants." Hermann's father, Jacob the butcher, could snatch up a huge sack of flour with his teeth. In his youth Hermann worked as a peddler carrying heavy loads on his back, and he served in the Austrian military where he rose to platoon sergeant. He remained a staunch Austrian patriot. He was literate in Czech and fluent in German. By suppressing his Jewishness in public, speaking good Czech or German to his customers as needed, he scrambled through Prague's ethnic divisions during a period of rising Czech nationalism when there were ugly tensions between Czechs and Germans and Jews. By the end of his life, Hermann was a proud grandfather and a successful patriarch who owned a block of flats and a warehouse on Old Town Square.

But assimilation was a tense daily battle that cost his family at home. He was verbally abusive and easily enraged. He demanded Julie's full attention at all times and pulled her away from her children so she could play cards with him late at night. He picked on them at meal time, criticizing their eating habits while picking his teeth at the table. He "put special trust," Franz wrote, in bringing children up "by means of irony." Most evenings, Hermann released his tension with a stream of bitter nihilism. "You were capable," Franz wrote to his father, "of running down the Czechs, and then the Germans, and then the Jews, and what is more, not only selectively but in every respect, and finally nobody was left except yourself."[4]

Hermann knew prayer book Hebrew and was called up to the *bimah* for *aliyot*, but attended synagogue primarily for social prestige, moving up from the lower-middle-class "Gypsy synagogue" to the historic Alt-Neu Synagogue, the oldest surviving shul in Europe. Even as a boy, Kafka knew his father's religion was perfunctory.

"I could not understand how, with the insignificant scrap of Judaism you yourself possessed, you could reproach me for not making an effort . . . to cling to a similar insignificant scrap. . . . Four days a year you went to the synagogue where you were, to say the least, closer to the indifferent than to those who took it seriously."

Kafka dreaded being called to the Torah; his bar mitzvah "demanded no more than some ridiculous memorizing. . . . It led to nothing." "This was the religious material that was handed on to me. . . . How one could do anything better with that material than get rid of it as fast as possible, I could not understand." But getting rid of it was not possible. Kafka never got rid of any Jewish material any more than he could be done with his father.

15

Borispol Airport

Thursday, September 25

With the prompting of that good Hasid Yaakov of Savannah, I had written in block letters that Rabbi Nachman would receive me in Ukraine. It was more in hope than certainty. What promise did Ukraine hold for me?

On the plane I thumbed through the Lonely Planet guidebook. I read that Ukraine is one of the poorest countries in Europe, the site of the Chernobyl nuclear disaster, an HIV epidemic, and a drug-resistant tuberculosis epidemic. Public transportation is crowded and there's an "almost superstitious local aversion" to fresh air; "you might also be astounded by all the passive smoking you're doing." The roads are dangerous with "crazy driving"; "it's nothing to find hundreds of plastic water bottles strewn over remote clear-looking rivers . . . and broken glass encircling idyllic picnic areas." Packs of dogs roam the streets; some are rabid; foreigners are often subject to attacks; xenophobia is rampant, along with sex trafficking and sex tourism. Women are one of Ukraine's chief exports; not unrelatedly, "since independence Ukraine's population has fallen more dramatically than that of any other country not affected by war, famine or plague."

The national anthem is "Ukraine Isn't Dead Yet."

Thank you, Rabbi Nachman. I was making a return, but to what? Ignorant of my grandfather's past, I didn't know which Kamenetz of several in Eastern Europe our family name derived from. As a kid I'd chosen Kamenetz-Podolsk from an atlas.

As I passed through security, I should have been wearing a badge, PROUD TO BE A ROOTLESS COSMOPOLITAN. To all three modern forms of Jewish identification: secular, religious, Zionist, I was ill defined, and a hundred years more uneasy and attenuated than Kafka.

Going east, I was reversing the direction my grandfather David Kamenetz had traveled more than a hundred years before. Rabbi Adin Steinsaltz says that because Jews change continents every three generations, the delicate things of the culture get lost. Someone in shul said it differently: exile is when you know the prayers but have forgotten the melodies. Was I Hasid or *mitnaged*, Litvak or Latvik? None of the above really. Just a typical American Jew, living with non-answers, negations, and nos.

When I thought about burnt books, the ones that came to mind were not by Franz Kafka or Rabbi Nachman. They were stacks and stacks of books piled up into bonfires in fifty cities across Germany, burned by students who were cheered on by their professors, books with "un-German ideas" including works by Einstein, Marx, Heinrich Heine, and Sigmund Freud. When Freud heard the news, he responded with dry irony, "What progress we are making. In the Middle Ages they would have burnt me. Now they are content with burning my books."

But the Nazis were not content with burning books. We read Kafka through the smoke of the flames that consumed

Jewish Europe and left it for ash. In that perspective the Jewish dilemmas of Kafka's generation acquire the urgency of the catastrophe they were moving toward.

Kafka's friend Bergmann left Palestine early, Brod late, carrying his Kafka manuscripts. They lived to witness the destruction.

Two of Kafka's sisters died in the Lodz ghetto; Kafka's favorite, Ottla, was murdered in Auschwitz after volunteering to accompany a children's transport. Kafka's Czech lover and translator, Milena Jesenská, joined the Resistance and died at Ravensbruck. The Jews of Czechoslovakia were all but exterminated. Jiri Langer, the Belzer Hasid, also escaped at the last possible moment, a mystical *luftmensch* lugging three heavy suitcases full of holy books to Palestine. But most of the Hasidim, following the advice of their rebbes, stayed and perished. They saw America as a non-kosher land, fatal to Jewish identity, but my grandfather Kamenetz thought differently and I am the grandson of that choice. I've rarely worried about my Jewish body, but do wonder about my Jewish soul.

Yet in the Borispol airport I joined a long line of Jewish souls who were waiting to be processed and stamped. Most were magnetized by Rebbe Nachman's call to join his Rosh Hashanah. I handed my slip of paper to a bored young woman in the passport control booth. She glanced at the Rebbe's name listed as my host, shrugged, and stamped. I was in. Outside, more pilgrims gathered in clumps. Jews of all kinds, shapes, ages, colors, with beards long and short, white, or nonexistent, with and without side curls and Hasidic hats, mingled. Two suave hip-looking Hasidim puffed cigarettes before piling into a minivan. The vans and taxis were out in full force to drive the faithful two hundred miles to Uman.

Wawa, a slight Ukrainian woman in tennis shoes, held up a sign with my name. She's a dear friend of my sister-in-law, Lisa Crone, who at that time was a professor of Slavic languages at the University of Chicago. (Lisa passed away about a year after my journey.) Wawa worked in the Fulbright office and when I contacted her, full of fears and doubts about traveling alone to Kamenetz and Uman, she became the angel of my trip and hooked me up to a second angel, a visiting Fulbright scholar, Professor Yohanan Petrovsky-Shtern. He in turn offered to accompany me on the train to Kamenetz and the bus to Uman.

After an hour's rest on her living-room couch, I followed Wawa to the Maidan metro to wait for Yohanan at the foot of the towering escalator. A two-fisted drunk swaying with liter beer bottles approached. He weaved dangerously and for a moment I admired his footwork, wondering how he was dancing with gravity, when Wawa flinched and grabbed my arm. He was right in her face. I waved him away, but he returned, shouting. Just then Yohanan showed up, in a trench coat, identical to the trench coat I was wearing. My brother. The drunk retreated: two trench coats were too many. Wawa lightly stepped up the astonishingly steep escalator, pride of Soviet technology.

Yohanan looked the perfect Jewish intellectual: late forties, short trimmed beard, intense eyes behind gold-rimmed glasses, a tie, maroon sweater. Born in Ukraine, educated at Moscow University, he founded a Jewish Studies program in the nineties at the university in Kyiv. He's written books in Russian and in English and is now an associate professor of modern Jewish history at Northwestern University. He is smart as hell and an expert on Ukraine, shtetls, and Rabbi Nachman's Uman. We became good friends on this trip.

For now, we had no time for words. He began moving immediately—we were late. We crammed into a crowded car and in minutes of metro travel had two hostile encounters. Our sin was wearing backpacks, a very grave offense to Ukrainian youths on crowded trains. Some glared at us, some bumped us: two different young men spoke angrily to us. Yohanan talked them down. On the steep escalator to the train station, a very insane man shouted behind me. I looked at his face. I did not understand his words, but his eyes were full of sharp glass.

I was on my way to the Kamenetz train.

16

Who by Water, Who by Fire

The night of the great fire taught Kafka the one way he ever wanted to write. But it also gave him his first and most important subject. He wrote it on the Sunday evening after Yom Kippur, a day when it's believed God seals a judgment on the whole world. There's a strong hint of the Jewish connection in the title, "The Judgment."

He was twenty-nine, living in his father's house. From childhood on, Kafka accompanied his father to synagogue every year during the High Holidays. But by 1911, Kafka was getting fed up, writing in his diary, "The Alt-Neu Synagogue yesterday. Kol Nidre. Suppressed murmur of the stock market."[1] The next year he did not attend.

When he sat down to write the evening after Yom Kippur ended, on the twenty-second of September, he may have felt some guilt. Even secular Jews feel a certain dread of Yom Kippur. "Polish Jews going to Kol Nidre," Kafka observed in his diary, "The little boy with prayer shawls under both arms, running along at his father's side. *Suicidal not to go to temple.*"

Suicide ends the story he wrote that Sunday evening.

As "The Judgment" opens, Georg Bendemann, an assured and confident young man, is writing a bachelor friend in

Russia. Should he tell him his news, that "he had become engaged a month before to Miss Frieda Brandenfeld"? Georg is a stand-in for a confident worldly Kafka who just a month earlier had met Felice Bauer and was wooing her in a furious correspondence.

Georg's father, by contrast, seems ill, decrepit, possibly demented. He seems dependent on his son, who lifts him in his nightshirt and puts him in bed, covering him with a blanket. "Am I well covered up?" the father asks. Just here the story shifts. The father furiously denounces his son for disloyalty to his dead mother and to him. He reveals that he has long been corresponding behind his back with Georg's friend in Russia, who in fact knows all about Georg's betrayals. He is scabrous about his son's engagement:

> "Because she lifted up her skirts," his father began to flute, "because she lifted her skirts like this, the nasty creature," and mimicking her he lifted his shirt so high that one could see the scar on his thigh from his war wound, "because she lifted her skirts like this and this you made up to her, and in order to make free with her undisturbed you have disgraced your mother's memory, betrayed your friend, and stuck your father into bed so that he can't move. But he can move, or can't he?"
>
> And he stood up quite unsupported and kicked his legs out. His insight made him radiant.
>
> Georg shrank into a corner . . ."[2]

The son shrinks, the father grows in power. It's an unnatural dramatic reversal. Then the father delivers his final judgment: "I sentence you now to death by drowning." The hallucinatory compression jumps the reader into the compulsive illogic of a dream, as Georg rushes out of the house and swings himself over the bridge railing. Just before dropping into the river, Georg calls out "in a low voice," "Dear parents I have always loved you all the same." That could have been Kafka speaking, too; he remained under his father's domination to his dying days.

Kafka's writing drew on his personal conflict with his father for its emotional resonance. The night he wrote it, the judgment he feared, and rightly, was his father's disapproval of his new romance with Felice Bauer. He dedicated the story to "Miss F.B." and Kafka noted the shared initials with Georg's fiancée, Miss Frieda Brandenfeld. The month the story was published, Kafka asked Felice to marry him.

Romance and marriage signaled independence from his father, but also heightened his guilt. Kafka knew of the Oedipal complex through Freud's work on the subject that had appeared four years earlier, and he cites Freud as an influence on his story. In Freud's thought, every boy wishes to marry his mother and kill his father, and unconscious guilt arises from these two desires. When the complex is properly resolved, the boy comes to identify with his father. But that never happened for Kafka, who all his life viewed his father as critically as his father viewed him.

"The Judgment" presents the conflict in reverse. It's Kafka's pleasure to punish himself for his wish to kill Hermann, by imagining a father who orders his son's death. Freud's fundamental theory uses the Greek myth of Oedipus, who killed his father, Laius, and married his mother, Jocasta. But "The Judgment" actually describes the tyranny of Laius, who in the backstory of the ancient myth once sought to kill his son.

Kafka acknowledged the influence of the Greek myth but

fails to mention another pertinent story he was entirely familiar with. Sitting beside his father every New Year, Kafka would have heard the Torah portion of another father who set out to kill his son. It is the sacrifice of Isaac, known as the *akeidah*. This story of dread and awe fits the theme of the High Holy Days: God alone has the awesome power to judge each human being for the coming year.

"On Rosh Hashanah it is written, on Yom Kippur it is sealed." This is "the power of this solemn day" in the words of the thousand-year-old prayer, the *unetaneh tokef*. The fate of each person is written in a great book, "who will live and who will die, who by water and who by fire." When Georg's father says, "I sentence you now to death by drowning," he's echoing the language of the prayer recited every Jewish New Year, and again on Yom Kippur. Here Scholem's "theological content" of experience emerges in Kafka's writing.

Kafka's "The Judgment" carries the feeling tone of Yom Kippur into an entirely secular context. It's an assimilated story, though: its connection to Yom Kippur can be felt by those who know the feeling, and completely missed by those who don't. It can be read simply as an Oedipal story, or a story of generational conflict. Except the father in Kafka is more terrible than God is in the *akeidah*. The father goes for the kill, while God, after testing Abraham's faith, substitutes a ram for Isaac.

That substitution was the kind of sentence modification we hoped for when we prayed in synagogue. We were told that prayer and repentance and charity (*tefillah* and *teshuvah* and *tzedekah*) can avert the evil decree. But for Georg there is no reprieve. "The Judgment" represents the emotional dilemma of the secular Jew who can't shake the feeling of being judged by God but no longer believes in the power of atonement.

Kafka remained highly interested in the Abraham and Isaac story. In his diary and in a letter, he proposed midrashic riffs on the story.[3] In one, Abraham is more than willing to carry out the sacrifice, "but cannot imagine he is the one meant, the repulsive old man and his dirty boy. . . . He is afraid that he will, to be sure, ride out as Abraham and his son, but on the way will turn into Don Quixote." Kafka's joking is complex and nervous. He was never acquitted of his guilt, so he never could leave off brooding over his father.

But what psychology underlies Rabbi Nachman's story, "The Rabbi's Son"? It, too, is the story of an obdurate father who causes the death of his son. Rabbi Nachman also knew that the father-son conflict is an old Jewish business.

17

The Rabbi's Son

The Rabbi's Son" stands apart, for more than any other it is a tale of the seventy faces, in that it closely resembles similar legendary stories told about other rebbes, for instance, those found in *In Praise of the Baal Shem Tov*.[1] Instead of being set in a mythical landscape like the other canonical tales, this one reflects Hasidic life in Rabbi Nachman's own time and place. It features travel in horse-drawn carriages, a typical Ukrainian inn, and three openly Jewish characters, the rabbi, his son, and a tzaddik. The realism extends to the plot: while the other tales promise a happy ending, this one ends on a pure note of woe.

A wealthy and learned rabbi has supported his son's religious studies, but the son feels a lack of inspiration. The son believes a certain tzaddik can help him, but his father is strongly opposed to their meeting. "Why should you go to him?" replied the father. "You are a more accomplished scholar than he is. Your family background is better than his. It is not at all fitting that you go to him. Give up this idea." The father continued in this manner until he stopped his son from going.[2] The son asks again, and this time the father insists on accompanying him on the journey. He tells his son that "if everything goes smoothly, then [the journey] is from heaven. If not, then it is not from heaven, and we will return home." Everything does not go smoothly. The horses slip on a small bridge, the carriage turns over, and so they return home.

But the son's longing to meet the tzaddik returns. Son and father set out once more. This time, the axles break, ending the journey. A third attempt ends when a merchant speaks ill of the tzaddik at an inn. The father insists that his son turn back.

Now the son dies. He appears to his father in three dreams. He is full of anger. "Go to the tzaddik," he says, "and he will tell you why I am angry."

The father stubbornly ignores the first two dreams. But after the third, he is shaken and journeys to the tzaddik. Stopping at the same inn as before, he encounters the merchant, who slandered the tzaddik. The merchant reveals himself now as Samael,* the Evil One. Had the tzaddik and his son met, "The Messiah would have come. But now that I have caused him to die, you may make the pilgrimage." When the father reaches the tzaddik, he wails in grief, "Woe! Woe! Woe is to those who are lost and can no longer be found."

"The Rabbi's Son" reflects, in part, Rabbi Nachman's early years as a rabbi. After his marriage, Rabbi Nachman's father-in-law set him up with an attic study, just like the son in the story. He would pray and meditate there. But his father-in-law took a second wife, following his first wife's death, and she was unfriendly. One day, while Rabbi Nach-

*Rabbi Kaplan offers this note: It is taught, The Evil Urge, the Satan, and the Angel of death are all the same (Bava Batra 16a).

man was on a journey, his new mother-in-law moved a bed into his study to reclaim the room. Rabbi Nachman was furious and quit the house in a huff.[3]

More broadly, "The Rabbi's Son" reflects family tensions arising from the spreading influence of Hasidism in Rabbi Nachman's time. This was Rabbi Nathan's story. He was a Sternhardt, son of a wealthy family of rabbis and merchants in Nemirov, near Breslov. His father-in-law was the chief rabbi of Sharogrod and a well-known *mitnaged*, that is, a firm opponent of Hasidism. Like the rabbi's son in the tale, Rabbi Nathan was not satisfied with his spiritual life and went looking for a rebbe. Later, he compared a Hasid and a *mitnaged* to a warm and cold knish. "Both have the same ingredients. Yet, the cold one doesn't taste nearly as good as the warm one!"[4] He wanted spiritual heat, he wanted fire. When he met Rabbi Nachman, he knew he had found it.

Rabbi Nathan was intelligent and learned, but he completely abandoned his own ideas for his teacher's. With complete devotion, he faithfully recorded his Torah teachings, and even his casual conversations. Though only eight years his senior, Rabbi Nachman became his spiritual father and Nathan became Rabbi Nachman's most devoted Hasid.

This devotion led to conflict with his father who, like the father in the tale, viewed himself as socially and intellectually superior to Rabbi Nachman. Nathan neglected his business and had to find excuses to slip off to Breslov. In 1803 he tarried three weeks there while his wife tended his shop in his absence. When he returned, she threw the keys of the store in his face and his father threw him out of the house. The conflict went on for years. In August 1807, Rabbi Nathan's "father was very angry with him for refusing the

rabbinical position that his father-in-law had offered him."
The tale was told a month later, perhaps as consolation.

"The Rabbi's Son" also provides hints about Rabbi
Nachman's feelings about his own father, Rabbi Simcha.
Thanks to Brod's publication of Kafka's *Letter to His Father*,
we know all we want to know about Hermann Kafka. But all
we know about Rabbi Simcha is that we don't know much
about him. Rabbi Simcha's father, Rabbi Nachman of Horodenka, was an important Hasid of the Baal Shem Tov, and
his two brothers were also prominent rebbes. But Rabbi
Simcha never became a public figure. It's likely he was a gentle soul, a highly reclusive mystic, given to wandering off in
solitary meditations. His wife, Feiga, the Baal Shem Tov's
granddaughter, was said to have psychic powers. One time,
when Rabbi Simcha wandered off too far, she used her powers to relocate him. Nine months later Rabbi Nachman was
born.

The son, too, was given to solitary meditations in fields
and meadows. Did his father guide him into these practices?
Or was the young Nachman alone in the woods, searching
for a lost father as he searched for God?

Sons with weak connections to their fathers often rebel,
and Rabbi Nachman was a rebel rebbe. After his successful
return from the land of Israel in 1799, he boldly moved into
the territory of an older man, Rabbi Aryeh Lieb, known as
the Old Man of Shpola. His age was the Old Man's chief
claim to fame, for at the time he was the last living contemporary of the Baal Shem Tov.

Their dispute was in part about money. When a Hasid
comes to see a rebbe, for advice or for healing, it's customary
to give a "ransom" known as a *pidyon*. That is, in part, how

rebbes make their living. Rabbi Nachman settled in the town of Zlotopolye, only two miles from Shpola. It was considered disrespectful to enter someone else's territory without permission.

But there was more than money to the conflict. Rabbi Nachman viewed the older generation of rebbes as dumbing down his great-grandfather's Hasidism. He was quite fierce in denouncing them. The "Old Man" returned the favor and branded Rabbi Nachman a heretic, and the younger man was driven out of town. He had to remove to Bratslav in 1802, into the domain of his uncle Baruch of Medzhibozh.

Rabbi Nachman's uncle Baruch was an imposing leader, one of the first rebbes to have a grand palatial court, with white horses, servants, and even a court jester. The materialism of the Hasidic courts was not to Rabbi Nachman's taste. Eventually uncle and nephew also quarreled. Rabbi Nachman was an ascetic and mocked the "schnapps Hasidim" who came to the Rebbe's courts for a drink or for the food. Unlike Kafka, Rabbi Nachman was never afraid to openly challenge fathers.

So who is the father and who the son in the tale? As in a dream, every character is an aspect of Rabbi Nachman, but read as autobiography, he seems to be the tzaddik who attracts the son from the father. The story then describes his own relationship to Rabbi Nathan, who indeed was a rabbi's son.

But another possibility comes to mind. Shlomo Ephraim is also a rabbi's son. Rabbi Nachman believed he had caused his child's death by publishing a book that revealed secrets, in which case one can hear in the voice of the anguished father crying out at the end of the tale the woe of Rabbi Nachman himself.

Rabbi Nachman believed that his visit to Kamenetz caused the death of his daughter. He believed that his writing and promulgating a book caused the death of his son. This is a way of thinking that does not allow for meaningless events. This sense that every action is judged governs Rabbi Nachman's feelings about the world.

Franz Kafka shared this outlook. For him every day was Yom Kippur. He brooded endlessly on trivial incidents that most people would forget. As pious Jews make a spiritual accounting before retiring, Kafka would judge himself in his diaries. "How do I excuse yesterday's remark about Goethe. . . ? In no way. How do I excuse my not yet having written anything today? In no way. . . . I have continually an invocation in my ear: 'Were you to come, invisible tribunal!' "

That invocation links Kafka to the kabbalist who believes in a celestial court that judges all the time and delivers sentences through illness, misfortune, even death. Joseph K. in *The Trial* knows little about the court that judges him except that it appears to be entirely separate from civil or criminal court, but Kafka would have known this "invisible tribunal" from Jewish folktales and Hasidic stories, or from the Kol Nidre prayer he heard every Yom Kippur, which opens, "By the authority of the court on high and by the authority of the court on earth."[5]

The kabbalist lives in a world where the court on high is always in session, and every moment of suffering represents a divine decree. So Rabbi Nachman understood the death of his children and the illness and death of his wife, Sashia. Nothing is meaningless, nothing is "just because." Each event reflects a divine judgment. Indeed Rabbi Nachman once told his Hasidim, "Everything done in this world, even among the gentile nations, down to the last details of their gait and clothing—everything has some purpose and nothing is meaningless."[6]

To an unusual degree Kafka was haunted by a constant sense of being judged arising from the unresolved guilt in his conflict with his father. It's driven so deeply it brings a metaphysical depth to his writing, beginning with "The Judgment." We sense something supernatural as the father rises from his sickbed and rapidly sentences his son to death. It's a tour de force of narrative acceleration that opens a disturbing rift in ordinary literary realism.

"The Rabbi's Son," more than the other tales, is set in a realistic framework, but it, too, has a cosmic backdrop. The father's stubbornness creates an opening for the devil to leap in; and the split between father and son reflects the shattering of the vessels.

Though the son's death means there's not even a promise of *tikkun* for him and his father, the larger plan of the repair of the world is still active. When the Merchant, who is the Evil One, mocks the father, he tells him that his son "was an aspect of the Lesser Light. The tzaddik was an aspect of the Great Light." The lesser light is the moon, the great light is the sun; moon and sun together represent the unification of the lower wisdom and the higher wisdom.

The Hasidim believe that in every generation these two tzaddiks exist. "Thus the Baal Shem Tov says that if he had come together with Rabbi Chaim ibn Atar . . . they could have brought the Messiah." This was also "the meeting of Moses and Joshua, as our sages teach, 'Moses' face was like the sun, while Joshua's face was like the moon' " (*Bava Batra* 75a).[7]

The imagery of lesser light and greater light reflects

Rabbi Nachman's deeper sense of his connection to Rabbi Nathan. When they first met he told him mysteriously, "We've known each other for a long time, but we haven't seen each other recently!" Their souls had met in previous lives. They were like Moses and Joshua. One implication is that Rabbi Nachman knew that Rabbi Nathan would live on after his death to carry out his mission.

Kafka's new style in "The Judgment" adds a fantastic depth to a realistic surface. But all of Rabbi Nachman's tales, at the fourth or secret level (*sod*), allude to a vast scope of time and space, the grand Lurianic myth of creation and redemption.

The lesson of Rabbi Nachman's tale is that the rift between generations allows the devil to leap in and cause a delay in redemption. And starting with Rabbi Nachman's time, there were a series of rifts between generations. First came the conflict between *mitnaged* fathers and Hasidic sons, then, with the *haskalah*, the rift between religious fathers and secular sons. And finally, the strange predicament of Kafka's generation: Jews who upset their assimilated fathers by becoming too Jewish.

18

In His Father's House

Kafka was intensively searching for a connection to Jewishness in the two years leading up to "The Judgment." In his diary in January 1912, he exulted in his recent Jewish enthusiasm. He'd just read "500 pages" of Pines's *History of German-Jewish Literature* "with such thoroughness, haste and joy as I have never yet shown in the case of similar books." Kafka took notes. "*Haskalah* movement introduced by Mendelssohn at the beginning of the nineteenth century, adherents are called *Maskilim*. . . . Principle formulated by Gordon: 'Be a man on the street and a Jew at home.' "

But within Kafka's lifetime, Judah Leib Gordon's old *haskalah* formula broke down completely.

"A Jew at home"—but what kind of Jew? "A man in the streets"—but the streets were full of Jew-haters. Already at age fourteen, Kafka could have seen Czech mobs in 1897 attacking "German and Jewish shops, houses and cafes" in the Old Town Square. "Thousands of windows were broken, including those of the Brod family." "Stones were thrown at synagogues." "Hermann Kafka's shop was spared because his surname was not obviously Jewish. "Leave Kafka alone," the rioters called, "he's a Czech."[1] Ominous political developments made assimilation seem increasingly untenable all over Europe. The fires that would eventually burn Jewish books and Jewish bodies could already be spotted in the streets of Europe, at least by some eyes.

In Paris, the journalist Theodor Herzl was shocked by the virulence of anti-Jewish mobs following the Dreyfus trial of 1894. The next year he saw an open Jew-hater elected mayor of Herzl's native Vienna. After these episodes, he gave up entirely on assimilation and devoted himself to political Zionism.

Similarly, Jewish students in Prague founded the Bar Kochba Society in response to the 1897 riots there. It became the most influential Zionist organization in central Europe. A year later, mobs once again "rampaged through the old city in Prague, overturning stalls and attacking shops," this time because of ritual murder accusations made against an unemployed Bohemian Jew, Leopold Hilsner. Pamphlets and newspaper articles declared that the victim's blood had been used in Passover matzos. Fourteen times, between 1867 and 1914, these weird medieval accusations roiled the Austro-Hungarian empire.*

Biographer Frederick Karl locates Kafka's plight in social terms: "The uncertainty he felt whenever he contemplated reality was matched by the uncertainty of the Jew in an enemy setting, among Germans, whose language he spoke, and among Czechs, whose nationalism had no role for the Jew to play."

But the Jewish community itself was badly divided.

---

*The 1911 Beilis case, a ritual murder trial in Ukraine, deeply impressed Kafka, who wrote a play about it while living with Dora; she burned the play.

"There were those who spoke no Czech"; there were Zionists and socialists, "hostile . . . to Zionism"; "those who sought assimilation as good Germans within the Czech setting; and those who, like the elder Kafka, straddled the fence" between Czechs and Germans.[2] "The question of assimilation . . . created in itself an ambiguous kind of reality, often more hallucinatory than realistic."

As a schoolboy Kafka flirted with socialism and became "almost fanatically opposed to both Zionism and Judaism." But in the year before the great fire, he became "deeply interested in both."[3] He imagined this new interest might heal the rupture with his father, but when Kafka spoke with enthusiasm about Jewish texts, his father became enraged. "Through my intervention Judaism became abhorrent to you, Jewish writings unreadable; they 'nauseated' you."[4] Hermann was a loyal veteran of the imperial Austrian army, a staunch assimilationist, and a successful one, too. He did not want his son to become more religious or more Zionist than he was.

Kafka's conflict with his father was exacerbated because he lived in his house through his twenties and thirties. This was not entirely unusual for a bachelor son in a bourgeois Jewish family at the time. So long as he remained unmarried he was not really free of his father's judgments. After his sister Elli married in the fall of 1910, Kafka shared the home with his parents, his sisters Valli and Ottla, and a servant. In a short comic piece published in the Prague literary journal, he describes himself in his room "in the headquarters of noise of the whole apartment." The oven door bangs, doors slam, and his father "bursts through the door" of his room and "passes through, his robe trailing." His sister Valli shouts about "whether Father's hat has been cleaned yet" and by the time he leaves, shutting the door "with a dull manly bang," Kafka imagines opening his door a tiny crack and slithering "into the next room like a snake."[5]

Kafka's metamorphosis into a reptile signals a disturbing breakdown of identity. He did not have a room of his own in the house until he was twenty-four, and the room he got then was more like a corridor from his parent's bedroom to the shared bath. He was squeamish and finicky, and felt constant disgust, loathing, and self-loathing. He was horrified by any intimations of his parents' sexuality, such as their bedclothes on their bed. His father's slurping and chomping food made a vegetarian out of him. His father's booming voice could be heard everywhere. To get away from the house, he made frequent short trips with Brod, or on business, to Germany, to Paris. His sex life was furtive: his first sexual experience was with a Czech shopgirl; he also frequented brothels and had short-lived affairs on his travels or at various sanatoria, well outside his family's purview. His two formal engagements to Felice were another matter, and Hermann strongly disapproved, believing his son was not financially ready to be married. In other words, Hermann did not believe his son was ready to be a man.

Hermann was big and solid, physically powerful, voluble and opinionated. Guests were received by the whole family and then judged. When Kafka brought home his closest friend, Max Brod, who had strong Jewish interests, Hermann denounced him in Yiddish as a *"meshuggener ritoch,"*[6] a crazy hothead. Kafka suppressed his reactions. He even felt guilty for recording the incident in his diary. "I should not have written it down, for I have written myself almost into a hatred of my father."

Kafka rarely responded directly to Hermann's tirades.

But when Hermann insulted another Jewish friend, the Yiddish actor Yitzhak Lowy, Kafka could not contain himself "and said something uncontrolled. To which Father with unusual quietness (to be sure, after a long interval which was otherwise occupied): 'You know that I should not get excited and must be treated with consideration. And now you speak to me like that. I really have enough excitement. Quite enough. So don't bother me with such talk.' I say: 'I make every effort to restrain myself' . . ."[7] After a similar incident: "Father quarreled on, I stood silently at the window."[8]

Kafka's father had high blood pressure and heart problems. No one was allowed to "excite" him. So he could attack his son, and then hide behind his medical condition. Because Kafka felt he could not respond directly, the wounds with his father festered. That is why even in his last year with Dora he still spoke of freeing himself from "ghosts."

The day he emanated into my study, I was reading Kafka's aphorism that begins, "It isn't necessary that you leave home." He never really did. Yes, he traveled frequently, spent summers in sanatoria, or with his beloved sister Ottla. But he did not move to a flat of his own until he was thirty-two, and two years later he was living at home again. Emotionally he remained a prisoner in his father's house.

That did not keep him from searching for a new Jewish home, a search that came as Jews from Eastern Europe were leaving theirs. Driven by persecution and pogroms, deteriorating economic conditions, and then World War I, Yiddish-speaking Jews from Hasidic backgrounds flooded into Berlin and Prague. They carried with them a wealth of *Yiddishkeit*, of religious practice, story, tradition, and lore. To Hermann and Julie Kafka the Eastern Jews were unwelcome reminders of a past they'd left behind. But Kafka and his friends were strongly attracted to them.

In fall 1911, Kafka became infatuated with a scruffy troupe of Yiddish actors performing in cafés in Prague. He fell in love with one of the actresses and became fast friends with the leader of the troupe. That is how Yitzhak Lowy came into his life. Lowy was from an Hasidic family in Warsaw and Hermann hated him. He once called him an *ungezeifer*, a vermin. Hermann disliked Lowy for his overt Jewishness and also compared him to a dog with fleas.

Kafka reacted to Hermann's harsh vituperation by doing all he could to champion Lowy, his troupe, and the Yiddish language his parents despised as "jargon." Kafka cataloged his activities on their behalf: "I spent a lot of time with the Jewish actors, wrote letters for them, prevailed on the Zionist society to inquire of the Zionist societies of Bohemia whether they would like to have guest appearances of the troupe; I wrote the circular that was required and had it reproduced; saw Sulamith [a Yiddish play] once more."[9] Kafka later gave an elaborate lecture on the glories of Yiddish at the Jewish Town Hall, as an introduction to the glories of Lowy's Yiddish theater. It was a public effort unlikely to please his parents.

Gershom Scholem wrote:

> The more we encountered the not at all infrequent rejection of Eastern European Jewry in our own families, the more strongly we were attracted to this very

kind of Jewishness. I am not exaggerating when I say that in those years, particularly during the war and shortly thereafter, there was something like a cult of Eastern Jews among the Zionists. All of us had read Martin Buber's first two volumes about Hasidism, the *Tales of Rabbi Nachman* and *The Legend of the Baal Shem*, which had appeared a few years earlier and had made Buber very famous. In every Jew we encountered from Russia, Poland or Galicia we saw something like a reincarnation of the Baal Shem Tov or at any rate of an undisguised Jewishness that fascinated us.[10]

Martin Buber, the Viennese-born philosopher and Jewish thinker, played a major role in this period for Kafka's generation as a bridge between East and West, and as a Zionist theorist. His grandfather Solomon Buber was a strong influence, an important scholar of midrash who lived in Lemberg (Lviv) where Buber spent most of his summers. In Prague Buber's version of cultural Zionism was a favorite of the leaders of the Bar Kochba Society, including Kafka's friend Hugo Bergmann. Cultural Zionism originated with Ahad Ha'am who emphasized the spiritual and cultural side of the return to Palestine, while Herzl focused more on the political. Buber adapted Ha'am's ideas but stressed that the renewal would have to come in Europe before emigration.

Buber delivered three of his early "addresses on Judaism" at the Bar Kochba Society from 1909 to 1911, and Kafka attended two, probably the last two. Kafka, so sensitive and abstemious about language, was not particularly impressed with Buber's public lectures, which were full of broad generalities and romantic fervor. But the third lecture on Jewish renewal was widely attended and well received: Brod in particular was enthusiastic.

Gershom Scholem spoke for a majority view when he reflected on the "considerable magic" of these addresses. "I would be unable to mention any other book about Judaism of these years which even came close to having such an effect . . . among a youth that here heard the summons to a new departure ."[11]

At the third lecture in Prague, Kafka would have heard Buber's call for a "Jewish renewal." "Propitious ground for the radical shake-up that must precede such a total renewal" would be provided by "the great ambivalence, the boundless despair, the infinite longing and pathetic inner chaos of many of today's Jews."[12] Buber knew his audience and when it came to "pathetic inner chaos" he could have been describing the state of Kafka's soul.

What Buber could not have known at that time was the narrow space within which Kafka struggled. He lived within his father's confines in every sense. The great fire and all its intensity was necessarily concentrated into the writing of a single night, while his family safely slept. How then could Kafka enact anything so grand as Buber's vision of reinventing Judaism, when he couldn't even leave home?

19

Annihilation of the Self

Because he could not openly rebel, Kafka's experience of being undermined by his father was bottomless. At any moment he could collapse, just as Georg does in "The Judgment" in the face of his father's withering attack. Or he could imagine himself being tortured and punished, or losing his human identity altogether and slipping into an animal form, a slithering snake, a dog, a mole. His soul lived loose in his body. His experience of emotional annihilation brought him near to the inner world of Rabbi Nachman.

In Hasidic thought, the "annihilation of self" (*bittul ha-yesh*) is a spiritual aspiration. The Hasid who desires nearness to God—*devekut*—must eliminate the "somethingness" (the *yesh*) of the self, for the solidity of the ego only gets in the way of complete communion with God. Being nothing in this sense was something—a desirable spiritual attainment. It was a complete surrender but it was also necessarily painful, for it meant discarding and separating from cherished parts of oneself, proud accomplishments, and beloved attachments. The similar Christian term gives a sense of the difficulty: dying to self.

Kafka knew the pain of dying. Whatever he gained in his nocturnal writing of the indubitable was constantly gnawed away by his daily sense of inadequacy. This gnawing carved out the "hollow space" that "divided" him from all things. In the letter to his father, he says that "this sense of nothingness that often dominates me . . . comes largely from your influence."

He traced this feeling back to childhood.

What I would have needed was a little encouragement, a little friendliness, a little keeping open of my road. . . . I was after all weighed down by your mere physical presence. I remember, for instance how we often undressed in the same bathing hut. There was I, skinny, weakly, slight; you strong, tall, broad. Even inside the hut I felt a miserable specimen, and what's more, not only in your eyes, but in the eyes of the whole world, for you were for me the measure of all things. But then when we stepped out of the bathing hut before the people, you holding me by my hand, a little skeleton, unsteady, barefoot on the boards, frightened of the water, incapable of copying your swimming strokes, which you, with the best of intentions, but actually to my profound humiliation, always kept on showing me, then I was frantic with desperation and at such moments, all my bad experiences in all spheres fitted magnificently together.[1]

Moments of intense inadequacy are normal feelings for boys. Normally such inadequacy can be relieved by a father's reassurance, but Hermann was more rough than tender. Franz the son also played his part. He had so much pent-up resentment that, even when his father did reach out, he was incapable of receiving him. Most people take

Joseph K.'s side in *The Trial*, and Kafka's side in the argument with his father. They take both men to be innocent victims. Readers tend to project their own trouble with fathers onto Kafka's.

Because Kafka found it "not necessary to leave home," he prolonged his "uncertainty" to the end of his days. He used his diary to track it. In May 1913 he opened a new notebook and wrote, "It has become necessary to keep a diary again. The *uncertainty* of my thoughts, F[elice]., the ruin in the office, the physical impossibility of writing and the inner need for it." The next day: "The terrible *uncertainty* of my inner existence." Six months later, "I am more *uncertain* than I ever was." In February 1914, Kafka observed, "The notebook begins with F. [Felice Bauer] who on 2 May 1913 made me feel uncertain; this same beginning can serve as conclusion too if in place of *'uncertain'* I use a worse word."[2]

Probably by "worse word" he means "suicidal." Uncertainty led Kafka down the avenue of masochistic fantasies and suicidal thoughts.

Shortly after his father so harshly condemned his two closest Jewish friends, Brod and Lowy, Kafka wrote, "This morning, for the first time in a long time, the joy again of imagining a knife twisted in my heart."[3] That is how Joseph K. is dispatched at the end of *The Trial*.

Joseph K. is laid out on a boulder in a quarry. The knife is passed back and forth above him. It very much evokes the hesitation just before the sacrifice of Isaac, when a divine intervention stays Abraham's hand, which also holds a knife. Kafka felt these scenes so deeply with his own pain that his writing reconnects us to the stark scene in Genesis.

Kafka frequently fantasized self-torture as a kind of

strange relief. One day he wrote in his diary: "To be pulled in through the ground-floor window of a house by a rope tied around one's neck and to be yanked up, bloody and ragged through all the ceilings, furniture walls and attics without consideration, as if by a person who is paying no attention, until the empty noose dropping the last fragments of me when it breaks through the roof tiles, is seen on the roof."[4]

The same kind of material found its way into his fiction. "In the Penal Colony," written in the first great period after "The Judgment," describes a torture device in which long needles slowly but inexorably write a sentence into the victim's back. The needles sink deeper and deeper as the clumsy machine vibrates, until as he expires the prisoner comes to understand what is being written on his flesh: the commandment he disobeyed.

In Hebrew a covenant is not written but "cut," and the original covenant or *brit* between God and Abraham is cut into the flesh of the penis. The circumcision Kafka observed may have seemed an outdated ceremony, but "In the Penal Colony" combines a covenant cut into the flesh with the High Holiday imagery of God writing a judgment in a book.

Kafka's exquisite and elaborated masochism gave him a sense of control over difficult feelings: the fantasies of punishment relieved the guilt, guilt arose from anger, anger was a reaction to inadequacy. His dreams in that period also display these feelings, such as the following from May 1912:

> I was riding with my father through Berlin in a trolley. . . . We came to a gate, got out without any sense of getting out, stepped through the gate. On the other

side of the gate a sheer wall rose up, which my father ascended almost in a dance, his legs flew out as he climbed, so easy was it for him. There was certainly also some inconsiderateness in the fact that he did not help me one bit, for I got to the top only with the utmost effort, on all fours, often sliding back again, as though the wall had become steeper under me. At the same time it was also distressing that the wall was covered with human excrement so that flakes of it clung to me, chiefly to my breast. I looked down at the flakes with bowed head and ran my hand over them.

When at last I reached the top, my father, who by this time was already coming out of a building, immediately fell on my neck and kissed and embraced me.[5]

Hermann dances up the wall, Kafka struggles. "There was certainly also some inconsiderateness in the fact that he did not help me one bit." But he doesn't ask his father to help. He doesn't want to feel his inadequacy as a son, so he covers it with resentment. Why is the wall covered with "human excrement"? This represents shame and guilt because of his anger.

The dream hints at reconciliation. After he climbs the wall, his father embraces him and kisses him. But Kafka can't accept his embrace; there's already too much shit on the wall, that is, he is too preoccupied with anger, shame, and guilt to receive his father's love.

This cycle of feelings animates his fiction, with its accusers and accused, its shamers and victims. By day, Kafka felt his "uncertainty." At night, he released the deeper feelings into the great fire.

Kafka's experience with his father was private, but its intensity reverberates with the social and religious uncertainty of his entire generation of Jews. Looked at from our perspective, these young Jews of Prague had reason to feel uncertainty; perhaps in some way they were sensing what was to come. Those who did not find it "necessary to leave home" died there; those who chose a new life in Palestine lived.

B uber hoped this "inner chaos" of Western Jews would lead them to a new Judaism.

Buber lived in generalities and had his eye on grand movements of religious history. In his version of "cultural Zionism" from 1909 to 1911, he called for a Jewish renewal as the first step Western Jews could take to the promised land. They could act as Zionists right away, where they were, before emigrating. Buber saw no point in preserving old religious forms in the "old-new" land of Israel. Before packing their suitcases, he wanted his audience of young assimilated Jews to skip back a generation and reconnect with the power of an absolute "ur-Judaism," a primal Judaism. Gershom Scholem observed that "in his Addresses on Judaism" Buber took Zionism in "a new markedly religious-romantic direction, confronting a 'religion' grown rigid in form with a 'religiosity' that would be creative and truly central."[6] This romantic approach was wildly popular for a time.

Buber recast the history of Judaism purely as a dynamic spiritual process. Instead of an age-old conflict between generations, he saw a conflict between forces and forms, "religiosity" and "religion." (Buber's abstraction is typical of his rhetoric.) By "religiosity" Buber meant the spiritual intensity of direct religious experience, by "religion" the rituals and codified practices. The prophets and the Hasidim were both models for "religiosity." He wanted to steal the fire of the Baal Shem Tov and Rabbi Nachman for a new generation, but without taking on their Torah way of life. (Of course, this would have seemed anathema to them.) To Buber, specific religious practices were merely "forms." Buber never practiced observant Judaism and as for Kafka, there was also no question of his becoming a *ba'al teshuvah* or any sort of practicing Jew.

Religiosity without religion was certainly an attractive formula for the children of assimilated parents who, like Kafka, had only "insignificant scraps" of Judaism handed on to them. Though as a schoolboy Kafka took an atheist position in an argument with Hugo Bergmann, he was closer to what today we would call a "spiritual person." Writing Felice in 1913 he echoes Buber's distinctions between direct religious experience and formal observance:[7] "Have you ever, without giving the slightest thought to anyone else, been in despair simply about yourself? Desperate enough to throw yourself on the ground and remain there beyond the Day of Judgment? How devout are you? You go to the synagogue; but I dare say you have not been recently. And what is it that sustains you, the idea of Judaism or of God?"

Like Buber, Kafka contrasts religion and religiosity, "Judaism" and "God." Real devotion arises from deeply felt need. Spirituality was not defined by synagogue observance, but by a relationship to God.

"Are you aware, and this is the most important thing, of a continuous relationship between yourself and a reassuringly distant, if possibly infinite height or depth? He who feels this continuously has no need to roam about like a lost dog, mutely gazing around with imploring eyes."

Kafka was dogged by his disconnection from his father or from God. He frequently felt that lost dog feeling. "Like a dog!" is Joseph K.'s dying exclamation at the end of *The Trial* and it seems like a verdict on his whole life, "as if the shame would outlive him." The dog reappears as a narrator in "Investigations of a Dog." Kafka also saw the dog in his constant "active introspection." He wished he could put up with himself more calmly, "to live as one must, not to chase one's tail like a dog."[8]

He certainly never felt "a continuous relationship" with the infinite. Yet he dreams of it, which suggests that his encounters with Hasidism must have struck home. As a man "made of literature," the deepest way he could have been touched was by story, and his deepest Jewish encounter was with the most compressed of all Jewish story forms, the Hasidic parable.

20

On the Train to Kamenetz

Thursday Evening, September 25

Kamenetz-Podolsk is 295 miles from Kyiv, about seven hours by "fast" train. But after our adventures in the Kyiv metro, Professor Yohanan Petrovsky-Shtern and I boarded the slow train that left Kyiv at 8:30 in the evening and would arrive eleven hours later. There would be plenty of time to talk and tell stories, if I couldn't sleep.

Yohanan and I shared a couchette, which sleeps four: two sets of narrow bunk beds, top and bottom. The conductor supplied us with blanket, pad, pillow, pillowcase, tissues. He had a round head, wide eyes, like a doll's head, and a perpetually astonished look. We were joined by a mother and daughter. The conductor brought hot tea in glasses in metal frames. The mother broke a chocolate and shared it. I shared dried fruit. Yohanan and I slipped out into the corridor to give them some privacy while they prepared to sleep. As we rocked along in the corridor, Yohanan told me he was writing a book about shtetls. He sees Uman as in some ways a reenactment of the nineteenth-century shtetl Rosh Hashanah because he feels it carries the original vitality of Hasidic enthusiasm.

I was carrying Franz Kafka with me, who is not known for

unbridled enthusiasm: the black coffee mug, and in my backpack, his first slim book, *Meditation*.

Kafka belonged to my grandfather's generation, and if fate had worked differently, they might have sailed together on the same ship from Hamburg in 1906. Instead of reading Rabbi Nachman's tales that year, Kafka and my grandfather could have struck up a friendship on board. But maybe not. In many ways my grandfather was probably more like Hermann than Franz: he came to America to work and left behind the old country as Hermann left Wossek for Prague. As a twenty-two year-old immigrant from Eastern Europe, my grandfather hit the American ground running. My grandmother lit Friday-night candles, but my grandfather went to work the next day. There was no sign of Sabbath in my house. My grandfather would say "thanks God" if something good happened, but I don't' recall hearing about God from my father, Irvin. As far as Jewish material went, if Kafka complained of "insignificant scraps" from his father, mine gave me broken threads.

My father shed any traces of Orthodoxy that my grandfather hadn't shed already. When we went to synagogue on Yom Kippur, it was a rare occasion of father-son contact. He liked the duet between our Reform cantor and an invisible, probably blond, choirist, which he compared to the movie duets of Nelson Eddy and Jeanette MacDonald. As a boy I loved to hear about the big book where our sins were written, and the solemnity of "who by water and who by fire." But looking around at the comfortable middle-class congregation, I didn't imagine any of us in danger of dying by fire. That had happened in Europe before I was born; that was not for us in Baltimore.

Martin Buber was big in Reform Judaism in the fifties and

sixties. Every year the rabbi would tell the same story out of Buber's *Tales of the Hasidim* about an ignorant boy from the countryside who didn't know enough Hebrew to say a prayer. He brought his shepherd's whistle to the shul. At a crucial moment in the Yom Kippur service, when all the prayers for repentance in the shul were stuck outside the heavenly gate, the boy piped loud on his whistle. Because of his fervent whistling, the gates of repentance opened and the stacked-up prayers of the congregation were received, or so said the Baal Shem Tov, who seemed like a wonderfully forgiving, lax and jolly Jewish Santa Claus. We were the latest generation to buy into Buber's neo-Hasidism, fifty years after he first gave it to Kafka. This was ironic, for the good celebrants in Baltimore Hebrew Congregation would have had nothing to do with the actual Hasidim who lived down the avenue with their dark clothing and pious ways. The rabbi was flattering us for our ignorance. Or perhaps he was secretly making fun of us. We may not know Hebrew like the Orthodox, the story seemed to say, but a blow on a penny whistle would show even more fervor than the Orthodox, and then the gates of prayer would open. As Reform Jews that was how we understood Buber.

My companion Yohanan did not suffer from ignorance. Because he'd been born in Kyiv, he was who I might have been, had my grandfather stayed and we'd somehow survived World War II. He knew Russian, Ukrainian, Yiddish, and Hebrew and was a hundred times more knowledgeable about the old country than I could ever be. Yet he was kind enough to accompany me and save me all sorts of trouble and embarrassments. We were pilgrims together, to Uman and to Kamenetz, where I was a pilgrim to my name.

Were we going up or down? The train seemed to be moving sideways when it moved at all, across flat territory. But in terms of the soul, you are always moving up or down: there is the descent and the ascent, the *yeridah* and *aliyah*. So properly, one is either a *yored* or an *oleh*, a descender or an ascender. Today making aliyah most often means becoming a citizen of the state of Israel, while *yeridah* means leaving that country. But in origin the terms are purely spiritual: wherever we are traveling there is a spiritual map that tells us our souls are traveling toward or away from the Holy Land, for as the Talmud says, "The Land of Israel is higher than other countries." The Holy Land is the ultimate ascent for the sake of which Rabbi Nachman made his initial descent into Kamenetz.

There's another wrinkle: after Kamenetz we were going to the grave of a tzaddik. According to a teaching of Rabbi Nachman's, the grave of a tzaddik has a status equal to the land of Israel. It's like the status an embassy has in a foreign country. Thus even in Uman, if one comes to the grave of Rabbi Nachman, one would be making an aliyah.

But what did I hope to see in Uman? "Even you have never seen the king," says the *maskil* to the messenger in one of Rabbi Nachman's tales.* No one alive has ever seen the face of Rabbi Nachman either.

So for the sake of burnt books that no one can ever read, I would travel with Yohanan to the grave of a rabbi who has no face. I wondered out loud to him what good it would do. I mentioned my encounter in Frankfurt airport with Yaakov of Savannah, who told me that Rebbe Nachman is the *tzaddik ha-dor*, the tzaddik of our time.

"In Uman Bratslavers like him are a minority," Yohanan

*Cf. Chapter 22, pp. 174–177.

said. "There are Sephardim, religious Zionists, other Hasidim, non-Hasidim, modern Orthodox, and oddball Jews like you and me."

—Why do they come?

"Some come because they are credulous. They believe the voice of Rabbi Nachman is the voice of God."

—And you?

"I don't come because I believe this. But I come because of them."

Those Yohanan called "credulous" were no doubt more like Rabbi Nachman's spiritual ideal of the simple Jew, the simple person of faith. Yet though a very accomplished scholar, Yohanan felt he had something to learn from them as well. Not only for scholarly reasons. He wanted to be near their passion, I think, their old-time vigor, their faith and belief in the Rebbe. Their fire.

To Rabbi Nachman the problem of modernity is that God is now doubly hidden. Not only, he teaches, is God hidden by God's very nature, but in addition, due to our intellectual sophistication, it is hidden from us that God is hidden. We can't sense the invisible anymore. Oddly, the only people who talk about consciousness are the physicists. Our psychology, which by etymology should be the "study of the soul," has given up the mind as well.

Then there's also our pain. Our Jewish history is painful and pain produces logic. Logic says, How can you ask me to believe in a good and mighty king, after the fires of the Holocaust? How can you talk about an invisible king, who is supposedly good and mighty and humble?

The Holocaust stops every movement toward faith in its tracks, as we were stuck just now, somewhere in Ukraine in the darkness.

Yohanan and I stood talking for hours in the narrow corridor so we wouldn't disturb our traveling companions. The train wasn't moving, yet we were still talking about God and rebbes, as two centuries ago Hasidim did on the long carriage rides from Medvedevka to Breslov, from Breslov to Uman. Were we both reincarnations, *gilgulim* of two old-time Hasidim? Rabbi Nachman believed himself to be a *gilgul* of Rabbi Simeon Bar Yohai, the author of the Zohar. As Yohanan and I talked, it came to me that there'd been one more turning of the wheel. Seeking to complete his mission to secular Jews, Rabbi Nachman got himself reborn as Franz Kafka. He hoped to continue his outreach to secular Jews as a literary master, embedding within his strange stories gleams of the mystical truth. Unfortunately, born in Kafka's body, he'd sunk further down and could no longer ascend to the higher wisdom. At the most, he could only stand outside the gate and point to the light.

I didn't share this heretical tale with Yohanan, but I told it to myself as the train lurched into motion.

21

Hasidic Parables

Walter Benjamin wrote, "Kafka had a rare capacity to create parables for himself." He was referring to Kafka's last notes to Brod, and to Kafka's propensity to get lost in mazes of introspection. But there's another sense of Benjamin's remark. Parable as a literary form is where Kafka found a home. Rabbi Nachman was also a master of parable and an innovator in the form. It so happens that they wrote parables on common themes: looking at them side-by-side, a deeper sense of connection emerges.

Did it come through a direct literary influence? Kafka first read Buber's version of the tales sometime after their publication in 1906, and it would be wonderful for the story of burnt books if one could prove that Rabbi Nachman's tales inspired Kafka. But that does not appear to be the case. Kafka read some of the tales, but Buber's reservations about Nachman's style, and Kafka's reservations about Buber's, put static in the transmission.

So in terms of literary influence, one would have to look more broadly. During his years of Jewish exploration Kafka read and reread Hasidic parables, midrash, Talmud, Yiddish stories, and Jewish folktales. He also encountered these texts through lectures, at the theater, in performances at the

Bar Kochba Society, in his correspondence, and through long talks with Max Brod, Yitzhak Lowy, and Jiri Langer. He became so interested in midrash that he told Brod in a letter exactly how he would rewrite a "Talmud story" in Tractate *Sukkah*.

All this immersion in the "Jewish writings" that so appalled Hermann brought one definitive result: Kafka completely absorbed the Hasidic parable and made it new. Auden rightly called him "the modern master of the parable." Since Rabbi Nachman also reshaped the Hasidic parable, the two men share a common root. To understand this more extensively, it's worth making a detour into the general importance of story in Hasidism, and the significance of story in Judaism in general.

Rabbi Nachman's love of story came in childhood in Medzhibozh, where he soaked in fabulous tales of rebbes from traveling Hasidim communing at his great-grandfather's grave. These miracle stories were "tales of the seventy," set in the shtetl, drawn from everyday life, very Jewish stories of rebbes and students, synagogues and prayers, kosher butchers, merchants, rich and poor. Rabbi Nachman believed that hearing tales of the tzaddikim was spiritually beneficial. But primarily—"The Rabbi's Son" is one exception—his own tales don't resemble these legends.

Instead, his tales are expanded parables, in some cases parables stuffed with parables. The last tale, the seven-part "Seven Beggars," bulges like a sack of jewels.

Rabbi Nachman believed he drew these concentrated "tales of the ancient of days" from a higher wisdom. They tap into a deep archetypal imagination, the underneath of dream and fantasy.

They are a last and luxuriant flowering of the storytelling impulse that was at the origin of the Hasidic movement. The rebbes, beginning with the Baal Shem Tov, understood the religious power of story, the essential importance to religion of literary imagination.

In the early years of Hasidism, this meant a return to oral teaching through tales. Most Hasidim were not fully literate in Hebrew. Stories traveled by word of mouth in Yiddish and spread the Hasidic spirit like wildfire through the shtetls of Ukraine. Stories, parables, and Torah teachings all blended in the work of the itinerant preacher, the maggid. Several Hasidic masters were professional *maggidim*. The Maggid of Tarhovitze, the Hasid of Rabbi Nachman's who was so enthusiastic about the burnt book's teaching, was a student of the Maggid of Mezritch. That an erudite kabbalist like Dov Ber was known by that title indicates the great shift in emphasis in early Hasidism from *halakhah* to *aggadah*, from law to story.

This requires a story. The Hasidim tell of a rebbe who has two visitors arrive at the same time. One was an important scholar, a *rov*, the other a wandering storyteller, a maggid. The rebbe told his attendant to send the shabby storyteller in first, while the *rov* cooled his heels. Later his attendant asked why the rebbe saw the storyteller first. The rebbe said, "I did it the way God does it in the Torah. First he tells stories, then he gives laws."

This story has a root in Rashi, the greatest Torah explicator. At the very beginning of his masterful commentary, he asks why the Torah begins with "In the beginning . . ."? Why does a book of laws begin with a story? Rashi answers that a time will come when Gentiles will say that the Jews

stole the land of Israel. The Jews will answer with Genesis
1:1. In the beginning God created the . . . earth . . . and he can
give it to whomever he chooses.[1]

Judaism is often seen as a dry legalistic tradition. But
Rashi's midrash shows how at the very beginning, story is a
fundament, not an ornament. In *Between God and Man* Rabbi
Abraham Joshua Heschel writes:

> It is impossible to decide whether in Judaism
> supremacy belongs to *halakhah* or to *aggadah*, to the
> lawgiver or to the Psalmist. The rabbis may have
> sensed the problem. Rav said: "The world was created
> for the sake of David, so that he might sing hymns and
> psalms to God." Samuel said: "The world was created
> for the sake of Moses, so that he might receive the
> Torah" (Babylonian Talmud Sanhedrin 98b). There is
> no *halakhah* without *aggadah*, and no *aggadah* without
> *halakhah*. We must neither disparage the body nor sac-
> rifice the spirit.
>
> To maintain that the essence of Judaism consists
> exclusively of *halakhah* is as erroneous as to maintain
> that the essence of Judaism consists exclusively of
> *aggadah*. The interrelationship of *halakhah* and *aggadah*
> is the very heart of Judaism. *Halakhah* without *aggadah*
> is dead, *aggadah* without *halakhah* is wild."[2]

Heschel is drawing on a 1916 essay by the Hebrew poet
Bialik who famously argued in "Halakhah and *Aggadah*"
that far from being opposites, "Halakhah and *Aggadah* are
two things which are really one, two sides of a single
shield."[3] Bialik is radical and deep in his view. To him
halakhah is not dry and dusty, for the precepts of the law are

rooted in earthy fact. Hidden in every *halakhah* is an *aggadah*, just as *aggadah* is the ground for *halakhah*.

Story and law alternate in all Jewish sacred literature beginning with the Bible; this is the marker for Jewish literary DNA. Even in the tiniest literary form, the biblical proverb, story and statement are compressed into a single gesture. The Talmud, conventionally seen as pure law, is also marbled with stories. Likewise, a two-part structure defines the classic Talmudic parable. The story element is called the *mashal* and the meaning is the *nimshal*.*

The Talmudic *mashal* is an oral form that arose from face-to-face teaching by the early rabbis, who drew on down-to-earth metaphors to describe heavenly realms. In Talmudic *meshalim*, God is a father, more often a king. In Rabbi Oshaia Rabbah's classic midrash on Genesis 1:1, God consults with the Torah to create the universe as a king consults an architect to build his palace. This is the preexisting supernal Torah, from which Rabbi Nachman drew down his own "*torot*."

The Talmudic *mashal* deploys stock characters: kings and messengers, wise man and fools. These reappear in the Hasidic *mashal*, but the most forceful examples turn these conventions upside down. In them, the beggar is a tzaddik, the fool is actually wise.[4]

According to Rabbi Aryeh Wineman's study, *The Hasidic Parable*, the signature of Hasidic parable is paradox. The rebbes took the old Talmudic parable tradition and shook it up. One Hasidic *mashal* retold by Martin Buber offers a thief

---

*Confusingly, "*mashal*" also means "parable" in general; the plural is *meshalim*.

as a spiritual model. "Every lock has its key which fits into and opens it. . . . So every mystery in the world can be unriddled by the particular kind of meditation fitted to it. But God loves the thief who breaks the lock open: I mean, the man who breaks his heart for God."[5]

Often during the third meal of the Sabbath, the Hasidic masters gave a Torah lesson, based on the weekly portion, weaving parables into their homilies. The *mashal* condensed and simplified the rebbe's Torah. While some rebbes viewed the *mashal* primarily as illustration, Kafka's favorite master, Dov Ber, saw something more profound in the form itself.

Parable to the Maggid of Mezritch is not an accidental literary flourish, but an essential process in the universe, for Dov Ber taught that just as a father condenses his wisdom into a story to help his child understand it on his own terms, so God the storyteller contracted the supernal wisdom into the stories and laws of the written Torah. The supernal Torah is as an ineffable, nonmaterial, black flame written on white flame. Only as written Torah might it begin to be grasped by the finite mind. In the Maggid's interpretation, this deliberate contraction of supernal Torah into written is a manifestation of the *tzimtzum*.

"Parable and *tzimtzum*, as understood by the Maggid, mirror one another and ultimately exemplify a single process."[6] The Maggid's interpretation of *tzimtzum* goes along with the Hasidic idea that in truth there is no place absent of God. But there's a dispute among Jewish mystics about this very point. In Lurianic kabbalah—and there's a similar sense in Rabbi Nachman's teachings—*tzimtzum* is felt as a complete absence of the divine, a "for real" emptiness. For Dov Ber, the absence is a perception from the human side only and *tzimtzum* is actually a concealment more than a complete absence. Thus for Dov Ber the *mashal*, like *tzimtzum* itself, is both hidden and revealed, concealed and manifest at once. The parable may appear entirely dark to those who cannot see into it, but it contains a light.

What appears to be an empty space between the human and the divine is actually filled by story. In psychological terms, the unconscious may appear to be an empty or dark and confusing space, hence Buber's "inner chaos" and Kafka's "uncertainty." Only when this uncertainty acquires a narrative does it become a *mashal*, which can be given a meaning, a *nimshal*. That is why hearing stories can become so significant, for they "give to airy nothing a local habitation and a name,"[7] they resonate with our own inchoate stories and so awaken us to inner experience. The rebbes' particular gift was to know the right story to tell to awaken the right person. Rabbi Nachman's insistence that stories can heal is shared by all the Hasidic masters. In this regard, Freud is himself a kind of rebbe who provides for his client a tale that resonates with an inner *mashal*, of which the client may be consciously unaware. While he viewed his theories, such as the Oedipal complex, as scientific truths, today we understand them better as healing myths. As James Hillman tells it, in *Healing Fiction*, psychotherapy can be seen as a dialogue between therapist and client that produces a usable fiction that shapes the client's inchoate pain into a story. For only then can the story change.

The rebbes worked more quickly and intuitively, for they believed they could look into the eyes of each Hasid and know the root of his soul. So perhaps Rabbi Nachman meant it when he met Rabbi Nathan and said, "We have met before."

With that knowledge, the rebbe could choose the right story to tell him. When Rabbi Nachman told Rabbi Nathan that they were like Moses and Joshua, he created a parable that bound their lives together as master and disciple. "The Rabbi's Son" must have been a special effort to heal his Hasid's pain over his rift with his family. Each of us is looking to understand an inner *mashal* that speaks across the "hollow space" of our uncertainties.

That is why Kafka's adaptation of the Hasidic *mashal* for modernity is significant. He lived so deeply and constantly in his uncertainties for so long that the stories he drew from his dreamlike immersion resonate with a theological depth. He found in his own relationship to his father metaphors for the relationship to God. And these stories resonate for others who live in uncertainty. This in itself may account for the worldwide adoption of the Kafkaesque as a byword. But what binds him to Rabbi Nachman is not merely that they both wrote parables. It's that their parables speak to one another in a call and response. There is a secret communication between the Rebbe and the writer, particularly because each wrote a parable about the same theme, that of the king's messenger whose message cannot be received.

22

King and Messenger

In its original form, the Hasidic parable of the king and the messenger explores how God communicates with human beings. But—reflecting a new situation—Rabbi Nachman and Franz Kafka both give this theme a twist: what if a message is sent but cannot be received?

It's conceivable that Franz Kafka and Rabbi Nachman both drew on Dov Ber's parable, "The King's Two Messengers," which tells of a king who sends an angry soldier to summon a fool and a wise man. The fool is terrified by the soldier's angry display, but the wise man sees past it to "the fear and the awe of the king." The main point for the wise man is to hurry to the king. Another time the king sends a very jovial messenger. The fool dawdles with the messenger, but the wise man once more "goes directly to the king."

In the *nimshal*, which he makes explicit, the Maggid explains that the "messengers" represent emotions. Feeling love or feeling fear, a wise person will "elevate all" to the highest level, that is, to God. Not so the fool, who will wallow in his feelings instead of seeking their ultimate root.[1] Hasidic depth psychology derives from this entirely spiritual viewpoint. All feelings have their deepest roots in God. Our own psychology has moved in the opposite direction.

We don't see souls on their way to God, just brains on their way to the pharmacy.

For Dov Ber's Hasidim, a path opens between human feelings and the divine realm. Fear or joy can lead us back to God. But the path is broken for Kafka. His Jewish generation could no longer receive anything about God from their highly assimilated parents. The issue of broken transmission defines Kafka's parable, "An Imperial Message":[2]

> The Emperor—so they say—has sent a message, directly from his death bed, to you alone, his pathetic subject, a tiny shadow which has taken refuge at the furthest distance from the imperial sun.

"Emperor" and "pathetic subject," "sun" and "tiny shadow," Hermann and Franz. The trouble with his father becomes a trouble with God. As the dying emperor whispers a message in his herald's ear and dispatches him, the pathetic subject waits. And waits. For just here Kafka's *mashal* stretches out, a note of delay we'd never see in the Baal Shem Tov, with his parable of a thief smashing a lock.* Kafka reshapes the Hasidic parable to speak to his own difficulty at the tail end of a long tradition, where "religious forms which have reached their final end have merely a historical character."

> The messenger started off at once, a powerful, tireless man. Sticking one arm out and then another, he makes his way through the crowd. If he runs into resistance, he points to his breast where there is a sign

*Cf. Chapter 21, pp. 170–171.

of the sun. So he moves forward easily, unlike anyone else. But the crowd is so huge; its dwelling places are infinite. If there were an open field, how he would fly along, and soon you would hear the marvelous pounding of his fist on your door. But instead of that, how futile are all his efforts. He is still forcing his way through the private rooms of the innermost palace. Never will he win his way through. And if he did manage that, nothing would have been achieved. He would have to fight his way down the steps, and, if he managed to do that, nothing would have been achieved. He would have to stride through the courtyards, and after the courtyards through the second palace encircling the first, and, then again, through stairs and courtyards, and then, once again, a palace, and so on for thousands of years. And if he finally burst through the outermost door—but that can never, never happen—the royal capital city, the center of the world, is still there in front of him, piled high and full of sediment. No one pushes his way through here, certainly not someone with a message from a dead man. But you sit at your window and dream of that message when evening comes.

In Dov Ber, feelings arrive as messengers; in Kafka the messenger never quite arrives. Instead there's struggle and exhaustion and no end of anticipation. One scholar of the parable reads Kafka as expressing the "futility of understanding, the hopelessness of our interpretative efforts."[3] The *mashal* supports the reading. But a *nimshal* in the last line troubles it:

But you sit at your window and dream of that message when evening comes.

Kafka, the "miserable specimen" in the bath hut with his father, can be identified with "the pathetic subject" in the parable. But he also "dreams of the message" at the end. Kafka occupies two positions at once. He awaits the message and yet dreams the whole parable: emperor, subject, messenger, and message. Is there a frail element of hope in that imagination?

Of course Kafka's parable doesn't quite lead us anywhere. It, too, just sits and waits. It certainly does not provide the spiritual intensity Buber spoke of that would lead to a religious renewal. No one will be reciting "An Imperial Message"[4] in a shul, though for many Jews it might be a very honest place to begin. Because of its sense of disconnection. Because of its longing.

23

Uncertainty Principle

With quantum mechanics, indeterminacy moved to the heart of the physical universe. But it was already at the heart of Kafka's emotional universe. Einstein resisted quantum physics with all his heart, believing that "God does not play dice with the universe." He taught physics in Prague from 1911 to 1912 as Kafka was deep in his Jewish researches. Kafka may have met him at Berta Fanta's soirées; the wife of a pharmacist, she hosted theosophical discussions that both men attended. Or perhaps as Kafka walked past Charles University intent on one of Lowy's stories, Einstein stepped down the street for a coffee. Kafka died just before Heisenberg's famous work was published, but as an assimilated Jew Kafka already lived an emotional and social uncertainty principle. That is why his parables exhibit wave-particle duality, Jewish if looked at one way, German if another. Harold Bloom calls this literary indeterminacy "evasion," but that doesn't mean that interpretation is hopeless. There's a probability curve of meanings: once the reader makes a choice, the other meanings collapse.

To the Jewish element of king and messenger, there's the German in the "dying emperor," which references Nietzsche's parable of the "Death of God." Kafka was an avid reader of Nietzsche, but you can't quite pin him down as an atheist, either. His Jewish soul is a spiritual electron, nowhere and everywhere at once.[1]

If the messenger represents a feeling from God, it pushes forward, but "never will he win his way through." A resistance gets played out here, a grave force of dark matter opposing any forward motion. How can you follow the messenger back to the king if he never arrives? Kafka's permanent irony blocked him from ever acting directly on his feelings.

Kafka never fully differentiated his psychological and spiritual struggles. But he never fully participated in them either. He approached Zionism and avoided it; approached marriage and avoided it. He speaks in his diary of "coming closer" to a "spiritual battle," but it is as though it "were taking place in a clearing somewhere in the woods. I make my way into the woods, find nothing and out of weakness immediately hasten out again; often as I leave the woods I hear, or I think I hear, the clashing weapons of that battle. Perhaps the eyes of the warriors are seeking me through the darkness of the woods, but I know so little of them, and that little is deceptive."[2] The battle of the soul is real, but takes place in a darkness he can't bring himself to face directly.

Kafka refers to the soul several times in his aphorisms, though always using the oblique term "the indestructible." He is aware of the indestructible within himself, he says, but very uneasy about defining it further. He kept his soul in a black box, like Schrödinger's cat. If you open the box to look at it, there's a half chance it might disappear.

He says, in one aphorism, that felicity was "to believe in the indestructible in oneself and then not to go looking for it." That's the metaphysical joking Kafka specialized in. But despite his claim, not "looking for it" did not lead him to felicity.

Rabbi Nachman understood the problem of joking as a problem of the soul. As a rebbe, he was in the soul business. He looked after the souls of others, communed with the souls of the living and the dead. He tried to save as many as he could, including the souls of sophisticates like Kafka. A hundred years before the fact, Rabbi Nachman spoke to Kafka's spiritual dilemma in his own version of the "king and messenger."

Rabbi Nachman embeds his *mashal* in a longer tale, "The *Hakham* and the *Tam*," first told after his sojourn among the *maskilim* and doctors in Lemberg.[3] Rabbi Nachman was already setting his eyes on his final mission: outreach among the *maskilim* of Uman.

At his master's insistence, Rabbi Nathan published Rabbi Nachman's tales in a bilingual edition, Hebrew and Yiddish. The title, "The *Hakham* and the *Tam*," is vexed because in Hebrew, a *hakham* is a sage, but in Yiddish the *khokhem* is a would-be sage who in fact isn't very wise. To make matters worse, while *tam* in Hebrew is a simple man of faith, *tam* in Yiddish is a fool.[4] So "The *Hakham* and the *Tam*" offers multiple puzzles for a would-be English translator. You could call it "The Wise Man and the Simpleton," "The Clever Man and the Fool," or "The Sophisticate and the Man of Faith."

Dov Ber's parable plays the traditional conventions of the *mashal* straight: the wise man is wise, the fool is a fool. But Rabbi Nachman does not equate wisdom with intellectual sophistication. A first stab at reading the story suggests the

Yiddish *khokhem* and the Hebrew *tam*. The *khokhem* in the tale only thinks he's wise, but the *tam*, while certainly a memorable simpleton, is no fool but represents a good Jew, a simple man of faith. But the ambiguity remains, as Nachman's meanings hover between Hebrew and Yiddish.

As the tale begins, we learn that the *hakham* and *tam* are childhood friends, sons of rich families who have fallen on hard times. They loved each other but have taken very different paths in life. The *tam*—the simple Hasid—is a cobbler in his home village. He's quite inept: his crude three-sided shoes look like duck's feet. He and his wife live in simple poverty but they enjoy their plainness. They eat but one food, bread, but they call it kasha or broth or meat, and even seem to taste these flavors. They drink one plain beverage, water, though they call it beer, wine, or milk. They do the same with the one garment they share: it's a simple pelt, but they imagine it to be a caftan or a sheepskin coat. The *tam* takes pleasure in every simple experience and therefore he is happy. In every dealing with outsiders, the *tam* has only one caution and then he's satisfied. "Are you joking?" he asks.

Meanwhile his childhood friend, the *maskil*, has left home to see the world. He travels to Warsaw, Italy, Spain; he studies philosophy and masters the crafts of goldsmithing and gem-cutting and the profession of medicine. When he returns to his hometown in triumph, his old friend the *tam* greets him with simple joy. But he also notices how unhappy his worldly friend is.

For instance, an important landowner commissions the sophisticate to engrave a gem. The landowner is delighted but the *hakham* obsesses with a minor flaw that he noticed and is "miserable because of his mistake. 'What good is my skill . . . if I can make such an error?' " He is prey to Kafka's "inexorable severity," to his artistic perfectionism.

Now the king comes into the story, just as in the parable of the Maggid of Mezritch. And he likewise sends two messengers, a simple messenger to the *tam* and a sophisticate to the *hakham*.

The simpleton asks the messenger to read the message for him.

> He answered him: "I shall tell you by heart what is written there. The king wants you to come to him."
>
> He asked immediately: "Without joking?"
>
> He answered him: "Surely, it's true, without joking."
>
> And immediately he was filled with joy and ran and told his wife: "My wife! The king has sent for me." And she asked him: "What is this? Why has he sent for you?" And he had no time at all to answer her, but, immediately he hurried with joy, and set out immediately with the messenger.[5]

By contrast, the *hakham* wants to think it over and invites the clever messenger to spend the night. He spreads a banquet and "shows off his wisdom and philosophy."

> He questions the messenger: "Why should such a king send for an insignificant person like me? And who am I that the king should send for me? What is the meaning? He is a king who has such power and grandeur, and I am so insignificant in comparison with such a great king! Is it plausible that such a king

should send for me? If I say for my wisdom, who am I in comparison with the king? Doesn't the king have wise men? And the king himself is probably a great wise man, too. And so, why should the king send for me?"

Finally he tells the clever messenger, "Do you know what I think? It is conclusive that there is no king in the world at all. And the whole world is misled by this nonsense when they think that there is a king. Can you understand how it is plausible that the whole world would give itself up and rely on one man who is the king? Surely there is no king in the world at all!"

The clever messenger answered: "But I brought you a letter from the king."

The first *hakham* asked him: "Did you yourself receive this letter from the king's own hand?"

He answered him: "No, but another man gave me the letter in the name of the king."

He stated: "You can now see with your own eyes that my words are true, that there is no king at all." And he asked him again: "Tell me—since you are from the capital city and have been raised there all your life—have you ever seen the king?"

He answered him: "No."

The first *hakham* stated: "Now see for yourself that I am right, that surely there is no king at all. Because even you have never seen the king."[6]

In his parable, the dreamer is awaiting the messenger. Nachman is saying that even if the messenger showed up, you would not be able to receive his message. Kafka once said, "When the Messiah comes, he will no longer be necessary." Rabbi Nachman said, "When the Messiah comes no one will recognize him."

Nachman understood the problem of "joking" as a spiritual problem, a state of mind that does not allow change or *teshuvah*. We would call "joking" irony.

Irony is the essence of the humble king's land, because irony allows sophisticated people to remain suspended above their feelings, so they can never lead anywhere, certainly not back to the king. What's daring here is Rabbi Nachman's sympathy for the *hakham*. He understands his plight, for he saw it in himself. Inside himself he saw the fool and the wise man, the simple man and the sophisticate. He saw Kafka, too, for the *hakham*'s argument is pure Kafkaesque.

Some see Rabbi Nachman himself as a sort of undiagnosed manic-depressive, a glib formulation that suggests a little Librium would have kept the angels out of his brain. But that gets it all backward. Our psychopathology is reductionist. Rabbi Nachman lived Dov Ber's *mashal*. For him every feeling was a messenger, and most especially feelings of despair and even total emptiness. He was not afraid of any of them for they all led back to the king, though the hardest one was emptiness.

The trick was how to descend to those feelings and then ascend, or, in the language of Dov Ber's parable, how to travel from the messenger back to the King.

"Joking"—irony—is a mark of sophistication in literature and in life. Yet the end result of irony is a separation from soul. Both Kafka and Nachman were divided between their sophistication and their yearning for simplicity. In reading the tale of the *hakham* and the *tam*, scholar David

Roskies notes that Rabbi Adin Steinsaltz "finds the depiction of the simple man 'rather flat' and 'stereotypical,' " while the clever man "is treated with greater depth and understanding."[7] His sympathy for the *hakham* shows that Rabbi Nachman was far from simple.

The earlier master, Dov Ber, writing in the heyday of Hasidic enthusiasm, taught his Hasidim how deepest feelings can carry them back to God. But Rabbi Nachman's Hasidim are more deeply torn—because of the new influence of secularism, they are already on their way to Kafka.

Yet when the *hakham* in Rabbi Nachman's tale questions the king's messenger, he does so in a style that would sound very familiar to Jewish ears. It's a Talmudic style. It's as if Nachman were saying to the *maskil*, You may have lost touch with your Jewish soul, but you still have a Jewish mind. Kafka noticed this Talumdic quality in his own thinking.

24

Talmudic Style

In his period of intense Jewish exploration, Kafka recollected in his notebook a schoolboy dispute with Hugo Bergmann about God, where Kafka took the role of the atheist. "At that time I enjoyed grappling with a comparison I had found in a Christian magazine . . . between a clock and the world, and between the clockmaker and God: the existence of the clockmaker was supposed to prove that of God. Against Bergmann I could refute that very well. Once I refuted it while we were walking around the clock tower of the town hall."[1]

That astronomical clock was built in the Middle Ages and is still a major tourist attraction today—as the hour chimes crowds gather below to watch four animated figures who flank the clock. One is a Jew lifting a money bag.[2]

Yet even under such a clock, Kafka recognized that he argued with Bergmann "in a Talmudic style which I had either evolved from inside myself or copied from him."

Kafka was hearing echoes of his own dialectical thinking in the voices of disputing rabbis. His reading went so deep that he made something new from it: the modern parable. First he went short, then he went long. He took the parable and blew it up into the novel, a trick also followed by his

Hebrew successors, S. Y. Agnon and Aharon Appelfeld. *The Trial* and *The Castle* are essentially book-length parables. And within the long parable of *The Trial*, Kafka set his most distilled parable, "Before the Law," like a gem. He wrote it in December 1914 at the very end of his first great period of writing.

Kafka was proud of "Before the Law,"[3] though interestingly he claimed at first not to understand it. He published it in the Zionist newspaper *Selbstswehr*, that is, *Self-Defense*. He reprinted it as a stand-alone piece in his collection *A Country Doctor*.

Perhaps because it puzzled him so, he decided to enter it into a novelist's version of the Talmudic process. He understood from his reading of Talmud how the rabbinic sages derived new meaning from a holy text through debate and discussion. This is the process of midrash. Starting with a given piece of oral law, a *mishnah*, the rabbis would debate back and forth, using logical arguments and intuitions, and citing proof texts from the Torah.*

Kafka treated the parable "Before the Law" in exactly this manner. After all, it had come to him as a sort of revelation—out of the great fire—when it arrived he himself didn't know what it meant. So he embedded the parable into a narrative of an extended argument between two characters. Like his old disputes with Bergmann, this dialogue parodies the sort of debate one reads in the Gemara.

Kafka conceals this Jewish operation so completely that a

---

*A good example is the argument Rabbi Ishmael makes about why it would be permissible to destroy an heretical book with God's name in it. See Chapter 10, pp. 95ff.

reader unfamiliar with Talmudic texts could completely overlook it. The discussion takes place in a cathedral. The "rabbis" are two Catholics: a bank vice president and a priest. To see the Jewish bones of this story, you have to peel back a very Gentile skin. But was this not exactly the dilemma of the assimilated Jew who, when acting as a "man in the street," can only express himself in disguise? Wasn't this Hermann's strategy of concealment?

In Brod's arrangement of *The Trial*, this scene comes one chapter before the final execution scene. After almost a year of the "process,"* Joseph K. is increasingly haunted by his failure to move his case forward. After consulting unsuccessfully with a "shyster lawyer," Huld, and a painter, Titorelli, who makes portraits of the judges, Joseph K. is looking for intelligence anywhere he can. He is at the end of his rope, increasingly distracted at work and perpetually distressed. Of the court and its "process," he knows only uncertainty.

He enters a cathedral to meet an Italian businessman who never shows. This is revealed as a pretext, for as Joseph K. turns to leave, a priest calls out to him by name. The priest reveals himself as a member of the court. At last Joseph K. has met a genuine gatekeeper of the law, one who knows him by name. Ominously the priest identifies himself as a prison chaplain.

The priest asks Joseph K. to turn himself around. That is what *teshuvah* means literally in Hebrew, the term for a spiritual rectification. The priest warns Joseph K. that with every step he's taken so far, he has made things worse because

---

*"*Der Prozess*" is the German title we translate as "The Trial."

he has a fundamental misunderstanding. To prove his point, the priest introduces "Before the Law" as a "scripture."

Let me summarize the parable here, as I've quoted it previously at length.* A "man from the country" comes to a gate of the law, guarded by a fierce gatekeeper. The gate is open, but the gatekeeper refuses to let him pass. "It is possible," he says, "but not at the moment." Years pass and the "man from the country" begs, pleads with, and bribes the gatekeeper, but to no avail. At the end, when the man from the country is feeble, he has but one question. "Everyone wishes to enter the law. Why has no one but me come to this gate?" The gatekeeper tells him, "This gate was meant for you. . . . I'm shutting it now." As the "man from the country" dies, he sees a "gleam of inextinguishable light" on the other side.[4]

The parable concentrates in a small space the entire plot of the novel. Joseph K. is the man from the country, the priest is the gatekeeper, and the gate is the parable itself. If Joseph K. can interpret it properly, he can find his way to the Law, which is what he seeks.

With this plot device, Joseph K.'s previous problems with the court become problems of interpretation. It's a very rabbinic gesture to make text interpretation the centerpiece of a novel. This alone makes *The Trial* essentially Jewish—even if, or precisely because—the rabbinic-style argument takes place in a cathedral. Kafka himself was very aware of mimicking the midrashic process. In his diary he takes satisfaction in this passage of the novel and refers to it as an "exegesis of the legend."

*Cf. Chapter 1, pp. 28–31.

There are more hints of the Jewish subtext. One is obvious: the man from the country seeks the "Law," and "Law"* references the Torah. And as the critic Hans Politzer first suggested, "man from the country" (*Mann vom Lande*) translates the Talmudic expression *am ha-aretz*—a person ignorant of Torah. Kafka was very aware of this usage, recording it in his diary.[5] We can hear the priest echo "Talmudic style" as he cites proof texts:

> He's well aware of the importance of his office, for he says, "I'm powerful"; he respects his superiors, for he says, "I'm only the lowest doorkeeper"; when it comes to fulfilling his duty he can neither be moved nor prevailed upon, for it says of the man "he wearies the doorkeeper with his entreaties" . . .
>
> In rabbinic fashion, every interpretation is followed by the citing of a proof-text from the original legend, always introduced by phrases such as "for he says."[6]

This shows the "Talmudic style" that Kafka either "evolved within himself" or copied from Bergmann. Was he born with it? Did he absorb it? In Talmudic disputes, Kafka must have heard an echo of his own frequent bouts of introspection where he chased his tail like a dog.

Primarily, the priest and Joseph K. argue about the gatekeeper. The man from the country waits his whole life to go through the gate, and at the end the gate is shut. Did the gatekeeper deceive the man? Joseph K. wants to know, for he, too, has sought out "gatekeepers" to help him in his trial.

---

*Gesetz. In German it carries both legal and theological senses.

He is actually standing before the last gatekeeper in the story, the priest himself. And he has some hope. For he appears a cut above the others: the slimy lawyer Huld, the painter Titorelli, the corrupt officers who steal his clothes, the magistrate who presides in a grubby attic and appears to be reading pornography instead of the law. They all appear corrupt incompetent "jokers." But perhaps the priest can solve his problem.

Joseph K. strongly identifies with the man from the country in the parable. So his first reaction to the "scripture" is that the gatekeeper deceived him. The priest counters that the gatekeeper merely fulfilled his duty. Then K. says, "So the gatekeeper did not deceive the man?" The priest denies that as well. "Don't misunderstand me, I'm just pointing out the various opinions that exist on the matter. You mustn't pay too much attention to opinions. The text is immutable, and the opinions are often only an expression of despair over it." The priest presents another long argument, this time to the effect that the doorkeeper is the one deceived. Joseph K. says, "So the man was not deceived?" "You run up against a contrary opinion there," says the priest.

In an imitation of the give-and-take of Talmudic dialectic, each conclusion Joseph K. lands on logically is countered by the equal logic of the priest. The Talmud itself recognizes the limits of mortal logic when it speaks of certain arguments that will only be resolved in Messianic times, by Elijah himself. But before then, all one can say about such logical contradictions is that "these and these are the words of the living God."

Rabbi Nachman was much concerned that logic by itself

can lead to paradoxes that can never be resolved. That is why he advised his Hasidim to avoid arguments altogether if they possibly could. Otherwise they might lose their simple faith. He believed logical paradoxes could only lead to despair, which is just what happens to Joseph K. At the end of the argument he is exhausted and frustrated. He cannot accept the paradox of a gatekeeper who deceives but is not deceitful. The priest's final statement about this question is highly paradoxical, "It is not necessary to accept everything as true, one must only accept it as necessary."

Joseph K. is stunned and appalled by this statement, which clearly recalls his own situation with the court.

"So lies are made into a universal system," he answers indignantly. He is being asked to accept the court's incompetence, its absurdity and seeming injustice. Its jokes. He can go no further. He lapses into despair.

The priest echoes here the concept in Lurianic kabbalah of the shattering of the vessels. There's an inherent design flaw in the universe. Evil and injustice are built in. In this world the "law" is inherently corrupt. This is the joke of the land.

But Joseph K. could never accept this sort of kabbalistic paradox. He is a bank vice president, cautious and logical, a man of common sense and propriety. He reasons from what he knows. Justice is justice, he believes. The court of his "process" must be like the courts below. Even though he's told from the beginning that the law of the court is not the law of the land, Joseph K. clings to the belief that all the ills he experiences, all the deceit and lies of the lower-level officials of the court take place without the knowledge of higher authorities. He thinks that if only he can reach the higher level, he can correct his mistaken arrest.

The priest, however, is saying that the deceptions are in fact "necessary." They are built into the very fabric of the system and are unavoidable. The world of the Law is simply incommensurable with human ideas of right and wrong, of just and unjust. They are what they are, built on necessities that go beyond human logic.

Joseph K. cannot go there. And who can really accept it? To believe that evil and injustice are inherent to God's universe goes against our deepest sense of justice and goodness. It requires a certain humility to grasp this concept. For instance, one would have to give up completely the idea of judging God.

But there's another reason why Joseph K. can't accept it. Because he has perceived the lower-level authorities to be dishonest, corrupt, to be jokers exactly in the sense of Rabbi Nachman's tale of "The Humble King," he has let himself off the hook. How could Joseph K. be guilty if the system is guilty?

It never occurs to him that at one and the same time, the lower-level authorities might well be jokers, and he himself might be guilty.

Joseph K. assumes that as in a criminal court, the accusations against him are for some previous crime. Since he is not aware of having committed any crime, the whole procedure seems to him a mistake or joke. But he's told again and again that this is no ordinary court. It resembles much more the celestial court invoked during the Days of Awe, but which, to the kabbalist, operates at all times. Every action of man is continually being judged by the "invisible tribunal," in real time.

The priest hints at this real-time nature of the Law when he tells Joseph K., "The proceedings gradually merge with the judgment." Joseph K.'s guilt is not for a previous act. His guilt arises in every moment, even from how he responds to the charges. And how does he respond? He blames others for his problems. He assumes his innocence and mocks his accusers.

Arrogance dominates all of his interactions. He presumes superiority in every encounter, from the arresting officer to the magistrates. He badgers them, criticizes them, exposes them, mocks them, and attempts to bribe them. He even tells the priest, "Perhaps you don't know the sort of court you serve." He has it just backward. Because in a worldly way he is sophisticated, he does not realize that in regard to the "invisible court" he is the ignoramus, the "man from the country," the *amhoretz*.

Joseph K. believes he is innocent, so he feels constantly aggrieved. He complains to the priest, "Everyone . . . involved with the proceedings is prejudiced against me." He has plenty of evidence of inept court officials. Yet he also believes that if only you go high enough with your complaint, reasonable officials will straighten things out. His search for such higher officials doesn't get very far, certainly not as far as the parallel search of the wise man for the humble king, or Job's search for God's justice, which leads him to hear the voice of the whirlwind.

We see the story of Job peeking through, especially when we realize how both *The Trial* and "The Humble King" reference the same issue. Joseph K. has no "strategy" to reach the higher authorities; he stumbles around in all ignorance. But in Nachman's tale the wise man does have a strategy, to enter the court system and deliberately lose.

At one point Job also imagines initiating a lawsuit against God so he might have an audience with the higher authority.

According to biblical scholar Ed Greenstein:

> Job introduces this topic by asserting that there is no way that a person could contend with God in a legal proceeding. First of all, who could compel God to reply: "If one wanted to litigate with him, / he would not answer—not one chance in a thousand!" (9:3). Moreover, how could one subpoena God to appear in court when:
>
> He is wise of heart and bold of strength—
> Who has ever challenged him and remained whole?
> He who uproots mountains unnoticeably, / who overturns them in his rage;[7]

When Job does finally succeed, he is answered by the voice of the whirlwind and utterly humbled.

"Then the Lord answered Job, and said, Shall a reprover dispute with the Almighty? He who reproaches God let him answer it."

The voice of God tells him how foolish he is to judge the Judge.

Job and Rabbi Nachman's wise man do succeed in getting a hearing with the higher authorities. But Joseph K. never reaches such a high level. He languishes at the first gate, like the man from the country.

Kafka's use of the term "man from the country" suggests

that he understands the irony: Joseph K.'s sophistication in the everyday world deceives him, for in the mystical realm of the Law, he is an ignoramus. He knows nothing of the Law but believes he knows more than anyone he encounters. In this he resembles Rabbi Nachman's *maskil*, who argues with the king's messenger that there is no king.

After his lengthy discussion with the priest, Joseph K. is exhausted and confused. He turns away, but now the cathedral is dark, and he is reduced to groping his way along the wall. His moment of possible *teshuvah* is over. By exiting through the cathedral door, he loses his chance to go through the door of the parable. It is a moment of utter despair. In Brod's version of the novel, it leads quickly to the last chapter, where he dies "like a dog."

Kafka wrote the *mashal* of the man from the country because it is his own *mashal*. He, too, hesitated all his life outside so many gates: marriage, Palestine, leaving home. He was paralyzed in expectation, like the man who dreams of the messenger. In his heart, he knew his sophistication was foolishness, for he wrote, "To see folly in every emotion that strives straight ahead and makes one forget everything else. What then is non-folly? Non-folly is to stand like a beggar before the threshold, to one side of the entrance, to rot and collapse."[8] The man from the country is the beggar before the threshold.

Kafka understood the folly of his non-folly, of his aloofness, hesitation, irony, and sophistication. And he might have read the same lesson in Rabbi Nachman's tale of the *hakham* and the *tam*.

But for all the rebbes he met, the readings he did, Kafka never found the wise man who could help him through the gate, and he could not pass through it by himself. He could not reason his way through. He could not write his way out of his predicament, either—only elaborate his basic *mashal*, with self-mockery, with huge irony, with monstrous joking.

25

Dirty and Pure

A keen self-observer, Franz Kafka watched the odd propensity of his own mind to turn on itself with a bemusement suitable to one who stands both within and without his situation, occupying two positions at once. "In my struggles with the world," Kafka wrote, "I want to hold the world's coat." This paradoxical position or non-position is the essence of Kafka's joking.

In rhetoric, a self-canceling statement is called "aporia." It asserts a negation and thereby erases itself. This way of joking was deeply ingrained in Kafka: one time called at the last minute to preside over a meeting, he announced, "I must begin this evening with regret that it is taking place." Aporia rules his writing. "This gate was meant for you—I'm closing it now," "The Messiah will come when he is no longer necessary." It's even in his dying words.

Robert Klopstock, his medical-student friend, had promised Kafka morphine to relieve his pain but kept putting him off. Kafka was exasperated and told him, "Kill me—or you are a murderer." How could Kafka have formed such words in extremis? He was either one of the bravest stylists of all time, or the most thoroughly literary man who ever existed. He was truly "made of literature."

Aporia is the rhetoric of the sophisticate. It erases exactly what it proposes, though at the same time it proposes exactly what it erases. Kafka became very good—the best—at describing again and again the suspended state of his soul.

Martin Buber thought the way to turn around jokers like Kafka would be exposure to the forthright spirituality of the Hasidim. Through his versions of the legends of the Baal Shem Tov and *The Tales of Rabbi Nachman*, he offered to lost Jewish souls the model of the Hasidic rebbe, of a teacher intensely interested in the soul of his Hasid, who could bring him nearer to God through story and parable. But Buber's "rebbe" was a literary and theoretical construct. Actual encounters with actual rebbes were more problematic for a sophisticate like Franz Kafka.

During a self-described spurt of "religious fanaticism," Max Brod had been taking the tram out to the Prague suburb of Ziskov to visit a Galician refugee there, the wonder rebbe of Grodek. One Saturday evening Brod and Jiri Langer persuaded Kafka to come along for a "third Sabbath meal" (*shalush seudos*). Kafka noted the children crowded on the pavement and stairs—women and girls in white kerchiefs, and the dark interiors as the Sabbath afternoon prolonged into evening. He had to grope his way up the staircase and into the room.

> We were pushed toward a table on the rabbi's right. We held back. "You're Jews too, aren't you?" A nature as strongly paternal as possible makes a rabbi. All rabbis look like savages, Langer said. This one was in a silk caftan, trousers visible under it. Hair on the bridge of his nose. Furred cap which he kept tugging

back and forth. Dirty and pure, a characteristic of people who think intensely. Scratched in his beard, blew his nose through his fingers, reached into the food with his fingers; but when his hand rested on the table for a moment you saw the whiteness of his skin, a whiteness such as you remembered having seen before only in your childhood imaginings—when one's parents too were pure.[1]

Dirty and pure—Kafka remained at the threshold. But the visit must have touched his incipient Jewish soul, for a few weeks later he sketched first paragraphs of a story about a golem-making rabbi.

Prague is the home of the golem, the legendary monster fashioned from the river mud by the famous Maharal, Rabbi Judah Loew. (Prague is also one of the few municipalities on the planet to have a statue of a rabbi outside city hall, though the Maharal looks uncomfortable with a naked woman at his left side.)

It's odd that the two most famous icons of mostly Czech Prague are Jewish: Kafka and the golem. The Alt-Neu Synagogue where Kafka squirmed impatiently as a boy houses the remains of the golem in its attic, so it is believed. Today the golem and Kafka have been safely reincarnated. A life-size plastic golem, like a muddy Michelin man, stands outside the Jewish tourist agency, and down the street tourists drink coffee in the Café Kafka.

Had Kafka completed a golem story, it would have been his first and only openly Jewish story definitively set in Prague. But the story remained unfinished. Kafka approached and avoided Jewishness.

On his way back from Ziskov that evening, Kafka sounded more like a cultural anthropologist than a potential *ba'al teshuvah*. "If you look at it properly, it was just as if we had been among a tribe of African savages. Sheerest superstition."

Kafka remained strongly divided within himself, eagerly absorbing Hasidic lore from Langer and Lowy, while maintaining his intellectual distance. Langer and Lowy were themselves moving in opposite directions. Lowy fled the rigidity of his childhood Hasidic milieu in Warsaw; Langer, a middle-class Prague Jew, horrified his parents by becoming a Hasid of the Belzer rebbe. When he came back from Galicia, reports his brother Frantisek, "the attitude of our family to Jiri seemed to us . . . to resemble the situation in Kafka's *Die Verwandlung* ['The Metamorphosis']."

Father told me with a note of horror in his voice that Jiri had returned. I understood what had filled him with dread as soon as I saw my brother. He stood before me in a frayed, black overcoat, clipped like a caftan, reaching from his chin to the ground. On his head he wore a broad round hat of black velvet, thrust back towards his neck. He stood there in a stooping posture; his whole face and chin were covered with a red beard, and side whiskers in front of his ears hung in ringlets down his shoulders. All that remained to be seen of his face was some white, unhealthy skin and eyes which at moments appeared tired and at others feverish. My brother had not come back from Belz, to home and civilization; he had brought Belz with him."[2]

Jiri's "exhibitionism" in the bourgeois Prague neighborhood of Vinohrady was "extremely embarrassing to all of us at home. Like the rest of the Jewish community, our family had completely assimilated itself to all the outward signs and customs of the neighborhood. . . . It seems to me that my brother's get-up scared my father and his strata of society in another way. It disturbed his feelings for security and permanence." As Jiri refused to bathe regularly—"dirty and pure"—and cooked his own food on a spirit stove, they essentially thought of him as an *ungezeifer*, the way Hermann thought of Yitzhak Lowy. Perhaps what attracted Kafka to both men was their open defiance of their fathers, which Kafka never dared directly.

Kafka could never have committed himself to become a *ba'al teshuvah*. Langer remained observant but had a remarkable range of interests. He fell under the spell of Freud and wrote a book on the erotics of the kabbalah. His book remembering his life with the Belzer rebbe is a classic, *Nine Gates to the Chassidic Mysteries*,[3] published in Prague in 1937. He wrote in Czech to explain to Czech readers the beauty of the Eastern European Hasidic world, a world about to be destroyed.

Langer took Kafka to the Bohemian spa of Marienbad to meet the ailing Belzer rebbe. Each recorded an account. To the devout Langer, every word the master spoke was full of hidden meaning and should be understood "metaphorically. The whole time his thoughts are concentrated exclusively on supernatural matters."[4]

Kafka, for his part, acknowledged the rebbe as "no doubt at present the chief representative of Hasidism" and was enthusiastic after meeting him.[5] But he expressed his ironic detachment with a typical lapidary aphorism: "Langer tries to find . . . a deeper meaning in all this; I think that the deeper meaning is that there is none and in my opinion this is quite enough."[6] Always protected by irony, Kafka remained the aloof *hakham* of Rabbi Nachman's story.

26

Blue Light of Dawn

Friday Morning, September 26

Strange stops in the middle of the night: loudspeakers blaring, then silence. Sleep came in the train's narrow bunk bed after twenty-four hours of traveling. A few hours of sleep, then no sleep. Some internal clock must have shifted back to U.S. time. I could hear the sounds of sleeping in the couchette. I was dead tired and wide awake. I was on my way to Kamenetz with my Kafka mug and I blamed it all on the story of the humble king.

To see if I could fall asleep, I retold it in my mind. One king sends a wise man to fetch a portrait of another, who is said to be mighty, good, and humble. The wise man has no more trouble getting into the kingdom than I did in the Borispol airport. But once he arrives, he seeks the essential joke of the land. This joke tells him that the land is full of deceit and trickery. So in order to make his way to the king he comes up with a brilliant strategy: he files a lawsuit, knowing the courts are corrupt and the judges are jokers. He sues and loses, appeals to a higher level, loses again. And in this way he works his way to the highest court of all, where the king sits behind a curtain. And there he does something totally amazing. He changes so much inside that he is able to cause the king to respond to him, to tear down the curtain and reveal his face. And that is how the wise man gets the portrait of the humble king.

There is a sense in which everyone can say, as Kafka did, I am "made of literature." Because our souls are made of the stories that we've taken in most deeply, that have become part of us. The literature we love mingles with our deepest substance.

That is also why telling tales, if they go deep enough, can transform the soul: why Rabbi Nachman turned to the telling of tales when he wanted to prepare his followers for redemption.

In our own time, with its easy nihilism, even the idea of looking for meaning feels like a joke. If we ever needed a portrait of the king, it's now, which is why "The Humble King" still appeals to me.

I like the wise man's plan.

He wants to reach the highest level of authority, the court of the humble king. So he will lose a case at the lowest level and appeal, lose again and appeal, and keep appealing until he reaches the highest level. It's a kind of joke in itself; you might call it active resignation, winning by losing.

When I first read "The Humble King," this absurd element made me feel a connection to *The Trial*. Both stories describe courts that are corrupt and seem contemptible. In both the higher authorities are either malevolent or indifferent. That is how most people read *The Trial*: they take Joseph K.'s view of his world, they identify with him as a victim. Everyone has experienced unfair authorities, lousy teachers, mean cops, corrupt judges and politicians. The world is Kafkaesque, isn't it?

I used to read *The Trial* that way, too, as a parable about the absurdity of believing in justice in a corrupt world. But the more I read it beside "The Humble King," the more I wondered about Kafka's intent, because each story seems to irradiate the other and subtly shift its molecules.

Both stories start from the same undeniable truth, taught in every spiritual tradition, Jewish, Christian. In Buddhism, it's called the first noble truth: the Nature of Existence is suffering, that is *dukkhah*, a Sanskrit word for a wheel with a wobbly axle. And in Yiddish we could say, Life is *tzuris*.

That's the truth of Job sitting on his dung heap, his skin covered in boils. On the street, it's said this way: the world is fucked up. In fact, the world is royally fucked up. So if we ever do find the king, he's got some explaining to do.

Isn't this why the sophisticate protects himself with irony, with his joking? To think at all is to see that the world is a joke. Kafka told that joke better than anyone in his time. When that pesky man from the country says to the gatekeeper,

> Everyone wants the law, but in all these years why has no one else come here but me?
> And the gatekeeper answers:
> —This gate is for you, I'm closing it now.

That's the perfect punch line. As a literary gesture it is "indubitable." It is also hilarious. The gate closes. And it was meant for you. Could it be any other way? Is there a better joke? That is death, Kafka says, and futility . . . and it's also funny. We know when Kafka read *The Trial* out loud to his buddies in Prague, they just laughed and laughed. They knew all about gates closing and doors in their faces. They were Jews living a constricted life in Prague with Czechs rioting in the streets and Germans looking down on them. So Kafka's stories joke around about futility and death and the shame just after.

But what about the just before?

Just before also needs attention. A thin thread of light irradiates Kafka's dark humor. When the man from the country has exhausted all his attempts at bribery, when he's fading out,

> Finally his eyes grow dim and he no longer knows whether it's really getting darker around him or if his eyes are merely deceiving him. And yet in the darkness he now sees a radiance that streams forth inextinguishably from the door of the Law."[1]

Rabbi Nachman taught, "It is impossible to tell stories of the tzaddikim, unless one is able to imitate God; that is . . . can separate between light and darkness. . . .

"For parallel to every story of a tzaddik . . . there is a parallel story about the wicked . . . for evil mirrors good."

Evil mirrors good, and light and darkness are harder to tell apart than you might think. We don't know how to see the difference, not ahead of time when it counts.

Isn't this true for Joseph K.? Once he's arrested, he goes from one adviser to another, from the lawyer Huld to the painter Titorelli, and he doesn't know the good guys from the bad. In the dark cathedral, the priest says, "Can't you see two steps in front of you?" It was "a cry of rage, but at the same time it was the cry of someone who seeing a man falling, shouts out in shock, involuntarily without thinking."

Evil mirrors good. The difference between the two kinds of stories, the stories that heal and the stories that don't, says Rabbi Nachman, is "discernible only to someone who can distinguish between light and darkness. Such a person knows the extent of the distinction and difference between the deeds of the tzaddikim and the deeds of the wicked."[2]

So are Kafka's stories evil, as he sometimes thought himself. Are they poison, not medicine? Are they darkness and thorns?

No. There's light in Kafka, a glimpse of light. Just before.

The man from the country sees it. Inextinguishable, radiant. Joseph K. sees it, too, in the last chapter of *The Trial*, as he is laid out on the stone like Isaac. The executioners have shown him the knife. They are passing it back and forth in some ridiculous ceremony and Joseph K. looks up and

his gaze fell upon the top story of the building adjoining the quarry. Like a light flicking on, the casements of a window flew open, a human figure, faint and insubstantial at that distance and height leaned far out abruptly, and stretched both arms out even further. Who was it? A friend? A good person? Someone who cared? Someone who wanted to help? Was it just one person? Was it everyone? Was there still help? Were there objections that had been forgotten? Of course there were. Logic is no doubt unshakable, but it can't withstand a person who wants to live. Where was the judge he'd never seen? Where was the high court he'd never reached? He raised his hands and spread out all his fingers.[3]

Okay, there are many interpretations of the window, of the light. Of those outstretched hands. I didn't care about all that right then. The train jerked into stillness. I needed to take a walk and didn't want to wake anybody in the couchette. I swung my legs down from the upper bunk and went out into the corridor, sliding the door as silently as I could.

The train was just sitting on the tracks. The windows in the corridor were so badly scratched I couldn't make out much more than dim outlines of trees. I heard the sounds of birds calling, though.

The light in Kafka is hope. It is elusive, for surely the parable of *The Trial* offers no big hope. That conversation everyone quotes between Kafka and Brod, where Brod asks if he is a Gnostic and Kafka says no, he doesn't think the world is pure evil and created by a malevolent being, the demiurge. Maybe it's not so drastic, Kafka says: maybe Creation is just a bad mood of God. "He had a bad day." So is there hope? asks Brod, who is more sentimental than his friend.

Yes there's hope, Kafka says, "Plenty of hope—for God—no end of hope—only not for us."

That's funny, too, isn't it? Kafka's way of joking is so permanent and perfect and so indubitable. Plenty of hope for God, just none for us. So if that is the real bottom of Kafka's thinking, no rebbe or wise man is going to save us or Joseph K., and that ignorant man from the country is going to see the gate shut on him, no *tikkun olam* is coming, at least not the grand general repair of the universe that Rabbi Nachman dreamed of and told his stories for.

No hope for us. Just the bitter humor, the irony, and the truth that this is the way things are, the way they are made. This is the Kafkaesque and you better wise up.

"But the hands of one man were right at K.'s throat, while

the other thrust the knife into his heart and turned it there twice."

Twice. You better understand that this is the way it is and will be, and this is how we laugh about it and move on. This is how we live in the world of the bitter joke. This is how we sophisticates get by.

Except for that thread of light. That inextinguishable radiance: blue light of dawn.

27

Kafka, Buber, Nachman

It would be curious to know what Kafka made of the "deeper meaning" of Rabbi Nachman's tales. But all we know for certain is how he felt about Buber's translation.

Though as Scholem noted, Buber's renderings of Hasidic tales had made him "very famous" and influenced the "Western Jewish love affair with Eastern European Jews." Kafka had a very negative impression of Buber's literary style in these early Hasidic works. (He much preferred Buber's later style in translating Dov Ber in 1922.) He called the early translations "tepid things" (*lauwarme Sachen*) in a letter to Felice in 1913,[1] and in a follow-up letter he criticized Buber's "drastic adaptation that makes his books of legends so intolerable to me."[2]

Kafka's literary instincts were always sure, rooted in his own "inexorable severity." About his version of Rabbi Nachman's tales, Buber himself admitted, "I have not translated these tales, but retold them with full freedom." Buber felt at the time that he could somehow intuit what the Rebbe intended and rescue it from the actual text, which he viewed as crude.

The tales in their original form clearly lack literary polish for they never aspired to it. Buber cast the blame for all the literary defects he perceived on the faithful amanuensis Rabbi Nathan: "The tales have been preserved for us in the notes of a disciple, notes that have obviously deformed and distorted the original narrative beyond measure. As they lie before us, they appear confused, verbose and ignoble in form." It was odd of him to judge these oral tales by German romantic literary standards, or to put the blame on Rabbi Nathan, whose overnight translation of the teaching on burning books so impressed the Maggid of Tarhovitze, and who served the movement so ably as the author, teacher, and leader for thirty-four years after the Rebbe's death.

Had Rabbi Nachman himself had a chance to reply, his critique of Buber might have cut deeper than Kafka's. One remarkable short parable, "The Chandelier," will have to do as Rabbi Nachman's defense.[3]

A son has returned to his father, after journeys where he has learned the skill of making chandeliers. The father invites all the expert chandelier makers in the town to appreciate a chandelier his son has made. The father later went to get the experts' opinions; each advised him the son's lamp was ugly.

The father returns to the son with this criticism and the son tells his father the experts have it backward. "In this lamp I included the shortcomings of all the local masters of this art. You did not realize that one considered one part ugly, but another part very well made. . . . I made this lamp out of shortcomings . . . to demonstrate to all of them that they do not have perfection. Each one has a shortcoming, since what is beautiful to one is deficient to the next. But if I want to, I can make a perfect lamp."

When Buber judged Rabbi Nachman's tales as "deformed"

"distorted," and "ignoble in form," was he another local chandelier maker? Rabbi Nachman understood that almost every reader would misread his tales, because he would necessarily read through the distortion of the evil that he mistook for the good. Damaged eyes could see only damage.

To his credit, Kafka—with his "inexorable severity" in literary matters—saw past Buber's late romantic aesthetic. But in the parable of the chandelier maker, Rabbi Nachman saw past aesthetics altogether because he was focused on the end result. The purpose of a chandelier is to carry light. "Every story," he taught, "has something that is concealed. What is concealed is the hidden light."[4]

28

Sleeping and Awakening

To judge him on his own terms, one would have to understand that Rabbi Nachman's purpose in telling tales arose from his diagnosis of the state of the Jewish soul in his time. Where Buber hoped for renewal in the "inner chaos" of secular Jews like Kafka, Rabbi Nachman had a more drastic premonition. He thought Jews had fallen completely asleep and needed tales to awaken them to their souls.

In "The Loss of the Princess," his first tale, "sleep" plays an important role. The princess represents the divine presence exiled in this world, that is, the *Shekhinah*. In Jewish mystical thought, after the destruction of the Temple, there was something of a divorce between the Holy One Blessed Be He and his bride, the *Shekhinah*. The *Shekhinah* goes into exile with the Jewish people. Wherever Jews wander, She is with them. The viceroy's job is to find her and restore her to her rightful place. But he keeps falling asleep on the job.

The first time the hero falls asleep for a very long time after eating an apple and thereby loses the opportunity to rescue the princess. The story alludes to the biblical story of Adam eating the apple. But mainly it is a critique of those who have fallen asleep in this world and are no longer awake to the possibilities of their own souls. A second time, the viceroy drinks from a spring that flows with red wine, an allusion to the drunkenness of Noah. The viceroy*[1] falls asleep once more, this time for seventy years.

What does it mean to sleep for seventy years? In Psalm 90, seventy years is the length of a person's life. By "sleep," Nachman means a consciousness wholly given over to the material world and lacking a spiritual dimension. To fall asleep one's whole life means to live entirely in a constricted consciousness. The lost soul of Kafka's letter to Felice, who is like a dog with imploring eyes, is asleep in just this way, unable to have a relationship to the infinite depth of the divine.

In a teaching Rabbi Nachman gave to explicate "The Loss of the Princess," he explains that sleep also means the loss of the "face" or countenance. Here we link back to the teaching on burnt books. A certain tzaddik knows "faces in the Torah." In the rabbinic tradition cited by Scholem, there are "seventy faces" to every word in Torah. But to fall asleep means to be in a consciousness that is unable to see these faces or to be awake to their meanings.

So there are many meanings for *sleep*. The loss of face means the loss of a person's vision of the divine, and the loss of a higher vision of oneself, a loss of soul. Another result is a loss of faces in the Torah, meaning an inability to interpret the Torah with depth. A shallow person will read a shallow Torah, a violent person will read a violent Torah. The inability to see all the faces and depths of Torah means that sleep rules.

Kafka, a few days after his visit with the Grodek rebbe,

*The viceroy represents successive incarnations of *tzaddik ha-dor*, including the very *tzaddik ha-dor* who is telling the tale; that is, Rabbi Nachman.

apparently tried to read Torah but could find no depth in it. "Opened the Bible. The unjust Judges. . . no significance in this, I am never visibly guided . . . the pages of the Bible don't flutter in my presence."[2] The Torah did not come alive for him at that time.

From Rabbi Nachman's point of view, to be asleep is to lose face, meaning losing the ability to be moved by the Torah or read it with spiritual depth.

The remedy to sleep is to tell tales. They will gently reintroduce the countenance and the light. "So too," Rabbi Nachman teaches, "when a person has been asleep and in the dark for a long time and we want to show him his countenance and rouse him, we must enclothe his countenance in the telling of stories so that suddenly seeing the light does not harm him."[3]

Thus "every story has something that is concealed. What is concealed is the hidden light"—the light that awakens the listener to his "face," that is, to his soul, and to his full spiritual potency.

Kafka, who wrote nocturnally and entered a dreamlike state, also writes "sleep" into his stories. "The Metamorphosis" and *The Trial* begin as the protagonist wakes from sleep, and in Joseph K.'s case, on his birthday. Given Kafka's "talent for immersing himself in a dreamlike state," the question arises: is the protagonist awake? Or is the story a dream?

This question reflects Kafka's own penchant for being the "daydreamer" in the window. While Rabbi Nachman's diagnosis of "sleep" leads him to tell tales to waken his listeners, Kafka's strategy is to deepen sleep and interpenetrate reality and dream, until the reader herself does not know the difference. Kafka's stories haunt me because I feel I have dreamed them already. Kafka's "talent" for dreamlike states leads to his capacity to imagine his death calmly. To live in this indeterminacy, this suspension of life in dream, more closely resembles an imagination of death than life. Kafka at the end of his life felt the horror of this dreamlike suspension, for it meant one could not properly live or die.

For Rabbi Nachman the whole matter of storytelling rests on the strong distinction between sleep and waking, between death and life, and ultimately, underlying them all, between good and evil, light and darkness. While superficially these would seem obvious distinctions, in fact they are not, for as Rabbi Nachman teaches, "Evil imitates good." In the matter of stories, the stories of the tzaddikim are very beneficial. But it's no simple matter to distinguish good stories from bad, because for every story about a tzaddik there's a very similar story about a wicked person. Therefore it requires a discernment, a divine gift, to tell stories correctly. This discernment can only be fully mastered by the tzaddik who makes the dangerous journey to the land of Israel.

29

A New Kabbalah

To the extent that Kafka carried out Buber's program of cultural Zionism, he never discovered the "ur-Judaism" Buber proposed. His direct contact with rebbes and Hasidim left him bemused but indifferent, aloof, or anthropological. All such encounters remained incomplete, suspended in irony, Kafka's "joking."

Like the sophisticate in Rabbi Nachman's tale, Kafka could argue himself into and out of any position. By January 1922 this tendency had led him to a profound crisis, which biographers describe as a nervous breakdown. He looked back on the previous decade of ventures into Jewishness as false starts, "with a feeling of fretfulness again. From what did it arise? From certain thoughts which are quickly forgotten but leave my fretfulness unforgettably behind." One such thought occurred "on the little path that passes the Alt-Neu Synagogue." He listed his "fretfuls."

Fretful because of a certain sense of contentment. Fretful that my life till now has been merely marking time, has progressed at most in the sense that decay progresses in a rotten tooth. I have not shown the faintest firmness of resolve in the conduct of my life. It

was as if I, like everyone else, had been given a point
from which to prolong the radius of a circle, and had
then, like everyone else to describe my perfect circle
round this point. Instead, I was forever starting my
radius only constantly to be forced at once to break it
off. (Examples: piano, violin, languages, Germanics,
anti-Zionism, Zionism, Hebrew, gardening, carpen-
tering, writing, marriage attempts, an apartment of
my own.) The center of my imaginary circle bristles
with the beginnings of radii, there is no room left for a
new attempt."[1]

Kafka was haunted by his uncertainty, the instability of
his thinking. He complained to his friends in long letters,
and to himself in his diary, where he reflected on the state
of his soul even if that introspection only led to more
fretfulness.

He was living back at home in Prague, desperately
unhappy. He had been through three broken engagements
(two with Felice and one with Julie Wohryzek) and was
winding down his most passionate, and most bittersweet,
love affair with his Czech translator, Milena Jesenská, a married woman who would not leave her husband. In the previous two years, he'd witnessed new anti-Semitic riots in
Prague (the "cockroach in the bathroom"), had bouts of
high temperature and difficulties in breathing. He was at a
low point and turned to his diary, listing his symptoms:
"First: breakdown, impossible to sleep, impossible to stay
awake, impossible to endure life, or more exactly the course
of life. The clocks are not in unison; the inner one runs
crazily on at a devilish or demoniac or in any case inhuman

pace, the outer one limps along at its usual speed. What else can happen but that the worlds split apart, and they do split apart, or at least clash in a fearful manner."

He blamed the wild pace of his inner life on the pursuit of new ideas, the ideas in "turn to be pursued by renewed introspection." But this pursuit "originating in the midst of men" could only isolate him further from humanity.

"Pursuit indeed is only a metaphor, I can also say, 'assault on the last earthly frontier,' an assault, moreover launched from below—from mankind—and since this too is a metaphor, I can replace it by the metaphor of an assault from above, aimed at me from above."

Was he pursuing his writing, or was his writing pursuing him from "above," from some otherworldly place? He sounds very much like Rabbi Nachman, who brought down his *torot* from higher worlds. Whether he was pursuing his ideas or his ideas were assaulting him, Kafka knew his writing was "an assault on the frontiers," and as such, had not "Zionism intervened," "it might easily have developed into a new secret doctrine, a Kabbalah."

"Though of course," he added, "it would require genius of an unimaginable kind to strike root again in the old centuries, or create the old centuries anew and not spend itself withal, but only then begin to flower forth."[2]

Kafka did not believe himself to have found a deep enough place within him where a new kabbalah could root itself. His writing was an "assault on the frontiers," but he felt himself turned away at the borders. Still, from this low point emotionally, he rallied one more time; in the nine months that followed it he wrote "A Hunger Artist," "Investigations of a Dog," and *The Castle*, his final, most enigmatic, unfinished novel.

What did Kafka mean, by 1922, by "a Kabbalah"?

Most people who know a little bit about kabbalah—a lot of people these days—think of it in terms of the schematics of the *sefirot*, the tenfold array of divine attributes. But these schematics are merely the end product of actual experiences of Jewish mystics: experiences of ascents into other worlds, through prayer, meditation, dreams. These meditative journeys were patterned on the original account in the book of Ezekiel of the descent of the chariot and followed through in the practices of rabbinic mystics, known as the "chariot riders." Whether the meditator was ascending to higher worlds or the higher worlds were descending to him is an ambiguity that runs through the tradition from Ezekiel to the kabbalists to Rabbi Nachman. Later kabbalists found these secrets of ascent hidden in the Torah text. But for Kafka, what was important was the actuality of the experience. I doubt he knew one of the *sefirot* from another, but he knew the great fire, in his own way and knew also of soul as something indestructible inside him, something separate from his experiences of everyday life "in the midst of men." Knowing that this part of him had a life of its own, he could so easily imagine it slipping into another body, even into the body of an animal.

30

Circus Acts

Kafka's uncertainty permeated his life and his writing. Or in old-fashioned terms, it reflected the state of his Jewish soul. Where other Jewish writers in his time and since have chosen between overt and concealed Jewishness, Kafka enacted both in a quantum uncertainty. In his writing, he's as Jewish as Dickens is English and as Jewish as Roth or Singer or Ozick, yet it's understandable why some readers could miss his Jewishness entirely. How, they ask, could Joseph K. be Jewish if he meets a priest in a cathedral? But Kafka showed here his most daring assimilation. Jews were so deeply assimilated that they could now inhabit outwardly Christian forms while remaining completely Jewish.

There are no rabbis in Kafka's published tales, no bar mitzvahs or synagogues.[1] There are no Jewish characters as such. You need Judah Leib Gordon's decoder ring of "man in the street/Jew at home" to penetrate the cover story. Kafka's stories are themselves "men in the street," but they are also "Jews at home," that is, at core. Ordinary code switchers migrate between two languages. But a genius code switcher like Kafka wrote German and Jewish into the same text, which goes one step beyond his father's assimilationism—into thin air.

Such writing is an acrobatic feat and Kafka knew that his predicament as an artist demanded a circus metaphor. Kafka writes a tale of a trapeze artist who always stays in the air, whose feet are never allowed to touch the ground. A second circus image appears in a letter to Felice after two early reviews of "The Metamorphosis" appeared. One reviewer saw his narrative art as "fundamentally German," the other, actually Max Brod, as one of "the most typically Jewish documents of our time." Kafka seemed anguished by this disjunction: "Am I a circus rider on 2 horses? Alas, I am no rider, but lie prostrate on the ground."[2] Prostrate also is the hunger artist's position on the floor of the sideshow cage, expired on the straw.

Kafka used another charged image in a late letter to Brod about his dilemma as a German-Jewish artist: "Most young Jews who began to write German wanted to leave Jewishness behind them, and their fathers approved of this, but vaguely (this vagueness was what was outrageous to them). But with their posterior legs they were still glued to their father's Jewishness and with their waving anterior legs they found no new ground. The ensuing despair became their inspiration."[3]

Here we meet the insect Kafka felt himself to be. It links Kafka's "uncertainty" as a Jew to Gregor Samsa; they share the wavering insect legs that can find "no new ground."

Gregor Samsa's "many legs, pitifully thin in relation to the rest of him, . . . threshed ineffectually before his eyes." The legs are "locked in what seemed if anything even fiercer combat than before, powerless to bring any kind of order into their chaos."[4]

Hermann had called that brashly unassimilated Jew,

Yitzhak Lowy, an *ungezeifer*. His son must have heard it as a curse, for three years later "The Metamorphosis" begins as if in fulfillment of his father's words: "Gregor Samsa woke from uneasy dreams one morning to find himself changed into a giant *ungezeifer*."

To Hermann, Lowy is too Jewish, and that makes him a vermin. But Samsa is not too "anything," he has lost his identity completely, submerged in his work and his family obligations. Gregor is the good assimilated son Hermann wanted Kafka to be, but his soul is so cut off from his body that he might as well wake up as an insect. In this reading, "The Metamorphosis" is a Jewish *gilgul* story, an extended parable on the "infinite longing and pathetic inner chaos"[*] of the Jewish soul trapped in an entirely assimilated body.

The plot is well known. Gregor Samsa works as a traveling salesman and is the sole support of his parents and his sister. In addition, his father owes a debt to his employer, further binding him to his job.

Gregor Samsa wakes as an insect with many legs and a large domed belly. No entomologist would mistake this for the description of a cockroach.[†] Somehow in the story, Hermann's curse has becomes Gregor Samsa's reality, though it's a portion of Kafka's art not to explain the mechanics of this transformation (*verwandlung*). Simply: a man wakes as

---

[*]Buber's phrase.

[†]Possibly Samsa is a bedbug or a sow bug. The maid calls him a dung beetle. Vladimir Nabokov, an expert on entomology, decides he is a brown beetle, and notes his large mandibles. But this requires Nabokov to argue that six legs is "many." As a beetle, he suggests Gregor Samsa is unaware that he has wings underneath his back. http://www .kafka.org/index.php?id=191,209,0,0,1,0.

an insect. This is the *mashal* with which we are presented, but the *nimshal* remains, as always, elusive. As in a dream, a single absurd premise begins the story, but what follows is quite logical.

Translations offer solace of interpretation. With "metamorphosis" the Muirs, a Scottish couple who did the first English translation, may have been thinking of Ovid. But the Latin poet's frolicking satyrs and nymphs seem far removed from Kafka's worldview. Perhaps they were thinking of entomology, too. "Metamorphosis" is the technical term for the instars of insects, as they molt from pupa to larva.

The Yiddish translation brings the story closer to the Hasidic world. The poet Melech Ravitch translated the title as *"Der Gilgul."* Kafka knew the concept of *gilgul* from his reading and contacts and notes it in his diary.[5]

A minor tradition in Jewish thought until the Ari, *gilgul* is mainstream belief among Hasidim. The Hebrew word means "to roll or cycle." *Gilgul* is a transmigration of the soul: some lofty souls recycle to complete spiritual missions, but most *gilgulim* are punishments for sins.

The Breslovers tell of Rabbi Nachman and Rabbi Nathan walking outside a Ukrainian village, when three dogs approach, barking furiously. Rabbi Nachman is unperturbed and says to the dogs in good Yiddish, *Ich weissn, ich weissn, ich weissn*—I know, I know, I know. What did the rebbe know? Who these souls were and how they had gotten trapped in dogs' bodies. And he would find a way to release them.*

---

*I heard Rabbi Ozer Bergman tell this story.

Gilgul seems like a charming fairy-tale sort of belief. In the vision of the Ari, Rabbi Isaac Luria, souls are constantly in motion: every rock, tree, flower, and bird is full of conscious life. And human beings can play their part in *tikkun;* the simple act of blessing bread can lift the souls trapped in the grain, and so Luria imagined each Jew playing a part in the grand restoration, *tikkun olam.*

But *gilgul* is also punishment and carries a huge weight of pathos, which is the sense of Kafka's story.

This sense of punishment comes from the suffering of human awareness trapped in nonhuman form. The transmigrated soul knows its former human potential but must endure time as a dog, or worse, a blade of grass or a stone. To be reborn in vegetable or mineral form is one of the worst fates of all. The only hope for release is through a sacred act.

Rabbi Nachman explains in a teaching that during a harvest, it's the custom to say "God's blessing" to the harvesters. This greeting alone, by mentioning God, can lift a soul trapped in the harvested grain to a higher level. But the Rebbe teaches, "There are wicked people who are reincarnated in grasses that grow on rooftops. They have no spiritual elevation, because these grasses are not harvested."

Lousy luck. To be trapped in a blade of grass or an ear of wheat, but with full human consciousness, is the horrific punishment Hasidim see all around them. They believe only the human being reincarnated in another human has amnesia about his previous life.

In Kafka's story, Samsa begins with full human consciousness in a bug's body, but he gradually forgets his true human nature. His soul succumbs to his body. Or perhaps the pain is too much and Samsa deliberately forgets his human part, following Kafka's advice in his aphorism that the best hope for "felicity" was "to believe in the indestructible in oneself and then not to go looking for it."

Gregor is a master of remaining unconscious, which is where the humor of the story is so effective. When he first wakes, his thoughts quickly turn from his weird plight to train schedules. He worries more about being late for work than his wriggling legs. He's lost to his basic feelings. How can they act as messengers to a king? He is so asleep to who he truly is that he might as well be an insect.*

Kafka conveys the gradual sinking of Gregor Samsa into an insect's consciousness. He prefers rotten food to fresh, and enjoys hanging upside down from the ceiling. When Grete, Gregor's sister, notices how the furniture in the room gets in his way, she enlists his mother to help her clear the bedroom.

Gregor is pleased. But then he hears his mother protest, "Isn't it as if by removing the furniture we were showing that we had given up all hope of improvement . . . ?"[6]

Hearing his mother's words, Gregory realized that the fact that no one had addressed him directly in the past two months, coupled with the monotony of life in the bosom of the family, must have considerably muddled his wits; this was the only explanation he could find of his seriously having wanted his room cleared. Did he really wish to have his warm, friendly room,

*Technically an insect has six legs. If Gregor is a beetle, he is an insect. However, "many legs" suggests he is a myriapod of some sort.

cozily furnished as it was with family heirlooms, transformed into a cave in which he would admittedly be able to crawl all over the place unimpeded but at the price of rapidly and completely forgetting his human past? Why, he was on the verge of forgetting already, and he had been rallied only by hearing his mother's voice again after all this time.[7]

Read through Rabbi Nachman's eyes, Gregor Samsa needs a rebbe to wake him up to who he is, and free his soul from his insect body.

31

The Turkey Prince

Rabbi Nachman's parable "The Turkey Prince" also depicts the plight of a soul trapped in an animal body.

In the parable, the prince has gone mad. He believes he's a turkey, and takes off his clothes. He lives under the king's table, pecking at crumbs. The king has consulted all the physicians of the land, and doctors in Rabbi Nachman stories can do no good. But a wise man shows how to cure the prince.

Only the wise man has the skill and courage to risk bringing him back from under the table. He acts like the best psychotherapist. Instead of diagnosing the turkey from a distance, he meets him where he lives. He descends under the table and shares his condition, stripping off his clothes. "Who are you?" says the prince. "I am a turkey," he tells him, for he cannot heal him if he remains above; only by descending to this low place can he heal him. With such empathy and compassion, the tzaddik "descends" to retrieve lost souls.

"Do you think," he tells the mad prince, "that a turkey can't wear a shirt? A turkey can wear a shirt." The wise man calls for a shirt, and puts it on, and calls for another, which the prince puts on. "Do you think a turkey cannot wear pants?" The wise man calls for pants and puts them on, and another pair for the prince. "Do you think a turkey cannot eat regular food?" Gradually, little by little, the story tells us, the wise man leads the turkey prince back to human dignity, to sanity.

Rabbi Nachman reframes *gilgul* as madness. To live as a turkey, to believe you are a turkey, is little different from waking up one fine morning as a turkey. The prince's descent to a turkey life, a life without awareness of his soul, is a form of madness. It is the furthest extension of the bifurcation of Jew at home/man in the street. The Jew at home forgets he is a Jew and the man on the street has forgotten his soul.

The story implies that the wise man knows how to cure the prince because he has been near mad himself. He's been under the table more than a few times and is willing to risk going back again. He's willing to descend for the sake of ascending.

In Kafka's story, Gregor's sister, Grete, plays an analogous role. She is the first family member who dares enter Gregor's room. She experiments to find which food her brother prefers. Noticing he now prefers rotten apples and spoiled milk, that is what she feeds him. But her efforts don't heal him. Instead of leading him back to humanity, she accommodates his new condition. And she can't sustain her love. More and more her empathy struggles with her disgust. Eventually she sees Gregor as less than human, an *ungezeifer*. She does not have the capacity of the tzaddik to redeem or heal.

Today's Breslovers read "The Turkey Prince" as a parable of Jewish assimilation. The prince is a secular Jew. He's "mad" because he's cast off the traditional clothing and dietary habits of the religious Jew. As a Jew, he's a naked lost soul, living in delusion. But the tzaddik knows the secrets of descent and ascent, how to descend to the level of the mad prince and restore his lost soul.

Rabbi Nachman's training as a rebbe of souls began early. As a child he stretched out on the grave of his great-grandfather to communicate with the Baal Shem Tov's soul. He yearned to enter the invisible realms, to have the gift of seeing souls, which he felt as his birthright. His impatience for direct spiritual experience was extraordinary.

Franz Kafka was by his own account a timorous child, but the young Nachman was bold. When a group of Hasidim stopped at Medzhibozh on their way to visit another rebbe, the four-year-old Nachman demanded to accompany them. They were reluctant to take charge of a child. So he put his foot on their carriage step and refused to move until they agreed to take him.

According to the stories collected by his Hasid Rabbi Nathan, the young Rabbi Nachman was very eager to learn Talmud and saved money his parents gave him for candy to pay his tutor for extra lessons. He had great trouble at first mastering Jewish texts and would cry and scream to God until he was able to learn. As he grew older he prayed constantly, not only the prescribed prayers in Hebrew but also individual prayers in Yiddish. He demanded some sign that God was listening and despaired that he wasn't. He wanted proofs, real results, real responses. He was looking for little miracles. He liked to pray in a certain spot in the country-side but was disturbed by a large roadside crucifix. He prayed to God for a miracle, and suddenly the crucifix collapsed. Another time, he wanted fish to swim up to his hand without a net. He prayed and it happened.

In the most dramatic instance he asked the favor of seeing a dead soul. One evening not long after his marriage, he locked himself up in his room and prayed. Suddenly the household heard him screaming in terror. A dead soul had appeared in the darkness, not a very good soul as it turned out. Nachman was so terrified he couldn't find the latch to let himself out of the room. They broke down a wall to get to him. "Subsequently,'" Rabbi Nathan writes, "he saw any number of dead souls and he was never afraid."[1]

To be a rebbe meant being open to the souls of the living and the dead. Sometimes it meant descending to a lower level in order to rescue souls. The Baal Shem Tov saw thousands, myriads of dead souls. Once, the story is told, he attempted to lift the soul of Sabbatai Zevi, the false Messiah. "The tikkun is done through the connection of soul with soul, spirit with spirit, and breath with breath." The Besht was afraid because Sabbatai Zevi was so wicked and he could not succeed. But he made the attempt because the false Messiah had a 'spark of holiness in him.' "[2]

To bind your soul to another soul, your breath to another breath, means to understand the consciousness intimately of one who has fallen to a lower level. The wise man in "The Turkey Prince" knew how to go under the table and even go naked, because he had been to such an extreme place himself. He, too, had lived under the table, and under the table you have no awareness of the king. You peck among crumbs while the full meal of the king is being served above you.

32

Movements of the Soul

Rabbi Nachman also suffered uncertainty, the uncertainty that comes from too much knowledge. Although he praised the simple Jew, the *tam* of "The *Hakham* and the *Tam*," Rabbi Nachman was a spiritual sophisticate. Within the realm of Jewish literature, he had a complete command of Torah, Talmud, the Ari, Zohar. There's no reason to doubt Rabbi Nathan's statement: "He could quote anything in the sacred literature as if the book was opened in front of him. It was like a table set before him, where he could see everything and choose what he desired."

Yet for all his knowledge, he warned his ordinary Hasidim against reading philosophy of any kind, Jewish or secular. Even Talmudic disputes could lead to questions that could not be answered. There was a certain kind of paradox that intrigued the mind but was ultimately meaningless. He led one around in circles; it led to despair. Rabbi Nachman could have been describing Kafka's whirlwinds of mad introspection.

But Rabbi Nachman read what he forbade others to read. As a tzaddik he had to know how to answer the heretic. But it was also a spiritual practice: he deliberately engaged in such explorations so he could find the area in consciousness where there was still emptiness to encounter. This is a remarkable project: a theist constantly reaching into the void to conquer it over and over.

In the realm of spiritual exploration, Rabbi Nachman has a great deal in common with the spirit of the "sophisticate" in his tale who extends himself into so many fields, who masters gold-smithing and gem-cutting. But his ultimate goal is medicine, which requires the study of philosophy. Rabbi Nachman's *hakham* resembles Maimonides, who was both physician and philosopher. He also resembles the *maskilim* of his own time, many of whom were doctors, including the physicians he consulted in Lemberg. The tale was told immediately after his return from that city.

In Lemberg, the reader will recall, Rabbi Nachman reluctantly agreed to burn the manuscript that had caused his son's death in 1806. By 1808 his wife Sashia had also died of tuberculosis, and he, too, had the disease. He was desperate to be cured. His followers knew he had accepted medical treatments, but Rabbi Nathan's faith was not shaken. He believed the consultations in Lemberg "involved deep mysteries. It was not for remedies that he made this trip, but for deep reasons known only to him."

Perhaps, but it's clear this venture into the realm of the *maskilim* deeply troubled Rabbi Nachman. Did he ask Rabbi Simeon to burn his book as a supreme sacrifice? Or was it expiation for consulting doctors, for his lack of simple faith? Or was it self-punishment? The burnt book represented his own pretensions to a much higher knowledge and perhaps in Lemberg he felt he had betrayed himself.

"Simplicity" and "sophistication" were warring poles of his consciousness. The tale reflects not only his social observation of Hasidim and *maskilim*, but his inner dialectic. The plot tells us that the *tam* triumphs and the sophisticate winds up in the mire. Intellectual sophistication leads to pride and contempt. "Through his wisdom, he had become a great craftsman, intellectual and physician and everyone in the world seemed like nothing."[1] But at the same time, Rabbi Nachman had moments when his own sophistication led him to feel greatly frustrated with simplicity. What he knew was often incommunicable and could not be understood by his Hasidim. Rabbi Nathan tells of a time when Rabbi Nachman had a new insight but told his Hasidim, "What has this got to do with you? What need do you have for any of this? And even if I were able to clothe this teaching in some moralistic lesson that would be of benefit to everyone for the present, I have no words."

The Rebbe paced back and forth inside the room and then he said, "I am more poor and needy than any of the great figures of our people. This one has wealth, that one silver, another has cities. But as for me, I have nothing! My only consolation is when I remember that in the World of Truth everyone will need me and they will all long to hear the original teachings I constantly give forth. What am I? Nothing but the original teachings my soul pours forth!"[2]

The Rebbe was a spiritual sophisticate who yearned for simplicity and not the other way around. Only a sophisticated soul could say, as Rabbi Nachman did, "The greatest sophistication is to work out how to avoid sophistication."[3] Yet Rabbi Nathan reported that the Rebbe "deeply yearned to serve God like the ignorant common people" and constantly emphasized simple faith and wholeheartedness to his followers. "My achievements came mainly through simplicity," he claimed. "I spent much time simply conversing with God and reciting the Psalms." How could Rabbi Nachman reconcile this contradiction?

The answer was to engage in a perpetual process of rising and falling.* He would constantly "begin anew" as if just beginning to devote himself to God for the very first time.

Rabbi Nathan writes: "This happened time and again, and each time he would start all over again. He would often begin anew many times in a single day. For even in the course of a day there were many times when he would fall away from his high level of devotion. But each time he would start again, no matter how many times it happened."[4]

He was never satisfied, even though he had practiced every sort of devotion, including fasting, praying, giving up all of his desires, and overcoming all his emotions. Already, according to Rabbi Nathan, he "attained the highest spiritual levels" in childhood, but "as soon as he achieved a new level, he would immediately begin anew. All his effort would be forgotten, as if he had not yet even taken the first step."

Sometimes Rabbi Nachman fell because he faced into questions philosophy asks, like the questions the *hakham* asks the messenger in the story. At other times, he sank even more deeply into a state of inanition and intellectual paralysis. He would tell his followers, "Now I know nothing, nothing, nothing at all."

These public declarations of Rabbi Nachman troubled his

---

*Zen Buddhists speak similarly of returning to "beginner's mind."

Hasidim, but they were actual moments in the "hollow place" Kafka described in his diary. They show up even in Rabbi Nachman's dreams.

Once he dreamed that it was Shavuos, which celebrates the giving of the Torah at Mount Sinai. Yet he has completely forgotten how to teach. In another dream, all his followers abandon him. No one comes to see him and outside the study hall rows of people are whispering and joking about him. He goes off to live in a forest, with five supporters, but an old man shames him and tells him he has disgraced his grandfather Rabbi Nachman of Horodenka and his great-grandfather, the Baal Shem Tov. There is no escaping his shame, even to another country.

"If that is how things are," Rabbi Nachman says, "and I'm a mere fugitive, at least I will have the World to Come."

"You think you'll have the World to Come?" the old man replies. "Even in hell you won't have any place to hide yourself after sinning like this."

The condemnations continue, though nowhere is the actual sin mentioned. The old man gives him a sign that he is from "The Upper World" and Rabbi Nachman in the dream remembers the Baal Shem Tov saying, "I love God even without the World to Come."

I threw my head down and turned away in great bitterness. As soon as I did so, all the different people the old man said I had shamed gathered before me—my grandfather and great-grandfather, the patriarchs. They said to me, "On the contrary we will be proud of you." They brought me all my supporters and my children (because even my children had left me when all

this started) and they spoke kind words like these—
the opposite of what had happened before.

Defeat turns to triumph. "As to my throwing down my
head in bitterness: if a person who transgressed the entire
Torah eight hundred times had thrown his head down
as bitterly as that, he would certainly have been forgiven."[5]
As in a psalm, just at the moment of extreme personal
anguish and isolation, there's a turning around from despair
to hope.

Some commentators have described Rabbi Nachman's
psychology in pathological terms, as a form of manic-
depression. But there are any number of manic-depressives
who are not religious geniuses, just as there are any number
of depressed people who never wrote a word approaching
Kafka's.

Rabbi Nachman was deeply sensitive to every moment of
his spiritual life, which included his words and actions and
his dreams. He did not reduce his spiritual experiences to
clinical categories; rather he viewed what we would regard
as symptoms as messengers from the king.* If he was
depressed, it was an encounter with nothingness that was in
itself an essential moment. To arrive at "nothing," to shed
for a moment all his knowledge and sophistication, was an
opportunity to begin anew, to become completely simple. It
was a moment of pain but also the first step to an even more
profound revelation.

Of this process, the Rebbe said, "My teachings are very
unique, but my 'I don't know' is more unique than all my
teachings."[6]

---

*As Carl Jung wrote, "God is in the symptoms."

Just a few weeks before his death, a large group had come to see him in Uman. The Rebbe said, "Why do you come? Don't you realize I know nothing at all now. I'm just a common simpleton." Then he broke bread, taught a Torah lesson, and "spoke with us at length with true grace and joy . . . cried out from the depths of his heart, 'Never give up! There is absolutely no reason to give up.' "

He said that whenever he fell completely he drew his inspiration from the memory of his most difficult journey. "The only thing that inspires me is the fact that I was in the land of Israel." On that journey he found a way to overcome every obstacle, including the obstacle of sophistication that tormented him.

But Franz Kafka found no such method of rebounding. When he was at the bottom, he was at the bottom, and in his moments of intense introspection, he seemed to pile on the pain, torturing himself even more. In some ways, his descents must have been more terrifying than Rabbi Nachman's, for in those low places he truly felt possessed by demonic forces beyond his control.

Yet he never stayed down for good. However sick Kafka felt physically, or desperate mentally, he always rebounded from his low points. Even at the end, in that cold apartment in Berlin, he was writing all night. He wrote his last story, "Josephine the Mouse Singer," on his last visit to Prague. Josephine could only "whistle," and Kafka said he wrote the story just in time, for his voice was going, too. Knowing all this explains again why Brod had difficulty believing his friend truly wanted him to burn his work.

Despite his self-flagellation, or perhaps because of it, in

his personal life, Franz Kafka was uncommonly kind, generous, compassionate. His thousands of pages of letters to his friends and family show his responsiveness and concern. Once in Berlin with Dora, he met a little girl on the street wailing because she had lost her doll. Kafka told her the doll was traveling. At night, he began writing letters from the doll and delivered them to the girl each day. The doll was traveling, she was having great adventures in foreign lands. He kept this up for three weeks, working hard each night, but then brooding about how to end it. He finally came up with the idea that the doll had gotten married and so could not return. In this way, the little girl came to accept the lost doll and even be happy for her.[7]

There was something within Kafka that could not be destroyed. He believed in the "indestructible" in himself—the soul—but did not want to look at it too carefully. Yet in his last two years, he did in fact speak of the kabbalistic concept of *gilgul*—of souls reborn—to describe his own spiritual condition. "If there really is such a thing as the transmigration of the soul," he wrote in his diary, "then I have not yet attained the lowest stage. My life is the hesitation before birth."[8]

Rabbi Nachman also taught that some souls cannot find a body in which to be reborn. These "naked souls,"* Rabbi Nachman said, "cannot enter a body at all. These souls are more pitiful than anyone alive. When a soul is born into this world, it can give birth to children and observe God's commandments. But these naked souls have no way of elevating

---

*A naked soul is a *neshamah artla'it*.

themselves and are most pitiful. They cannot accomplish anything on high, and also cannot clothe themselves in a body."

Rabbi Nachman believed that the Jewish victims of the massacres in Uman were naked souls. That is why he picked Uman as the place to die.

In 1768, several thousand Jews were murdered by rebel Cossacks (known as Haidamaks), men, women, and children. Their corpses were tossed to the dogs and pigs. It was a horrific massacre, though we now understand it was only a premonition of what was to come in Ukraine during World War II.

When Rabbi Nachman first visited Uman on his way from Medvedevka to Breslov, he saw the mass grave and called it a "Garden." He declared that he wanted to be buried there to help them. He himself would be the Master of the Field who would descend to these naked souls, bind them to his, and clothe them in his own spiritual garments. His mitzvahs—his merits—would cover for their lack.

When the Rebbe returned to Uman at the end of his life, he said he could see these souls appearing before him in the thousands, pleading. He knew this would be his mission even after his death, for a tzaddik's soul retains the capacity to rectify souls, even after death.[5]

Rabbi Nachman was particularly anguished about the naked souls of Jewish children who had been martyred in Uman. It's poignant that he first began speaking about doing this work with children's souls after the death of his infant son, Shlomo Ephraim.

In his discourse about naked souls, Rabbi Nachman spoke

of other states of the soul, other difficult "incarnations that have not yet been revealed."

He said, "One's incarnation can also cause him to constantly desire to travel. He makes plans to travel, but they do not materialize, and he ultimately remains at home."

That is the story of Kafka's failed journey to Palestine. But it is not Rabbi Nachman's story.

The first Jewish traveler, Abram, heard a divine voice that said, Take yourself out of here. *Lekh lekhah.* The simple meaning is "take yourself out," go away from where you live, the land of your fathers, the land of your birth, to the place I will show you. But *lekh lekhah* is not really about moving from point A to point B; if it were that, the traveling would be pointless. The journey is inward, and so the Hasidim read *lekh lekhah* another way, to mean "take yourself out," that is, get over yourself, for there's no way to find your way to God without some complete inner transformation. Something has to change on the inside, or all your miles are worthless.

All the discomforts and unfamiliarity of travel, the strange hours we keep, wear down our old pretensions and self-conceptions. By plane and by train, I did my *lekh lekhah* on my way to Kamenetz. It was hard for me to be me anymore after twenty-five hours of travel.

Abraham the father of nations is the father of journeys. Real journeys and fantasy journeys, in daydreams and in stories: Rabbi Nachman's journey to Kamenetz and my journey to Kamenetz, Rabbi Nachman's pilgrimage to Israel and all the pilgrims coming to Uman, the journey of the man from the country who sought the law, and the journey of the wise man sent to find a portrait of a humble king.

All of my journeys, and all of Rabbi Nachman's journeys, and Kafka's daydreams of journeys, the stories of all these Jewish souls wind around that old *mashal* of *lekh lekkah*. What remains is to tell how in the end I did arrive in Uman, at the tomb of Rabbi Nachman, with my Kafka coffee mug in hand.

PART III

Journeys

33

Aliyah

Franz Kafka loved to peruse guidebooks and daydream about journeys. When he was younger he wanted to emigrate to Spain and South America, and in the year of the great fire he wrote a novel about emigration to America. But increasingly in the last third of his life, all his dreams centered around Palestine, a destination inextricably bound up for him with love and marriage.

That connection was forged the night Kafka met Felice Bauer at the apartment of Brod's parents. Kafka was feeling his oats that evening, bearing the page proofs of his first published book, *Meditation*. He invited Felice to travel with him to Palestine, which became a running joke between them.

In his first letter to her, he reminds Felice of "a promise to accompany him next year to Palestine" and in the next, "But oh, what has happened to the trip to Palestine?" It was always a plan, and always put off, as he wrote to Felice, "in the near future, or the not so near future, by next spring or autumn for certain."* This ever-expanding postponement

---

*In the same way he frequently charted out complex train schedules allowing him to meet Felice, trips that often collapsed of their own complexity.

recalls the expanding topography in "An Imperial Message": the courtyard, the second palace encircling the first, stairs and courtyards "and then once again, a palace, and so on for thousands of years." Though the messenger is a "powerful tireless man," there's too much resistance, "how futile are all his efforts. . . . Never will he win his way through. And if he did manage that, nothing would have been achieved."*

Behind all the postponement was his father. Hermann had criticized his engagement to Felice, and later when Kafka was briefly engaged to Julie Wohryzek, the daughter of a shoemaker, Hermann was furious. The father in "The Judgment" mocked Georg for falling for a woman because she "lifted her skirts." Hermann spoke of Julie as if quoting from the story. "She probably put on a fancy blouse, something these Prague Jewesses are good at, and right away, of course, you decided to marry her. And that as fast as possible, in a week, tomorrow, today. I can't understand you: after all, you're a grown man, you live in the city, and you don't know what to do but marry the first girl who comes along." These words still stung when Kafka composed the *Letter to His Father*. There he imagines Hermann blocking all his paths, sprawled across a map of the world, "and I feel I could consider living openly in those regions that either are not covered by you or are not within your reach. And in keeping with the conception I have of your magnitude, these are not many and not very comforting regions—and marriage is not among them."

---

*The parable was written sometime in February or March 1917, as Kafka was renewing his engagement to Felice, after having previously broken it off. It was published in 1919 in *Selbstwehr*, the Zionist paper.

Marriage was not possible in Prague, under his father's purview, but perhaps in Palestine it might be. Whatever Buber intended at the time, his romantic brand of cultural Zionism provided Kafka's generation with the privilege of imagining emigration while making it "not necessary to leave home." First Western European Jews could prepare themselves for the promised land by discovering a more urgent Judaism. And they could do practical work for the Zionist cause "in the here and now" (*Gegenwartsarbeit*)[1] by aiding the Eastern European Jews flooding Western cities in the years before World War I.

As Jewish refugees arrived in Prague by the trainload, Kafka personally helped distribute food and clothing. But he generally preferred action at a distance to direct involvement. He observed classes for Jewish refugee girls taught by Brod, mused about Jewish education, and encouraged his sister Ottla to attend a Zionist agricultural school in Cologne. He likewise barraged Felice with letters encouraging her refugee work in Berlin, at the Jewish People's Home there.[*]

Gershom Scholem visited this same Jewish settlement house. There was a portrait of the Virgin Mary hanging in the house and he overheard the well-meaning "Western Jews" debating at length whether or not to take it down. They "had only a rudimentary knowledge of Jewish affairs" but were "utterly devoted to their work." At nineteen, Scholem also observed that "many of the girls were extremely charming, even beautiful."

And Felice Bauer observed Scholem in turn, engaged in

---

[*] *Jüdisches Volksheim.*

pointed debate with the leader of the home, Dr. Lehmann. Scholem disdained a "lack of seriousness which expressed itself in the group's interpretations of Buber's interpretations of Hasidism. . . . 'To Lehmann's understandable annoyance I demanded that people learn Hebrew and go to the sources instead of occupying themselves with such literary twaddle.' "

Felice Bauer wrote Kafka about the debate. True to form, he replied, "Theoretically I am always inclined to favor proposals such as those made by Herr Scholem, which demand the utmost and by so doing achieve nothing."[2]

For Scholem, learning Hebrew was the way to Palestine, for Kafka a wonderful detour. He agreed heartily with Scholem that Hebrew was vital, yet his motives were far from practical. Though Kafka began studying Hebrew a few months before his diagnosis of tuberculosis in August 1917, his studies became even more intensive after that illness made emigration implausible. The diagnosis also led to a final rupture with Felice. Marriage was temporarily off the map, but Palestine loomed larger. "As Kafka's health began to fail, his dreams about going to Palestine grew stronger and his Hebrew studies intensified." Kafka quickly worked through the first forty-five lessons in Moses Rath's *Textbook of the Hebrew Language*. Convalescing in the Bohemian town of Zürau* shortly after his diagnosis, he continued his Hebrew studies through spring 1918 and in the fall proposed to Brod that they correspond in Hebrew. At the sanitarium in Schelesen in 1919 he "studied Hebrew with another patient using Moses Rath's textbook."[3] There he also wrote

*In Zürau he wrote his aphorisms and read up on Kierkegaard.

the *Letter to His Father*, bitter after the failed engagement to Julie Wohryzek. Returning to Prague he studied Hebrew with Friedrich Thieberger, and quite probably Jiri Langer.

Later it became more enticing to learn the language from Puah Bentovim, a nineteen-year-old Jerusalemite, sent by Hugo Bergmann to study graduate physics at Charles University. She tutored Kafka in Hebrew every day for five months in early 1923. Kafka fell for her and, as with Felice a decade earlier, sought to accompany her to Jerusalem. She proved elusive. Then in April, Hugo Bergmann himself, by now a leading cultural Zionist, arrived in Prague and lectured about "The Situation in Palestine." Though in a weak condition, Kafka attended and his old friend encouraged him to make aliyah, even offering Kafka a room in his apartment in Jerusalem. Kafka was still mulling over the offer that summer in the Baltic resort of Müritz, where a letter from Bergmann found him. His reply is touching,

"This was the first letter in Hebrew I have received from Palestine. Perhaps the wishes expressed in it have great force. To test my transportability after many years of lying abed and of headaches, I pulled myself together for a short trip to the Baltic Sea."

Kafka described to Bergmann his pleasure in living near "a vacation camp run by the Jewish Peoples Home of Berlin," where Felice had volunteered seven years before.

"Through the trees I can see the children playing. Cheerful, healthy spirited children. Eastern European Jews whom West European Jews are rescuing from the dangers of Berlin. Half the days and nights the house, the woods and the beach are filled with singing. I am not happy when I'm among them, but on the threshold of happiness."[4]

On the threshold he would remain, a daydreamer in a window. He had one last flirtation left in him.

Dora Diamant was scaling a fish in the camp kitchen when Kafka first saw her. "Such gentle hands," he said, "such bloody work." Kafka, she said, had "long ethereal fingers, speaking fingers that took on shapes while he was telling a story." He made her laugh making shadow puppets on the wall. "He had shy brown eyes," was tall, and walked with a loping gait; he was so dark she thought he might have been a Native American. She was struck by his gentle manner with a young boy embarrassed because he took a spill. "What a clever way to fall," he told the boy, "And what a clever way to get up again."[5] By summer's end they made plans to move in together. She was nineteen, he was forty.

A month before Kafka arrived there with Dora, Scholem left Berlin for good, shipping ahead to Jerusalem his substantial collection of Hebrew books and his slim Kafka volumes. Hugo Bergmann gave him the room once promised to Kafka. In the end, Scholem took Kafka's place in the promised land.

Palestine represented Kafka's dream of normalcy, a simple life, and a humble profession (gardening, bookbinding). It was not about being a writer. He wrote his sister Ottla that Palestine was just a way to "give myself something to hope for."[6] With Dora he fantasized about starting a restaurant together in Tel Aviv. "He loved to play with great seriousness and carry the role of the waiter for me. He had an entire room to serve and the game lasted sometimes fifteen minutes while the meal got cold."[7] They "constantly played with the idea of leaving Berlin and immigration to Palestine to begin a new life."

It was a daydream, but his real life was at night, when he

wrote in the cold apartment, still holding to the demands of the great fire. All of his fantasies about Palestine constituted a delaying action. Kafka always remained outside the promised land, or the land of any of his promises. He identified with Moses on Mount Nebo when after forty years of wandering, he saw the land of Canaan spread before him. "He is on the track of Canaan all his life: it is incredible that he should see the land only when on the verge of death. This dying vision of it can only be intended to illustrate how incomplete a moment is human life, incomplete because a life like this could last forever and still be nothing but a moment. Moses fails to enter Canaan not because his life is too short but because it is a human life."[8]

In Berlin with Dora, Kafka was at his most human, his most vulnerable. At last he tasted domesticity, which softened his severities. Though Kafka never became a religious Jew, he loved it when Dora, the daughter of an Hasidic rabbi, recited *Got fun Avrum* (God of Abraham), a Sabbath prayer of Rabbi Nachman's contemporary, Rabbi Levi Yitzhak of Berditchev. In their last months together they studied Rashi's commentary on the Hebrew Bible. By spring 1924, he'd reached lesson 105 in Rath's textbook.

But the final bed at Kierling lay just ahead. Writing Klopstock from his sickbed, Kafka confessed that "Palestine would have been beyond me . . . Berlin too is almost beyond me. (My temperature has gone up, and there are other problems.) And the danger remains that the voyage to Palestine will shrink to a trip to Schelesen.* May it at least remain that, rather than end up as the elevator trip from the

---

*The sanitorium/spa where he studied Hebrew in 1919.

Alstädter Ring to my room." Kafka pictured himself dying in his old bedroom, not far from the Old Town Square where he once argued about God with Bergmann under the clock. He had run out of time.

Kafka's romance with Dora was the last chapter of Palestine, Eastern European Jews, and Hasidim. Kafka must have admired Dora's spunk, for in coming west she had rebelled against her traditionalist parents. But Kafka never told his own parents about her. Hermann would not approve of unmarried love or Polish Jewesses. Though Dora accompanied him on his last visit to Prague, she was not invited into Kafka's home.

Yet a month before he died, he wrote Dora's father proposing marriage. He confessed to the rabbi that "although he was not a practicing Jew" he was "a repentant one, seeking to return."[9] Dora's father consulted his rebbe, the Gerer, who gave a one-word answer.

No.

That gate was closed.

34

Rabbi Nachman's Journey to Kamenetz

Kafka viewed Palestine and marriage as part of life, and life was inimical to writing. But for Rabbi Nachman, the journey to Palestine was the path to his storytelling and the basis for his whole mission as a rebbe.

For him the journey was a *mashal* and the *mashal* in turn is a journey. That is the basic plot of so many of his tales, beginning with the very first, "The Loss of the Princess," which is about a journey to find a lost princess. But the tale is also first told "along the way" in a horse-drawn carriage traveling east from Breslov to Medvedevka, a trip of about 125 miles.*[1]

When Rabbi Nachman came to Uman at the end, he understood how mystifying his frequent relocations were. "He was constantly moving from place to place like a wanderer," writes Rabbi Nathan. "In Medvedevka he had had everything he needed. It would have been quite satisfactory if he had stayed there permanently. There he had peace and

---

*A day's journey in a coach could be as much as fifty miles though sometimes far less.

quiet. But he had not wanted a peaceful life. He left and went to settle in Zlotopolye where he endured so much opposition and suffering. Then he left [Breslov] and finally came to settle in Uman."[2]

Other people criticized him and thought him mad, but the Rebbe laughed and said, "It is very good to let a madman loose among the people. Everyone fools somebody and that somebody is himself. He deceives himself and makes a fool of himself. The one who takes care not to deceive himself, deceives the whole world."[3]

Rabbi Nachman's point is that in a world mad with self-deception, a person who follows the dictates of his soul will appear insane to others. They cannot hear the music he is dancing to. The general self-deception in the world, the disappearance of even the language for a spiritual life, is one more symptom of the shattering of the vessels. The more unbelief spread in his time, the more likely people with wholly secular values would view a rebbe as merely insane.

But Rabbi Nachman understood this completely. He once told a parable to this effect, "The Tainted Grain."

The king foresees that whoever eats the grain in the coming harvest will go mad, so he asks advice from his prime minister who answers, "We must put aside enough grain so that we will not have to eat from this year's harvest."

The king objected. "But then we will be the only ones who will be sane. Everyone else will be mad. Therefore, they will think that we are the mad ones."

Because it is "impossible to put aside enough grain for everyone," the king and prime minister must also eat the tainted grain.

"But we will make a mark on our foreheads, so that at

least we will know that we are mad. I will look at your fore-head, and you will look at mine, and when see this sign, we will know that we are both mad."[4]

Rabbi Nachman knew how mad he looked to others and took on the burden of their misunderstanding. That is why it makes sense in a way that he left no "image" of himself behind, just an empty chair. He was a hidden tzaddik in plain sight: if we look through the goggles of clinical catego-ries, like manic-depressive, his substance disappears.

And perhaps there were times he wanted to disappear. In late winter 1807, he completely abandoned his wife and family to become a voluntary wanderer, a spiritual practice the Hasidim called "undertaking exile" (*oprikhtn golus*).

Did he learn this practice from his father, Rabbi Simcha? As with most of his gestures, the Rebbe expected to be taken with utter seriousness. He said, "If people only knew why I am going on this journey, they would kiss my foot-steps! With every step that I take, I shall be turning the world's balance toward the side of merit." His aspirations for the journey were huge, Messianic. "I have the power to change the whole world for the better, not just simple peo-ple but even Tzaddikim, and I could even bring non-Jews close to God."[5]

Rabbi Nachman wrote a mournful farewell to his follow-ers in Breslov. "I shall henceforth be a wanderer from tent to tent, settling nowhere permanently but only sojourning." He would be sharing the exile of the *Shekhinah*, becoming a character in his own tale, the viceroy who pursues the lost princess. But by the end of the summer, he'd returned to Breslov. He was not destined to end his life as a solitary wanderer.

The first journey, the template for all of them, was the visit to Kamenetz in early spring of 1798. He took off with his faithful companion Rabbi Simeon, telling him, "I have a journey to go on."

"Where to?"

"I myself do not know."

"How long will it take?"

"Perhaps a week, perhaps two; perhaps a month, perhaps a quarter year, half a year, or an entire year."[6]

Rabbi Simeon thought it was a joke, but when he saw Rabbi Nachman was serious, he got a horse and wagon together. They set off for Medzhibozh, where the Rebbe was raised, and visited his parents. His mother asked if he was going to see the Baal Shem Tov at his grave. Rabbi Nachman said, "If Grandfather wants to see me, he can come to me."

That night he must have had a dream visitation. The next morning he announced that the Baal Shem Tov had given him his destination, Kamenetz. Rabbi Simeon fell ill, so Rabbi Nachman came to Kamenetz with a servant. That night, he stayed alone in the town, and when the servant appeared the next day, they visited many homes.

According to the speculation of his biographer Arthur Green, the Rebbe entered homes once owned by Frankists. He poured a schnapps and recited a *l'chaim* and a blessing. The mere act of a rebbe reciting a blessing had the power to lift up souls. Was he lifting fallen Jewish souls, or somehow purifying the homes they'd contaminated so that Jews could return to them?

About all this, Rabbi Nachman said, "Whoever knows why the land of Israel was in the hands of Canaan before the

Jews conquered it also knows why I was first in Kamenetz, and only afterward in the land of Israel." Perhaps he means that just as the promised land was first in the hands of the Canaanite idol worshippers, and only then in the hands of the Jews, so in some way, Kamenetz, once in the hands of Jewish heretics, would return to the hands of good Jews.

But there was another ritual impurity in Kamenetz that may have drawn him. Jews had been banned from Kamenetz for the previous fifty years by the Polish king Augustus. "Their houses passed to the town council and the synagogue was demolished." This was mainly due to complaints of rival merchants—the Jewish market offered tough competition to the other three nations. In addition, as Yohanan points out, the Poles knocked down the Jewish cemetery walls, making the town ritually impure. But after the 1795 partition of Poland, there was a new ruler in the land. Gone were the Poles, in their place, the Russians, for which the Jews were very grateful. A year before Rabbi Nachman's visit (in 1797), Czar Paul of Russia decreed that Jews could return to Kamenetz. But it wasn't until a year after the Rebbe's visit that the czar decreed that they could rebuild their cemetery walls. This change allowed them to settle in full force. The Breslovers attribute these beneficent changes to the holy work of the Rebbe.[7]

On the Shabbat after his return from Kamenetz, Rabbi Nachman gave a Torah lesson that he exulted in. "If this is the kind of teaching I give after returning from Kamenetz, how much more awesome will be the Torah teachings I will be able to reveal when I come back from the Holy Land."[8]

To us this would sound like boasting, as do similar statements he makes throughout his life. But these have to be balanced against other moments when he would declare himself to be in a state of complete simplicity, where he would openly say he had absolutely nothing to offer.

When he felt he was drawing from a higher wisdom, he had to honor that source. But he also knew, as a master, that to go higher, he would have to face going lower. Kamenetz, my eponymous hometown, was the lowest of the low places, and this marks the explicit spiritual dimension of his visit there. In Kamenetz heretics had triumphed, the Talmud had been burned. His great-grandfather had his heart broken by Kamenetz. To deliberately enter that polluted space was what the Hasidim called a "descent for the sake of the ascent," *yeridah le-tzorekh aliyah.*[9]

This concept has many applications. In simple terms, to descend and then ascend is an emotional movement, something everyone would like to master: how to descend to the lowest places, and then rebound, higher than before.

The goal for the Hasid was constant communion with God (*devekut*). But the Baal Shem Tov taught that the human being could not stay this high forever. There was always going to be a falling off, *yeridah*, a descent. And *yeridah* had its uses: you can be a regular person, have ordinary conversations. You can do your taxes in *yeridah*.

To some degree, *yeridah* was a necessary relief from spiritual intensity for the ordinary Hasid. But the tzaddik differed in one respect. He descended deliberately for the sake of communicating with his Hasidim. But maybe this was only an apparent descent.

Once Rabbi Nachman's brother observed him in casual conversation with his Hasidim. He took him aside later to chastise him. Rabbi Nachman spent hours with his brother explicating the hidden depths of each and every word and phrase, and at the end of it his brother wept for a long time and was astonished. Even in *yeridah* the Rebbe had his eyes on God.

Kamenetz was a far deeper and more dangerous spiritual descent, and Rabbi Nachman's success gave him confidence to make the next step. He viewed Kamenetz as part of the journey to the land of Israel. He knew from his own great-grandfather's history that it was a difficult spiritual journey and that there would be a high price to pay. He learned that as soon as he returned from Kamenetz for, in his absence, a daughter was born. Shortly after his return she died. There was not even time to give her a name. In a spiritual economy very difficult to understand, every ascent was at the price of death of those close to him.

To reach the land of Israel, he would deliberately experience a descent even more profound. It was not simply the idea of a falling off from a spiritual attainment, or even of contact with people or places at lower levels. It was a more radical inner transformation. According to the research of Zvi Mark, the process is alluded to in the mystical literature, in the writings of Rabbi Isaac Luria, the Ari, of whom Rabbi Nachman was a careful student. The practice was called "smallness."

To enter the state of "smallness" resembled dying, it resembled returning to a childlike state, it was like becoming a fetus.[10]

"Smallness" would allow Rabbi Nachman to succeed where his great-grandfather the Baal Shem Tov had failed, in overcoming every obstacle to reach the land of Israel.

35

The Narrow Bridge

Friday Morning, September 26

Kamenetz-Podolsk* was cold, gray, and raw. The train station is in the new part of town northeast of the old. It was 7:35 a.m., on time. Nick, a friendly burly guy with dark hair, grabbed my suitcase. He is the chair of the Department of Journalism and Language at Kamianets-Podilsky National University. As reward for Yohanan's lecture there, we were put up at the student dorm, which did not have hot water but did have laundry hanging out the windows. After we rested, Nick returned. At first the streets were rough and patchy. Two workmen with drills dug up the asphalt, while a third supervised. Down the street was the pink PLAYBOY club.

But as we headed for the university, the streets widened, lined with tall chestnut trees; we passed colorful pastel painted houses, many parks, many monuments to World War II dead, Soviet tanks that put a stop to Nazis. I stopped at one of the monuments to read the names of those who

*The Ukrainian transliteration is Kamianets-Podilsky, but for obvious reasons I prefer the Russian spelling.

died defending the town. I was looking for a Kamenetz, looking for a name, a sign. Dogs ran free, most without collars.

After the lecture, Nick led us west across the modern bridge on Prince Koriatovich Street over the Smotrych River. It was impossible to cross from this direction in the time of Rabbi Nachman. We stopped on the bridge and looked down a deep gorge. Three hundred feet below the river flows between grassy banks.

We came directly into the Polish market square, where the Talmuds were burned. Cobblestone streets, and a nice reconstruction project. The town was being spruced up for tourism. The tourist brochures and placards mention the "three nations" who traded in the town: Poles. Ukrainians, and Armenians. A fourth nation goes unmentioned. So does the site near the restored Polish market square where Bishop Dembowski had the Talmud burned in 1757.

Erasure is a multicultural game. Poised on the minaret next to the Catholic cathedral is a golden statue of the Virgin Mary. The minaret dates to the years of Turkish rule; Mary was put up there by Bishop Dembowski; his bust sits on a plinth, his large bishop's hat, his eyes tilted heavenward, a big simple cross on his chest. I walked into his cathedral, a word that is accurate but misleading: the church space is small with simple pews. How intimate it must have been, the Talmud Jews and the heretical Jews arguing back and forth in front of the altar; the bishop and priests observing a few feet away. They could smell one another's wasted breath.

In the rose garden, I looked across the way to the miniature blue onion domes that crown the Uniate church; for a small town Kamenetz has been full of religious conflict: Polish Catholics and Ukrainian Orthodox, Turkish Muslims and Jews.

Were there any signs of my ancestors in Kamenetz? Any signs of Jews at all? To walk through Kamenetz in my current incarnation was to go shopping for ghosts. Near the riverbank, Yohanan spied a churchlike building suspiciously bare of all external Christian symbols. We scrambled up the hill to get a closer look. A tall sanctuary and a long annex building that could have been a *beit midrash*. Yohanan pointed to the rusty iron cross set on top that sits, he said, "like a saddle on a cow." We went inside to investigate further. Again remarkably, this sanctuary has no Christian symbols carved in the outer walls. Inside, men cut sheets of plywood on a table saw; sawdust climbed into the light. The former sanctuary is a woodshop.

The old town is shaped like a kidney; the river forms a loop around it. Where the north and south loops nearly touch there's a narrow bridge. All the world, Rabbi Nachman said, is just a narrow bridge; the important thing is not to be afraid. This bridge leads to a fortress on a rock promontory guarding the town from its enemies, for this was the only approach. Some workmen were repairing a stone wall that lines the road to the bridge. Below, near the banks, is an archery concession. Lots of arrows must have flown in the past, when the Turks attacked and took over from the Poles, when the Poles regained it from the Turks. The fortress protected Jews in two Cossack attacks in 1648 and 1652, during the Chmielnicki uprising. A fierce-looking costume Cossack with a partially shaven head manned the archery concession. He had a lock of raven hair swept around one ear, wore a white blouse and gray vest and rose-colored pantaloons. He watched a young woman in an appliqué blouse pull back a bow and aim. Wherever I went in the town that day I saw him, this same Cossack—at a museum, posing in a courtyard with visitors, on the streets. I stared at him, he glared at me. I'd traveled six thousand miles and now I had my own personal Cossack.

As I crossed the narrow bridge, a wedding procession streamed away from the fortress. Bride beautiful all in white. Rabbi Nachman might have entered the town from her direction. The narrow bridge, the cannon and the arrows that once protected it, reminded me of the description the first king gives to the wise man about entering the land of the humble king:

"There is only one small path upon which only one man at a time can go. This path is also defended with cannons and if anyone attacks they fire the cannons. It is impossible even to come close to [his land]."[1]

Did Rabbi Nachman visualize the bridge into Kamenetz when he told that tale?

My first summer in Prague ten years ago I visited sites trying to connect in some deeper way to Kafka's stories. I walked across the Czech bridge (*Čechův most*) over the Vltava River. Above me, proud imperial eagles on Corinthian columns painted gold. The bridge is splendid—sleek and modern, pure art nouveau. Prague is a jewel box of architecture with every style from Romanesque to Cubist. I ran my hand along the railing, imagining Georg Bendemann's hand on it just before he leapt over, at the end of "The Judgment." "Dear parents, I loved you all the same." For three years from his room, Kafka watched the Czech bridge being built, joking how the street ended abruptly at the river. He called it a "running up ramp for suicides." In the same room, he wrote "The Judgment."

On a cold rainy evening—Prague summers can be autumn cool—I stood in front of Charles University and looked up as the Prague castle loomed overhead in the mist. Who could not think of the mournful land surveyor K., though for him, "there was no sign of the Castle hill, fog and darkness surrounded it, not even the faintest gleam of light suggested the large Castle. K. stood a long time on the wooden bridge that leads from the main road to the village, gazing upward into the seeming emptiness."

Another time, I found a tall rococo door with a security guard and was delighted to learn that this was the building where Kafka studied law. Voilà, the setting for the parable "Before the Law."

But these ventures came to feel like reductionism, tourist-class. Kafka was no realist, except of unreality. The last thing he wanted was to be a writer of local color. His feelings about Prague ranged from ambivalence to aversion. It took a long time, but these days Prague finally celebrates Kafka properly with a new museum and a statue in his honor. But Prague never loved Kafka when he was alive. He did not write in Czech and is not really seen by most Czechs as a Czech writer. He's a Jew, and despite the devastating destruction of Czech Jewry in the Shoah, the anti-Semitism in Prague remains unembarrassed today. You can buy a bearded rabbi marionette if you like, complete with huge nose and black beard. At the Golem restaurant in the Jewish quarter you can order "rabbi's pocket," which turns out to be a pastry filled with ham and cheese; in the Café Kafka there's an unsettling glass case display of Jewish ceremonial objects: a tallis and a menorah, particularly weird when you consider Kafka's indifference to Jewish religious ceremony. But then again, why should we expect Czechs to understand a struggle we Jews don't always understand ourselves?

The most painful thing for me about the Jewish Quarter of Prague is how much it fulfills Hitler's plan for it. He envisioned the Jewish Quarter as the site for a museum of an extinguished race, with actors strolling the cobblestone streets in beard and Hasidic costumes. As his troops swept through the Bohemian and Moravian countryside they collected and tagged Torah scrolls, silver Torah pointers, circumcision instruments, Shabbas candles, Passover plates—all for a planned museum. Today that collection is known as the "precious legacy" and is housed in the Klausen Synagogue. All of the synagogues in the Jewish Quarter are museums, apart from the Alt-Neu Synagogue. The walls of the Pinkas Synagogue are covered with the names of the dead in red letters. At the altar, strangely and unaccountably, the names of concentration camps are inscribed, where the holy ark would be.

If you have any knowledge of absence, it's easy to be a melancholy Jew in the Jewish Quarter. One time I walked past the Café Kafka in the Jewish Quarter and a German tourist pointed to the display case and said, "What is that candelabra called?" I felt so much pain in that moment, I could barely speak. But I told him. And he said, Ah yes, yes, a menorah, pronouncing the unfamiliar Hebrew word slowly. A menorah in the Café Kafka, but no Chanukah candles will ever burn in it. With its Japanese and Germans, the Jewish Quarter in Prague probably has more tourists from the former Axis powers on any given day than Czech Jews.

Jewish history in Europe is about absence and silence. Books burned and their smoke disappeared into the air. People burned and left names written on a wall. Recovering presence is an effort of the imagination. So I thought when I came to Kamenetz to trace Rabbi Nachman's old footsteps. But even more than with Kafka, Rabbi Nachman's mode is not literary realism. His tales are not intended to be read as travelogues or journeys into the past, but as interior journeys, journeys of the soul.

The wise man makes his quest through the corrupt court system to get a portrait of a king no one has ever seen. At the secret, deepest level, it can be read as the story of the tzaddik's spiritual ascent, the obstacles he encounters on the archetypal journey, and the revelation he receives of a very high level of God. The history of absence creates a taste for the invisible.

36

Two Kings

In most Jewish parables the king represents God. Our first problem with the tale of "The Humble King" is that there are two kings.

The first king sends the wise man on his journey to a second king "who designates himself 'a mighty hero,' 'a man of truth,' and 'a humble person.' As to his might, I know that he is mighty. . . . But why he designates himself 'a man of truth' and 'a humble person,' this I do not know. And I want you to fetch me the portrait of that king."

What is a portrait? In one of his lessons,[1] Rabbi Nachman explains that "God's portrait consists of the representations by which we depict Him: merciful, compassionate . . . and the other representations with which we address Him. All these representations were revealed by the prophets."[2]

The wise man then is on a quest to find a new portrait of God, that is, a deeper concept or understanding of the mystery of God. In a sense, wise or not, we are all on that same quest.

We, too, collect portraits of God throughout our lives, beginning in childhood. And often we become dissatisfied with our old portraits and seek new ones. Child or adult, atheist, agnostic, or just plain confused, we can never feel satisfied with our portraits of God.

Some of our portraits fulfill our own need for relationship, as when the young Kafka and his father sat side-by-side at Rosh Hashanah in the Alt-Neu Synagogue and recited the prayer *Avinu Malkeinu*, "Our Father, Our King." Even though we know ultimately that the portrait of God as a man or a king is not accurate, such portraits help close the gap between our human longing and the divine. Over the past decades, there's been a strong effort to include female portraits as well. Often these borrow from the feminine language of the kabbalah, which speaks of the female aspect of the divine as the *Shekhinah*.

All these portraits are useful and problematic. We speak of God as a king, but we don't believe in kings anymore. And if God is a parent, a mother or a father, what if our relationships with parents are difficult or fractured? Here is the dilemma that underlies Kafka's story "The Judgment." If God is portrayed as a father, what if your own father is terrifying or distant? How can you feel close to God as a father if you feel about your father the way Franz felt about Hermann Kafka?

Then there's the problem of the atheist or nonbeliever—including the atheist within each of us—for whom God seems entirely remote. Even a confirmed atheist carries a certain portrait of God, the God he doesn't believe in. As my teacher Rabbi Zalman Schachter used to respond when confronted by an atheist, "Tell me about the God you don't believe in—I probably don't believe in Him either."

The portrait the wise man is sent to find is of a reclusive, hidden God who rules an unjust land. This tale speaks to our own atheism, our own difficulty in believing there's a God in a chaotic, unjust world.

Why does Rabbi Nachman's tale speak of two kings?

About the first king, we learn that he "had all the portraits of all the kings, but no portrait of the king who had designated himself (with these titles) was available because he is hidden from men." The first king is someone the wise man evidently knows, but the second king is entirely recondite.

Rabbi Kaplan's note to the Breslov Research Institute's edition of the tales explains the matter of two kings in kabbalistic terms: "Kabbalistically the first king is Malkhuth. All the other sefiroth shine on Malkhuth and are seen through Malkhuth. Therefore, the 'portraits of all the other kings,' which are the lights of the other sefiroth, are found in Malkhuth. The sefiroth are known as 'kings' from Genesis 36."[3]

The ten *sefirot* are ten divine portraits. Each describes a different name of God, a different way of feeling God or experiencing God, a different way to address prayer or imagine relationship. The ten *sefirot* are not actually different Gods, there is only one, but they are different relationships or attributes or depictions. They might also be seen as different levels of perception.

The wise man's journey from the first king to the second is the meditative journey from *Malkhut* to *Keter*, from the lowest *sefirot* to the highest, and from the lower wisdom to the higher wisdom.

The lower wisdom, though, for most of us, is already incredibly high. Though in this tale *Malkhut* is described as a king (and *Malkhut* means dominion or kingship), to the kabbalist this *sefirah* corresponds to the *Shekhinah*. She is identical to the lost princess that the viceroy is always seeking in Rabbi Nachman's first tale. Of all the *sefirot*, she is closest to our world.

Yet we know how elusive the lost princess is in that story, how difficult for the viceroy just to get a glimpse of her. We, too, might spend our whole lives looking for her and fall asleep just before we are about to see her again. Or we might only glimpse her when it's too late, in some moment of inner illumination like the gleam of light streaming from the Law that Kafka's man from the country sees just before the gate is shut.

Seeing her is like collecting moonlight. And in kabbalistic symbols, *Malkhut* is the moon who receives the reflected light of the higher *sefirot*. We, too, receive in this way, by indirect reflection, as Rabbi Nachman teaches that "only through the lower intellect, which is *Malkhut*, can we even begin to perceive the higher intellect (*Chokhmah*). Hence it is through *Malkhut*, the revelation of His kingship and His attributes, that we perceive God and peer at his Portrait."[4]

To some degree this "lower wisdom" is the wisdom of the world, the wisdom of philosophy, or the knowledge of God we could find through intellectual contemplation and study of the Torah. However deep and profound this wisdom is, Rabbi Nachman was not content with the lower wisdom, which he already had attained living in Ukraine. He was not content with the reflected light. He wanted another look. He had seen the light of the moon, but now he wanted the sun. It's like the yearning of the "Rabbi's Son" who through study has attained the lesser light but now yearns for the greater. The rabbi's son wanted to journey to the tzaddik.

And Rabbi Nachman wanted to journey to the land of Israel, where he could attain the higher consciousness, the greater wisdom. The direct sun, not the reflected moon-light.

"The Humble King" can be read schematically as a meditation diagram, the journey in meditation from the lower *sefirah* of *Malkhut*, with its lower wisdom, to the highest conception of the divine that is attainable. In a sense, both kings are ultimately the same king, as the light of the moon is ultimately the reflected light of the sun. It is the dissatisfaction of the wise man that leads him on a risky journey to a deeper or higher understanding. I feel that dissatisfaction arising from the doubt about God when we contemplate how broken this world is.

Yet the tale is not only a metaphysical quest. It also reflects, as so many of his tales do, Rabbi Nachman's personal experience of a journey, and especially the journey of all journeys, his journey to the land of Israel.

Rabbi Nachman did not make a distinction, as we might, between the contemplative journey and the actual journey.

Rabbi Nathan tells the story of a lesson that Rabbi Nachman gave on the spiritual power of the land of Israel. Afterward, Rabbi Nathan took him aside and asked his master which spiritual "aspect" of the land he meant, as if he were referring to the land symbolically. Rabbi Nachman became quite irritated. "I mean Israel quite literally with its houses and apartments," he insisted.[5]

On all his journeys, every step and every obstacle was immensely significant. Near the end of his life, he spoke to his disciples with feeling about the traveling he used to do in Ukraine to give Torah lessons. Just sitting in the coach was something all by itself, he explained. "Then when he arrived at the edge of the town he was traveling to and the people would come out to meet him and pay their respects, that was something different. When he went into the town, that was something else. When he gave his discourse there, that was something different again. When he was given money, that was something else again." Every aspect of the trip "was something separate all by itself. The inference is that in every single detail of each journey there was an awesome and mystical task which he had to fulfill."[6]

Living with this intensity, every moment becomes a *mashal*, with a deep *nimshal*. That is why wherever he was traveling—to Breslov, Uman, Kamenetz—he could say, "I am always journeying to the land of Israel." The *nimshal* was in every gesture: if he burned a piece of paper or casually announced, "Today I will begin telling tales." The mere movement of his pen could stir the air and make it holier. Certainly if he traveled in a carriage from one town to another, or gave a blessing in a house in Kamenetz, or if he lived in Lemberg and saw a physician, or lived in Uman and played chess with a heretic—each of these acts was intensely significant. His life was like a huge archetypal dream in which every object became a symbol, and every encounter, a meaning.

The life of Rabbi Nachman interprets the tales of Rabbi Nachman and vice versa. Each becomes a *mashal* for the other, each a *nimshal* for the other. And the centerpiece and template of all his journeys was the journey to the land of Israel.

That journey became the template for the journeys in his tales.

In that sense, the story of his journey to the Holy Land is completely identical with the story of "The Humble King."

That is, in traveling from Ukraine to Israel, Rabbi Nachman was traveling like the wise man from the lower wisdom to the higher, from *Malkhut* to the unaccountably highest *sefirot*. And he was seeking a portrait of the hidden king.

In all the years that followed, in each of his moments of despair and loss, the very fact he had made that journey gave him solace. No matter how low he descended spiritually or psychologically, he could always renew himself by the thought of that journey and its obstacles.

The most difficult obstacle came after he arrived in Istanbul and was seeking to cross the Mediterranean Sea. To overcome it, he used a difficult, even life-threatening practice, which he called "smallness."

37

Rabbi Nachman's Journey to the Land of Israel

Rabbi Nachman was one of a number of Hasidic rebbes whose journeys to the land of Israel paved the way for the practical Zionism of Kafka's generation. The Hasidic aliyah began with leaders in the Baal Shem Tov's circle, among them Rabbi Nachman's paternal grandfather, Nachman of Horodenka, who settled in Tiberias in 1764. His grandson had many motivations to follow in his footsteps. One was to commune with his grandfather buried in Tiberias "so that he would always have access to that which he is to know through him."[1]

But that was not the whole story. He was also in many ways completing a failed mission of his great-grandfather. For the Baal Shem Tov had set off for the Holy Land, gotten as far as Istanbul, and took off in a ship. But a storm raged at sea, and for the sake of his daughter's life, he turned back. At that moment, the storm abated.

So that was also on his mind, in some way doing what his great-grandfather could not have done, though he had already paid a high price: just for journeying to Kamenetz, his daughter had died.

But there's more. Every step of the journey was a meditation in action, a myth in life. It's also a great adventure story that in some alternative universe would make a great road movie.

Not long after Rabbi Nachman returned from Kamenetz he took off once more with Rabbi Simeon, his Sancho Panza, his *tam*. It was late spring,[2] a month after Passover, and they rode a barge down the Dnieper loaded with grain to Odessa. Four days by ship in stormy weather took them across the Black Sea to Istanbul. He'd come as far as the Baal Shem Tov had in his own abortive journey to the Holy Land.

In the port of Istanbul he found obstacles. The Jewish community had banned travel by ship because Napoleon's navy was fighting in the Mediterranean. In the tale "The Rabbi's Son" the father interprets every obstacle as a sign from heaven to reverse course. But Rabbi Nachman viewed every obstacle in the exact opposite sense. External obstacles drove him inward. In this case, seeing the opposition to his journey, he found a remedy, in a strange spiritual practice that baffled everyone, including Rabbi Simeon.

He ran the streets "barefoot," "without a belt," in torn clothes. He played elaborate war games with boys, calling himself "France," and the others Turkey and England. He had a run-in with pious emissaries from the land of Israel, Hasidim from Tiberias, where his grandfather Nachman was buried. They were in Istanbul to raise funds for their community.

When they asked his name, Rabbi Nachman gave a different answer each day. He knocked on their door late at night, making prank visits. One Friday evening, he barged in on their Shabbat meal. He exasperated these pious Hasidim so much, they insulted him on the streets. Behind his back, they plotted to block his passage to the Holy Land.

All this strange childish play bewildered everyone. But Rabbi Nachman was not playing.

About the matter of smallness, Rabbi Nathan wrote:

> Before one can come to greatness he must first fall into smallness. The Holy Land is the greatest greatness, and therefore it is first necessary to fall to the smallest smallness. The reason why the Baal Shem Tov failed to reach the Holy Land was because he was unable to descend to this degree of smallness. The Rebbe, however, was able to reach the Holy Land through the extreme smallness he descended to by means of his formidable wisdom. He descended to the ultimate smallness, the smallest smallness, until he succeeded in reaching the Holy Land, which is the greatest greatness, the very essence of greatness.[3]

The key point was to be humiliated by others. "For several days running they insulted him in every way. The Rebbe patiently allowed himself to be insulted. Indeed he even manipulated them so that they would insult him. The Rebbe said that without his childishness and these insults, it would have been impossible for him to reach the Holy Land on account of the obstacles confronting him."

Zvi Mark, in his discussion of "smallness" in *Mysticism and Madness*,[4] emphasizes that this was not merely a moral question of achieving humility. Rather the purpose was to taste death itself by being publicly shamed. What might otherwise look like high jinks, immaturity, or insanity takes on a different coloration if understood as a deliberate spiritual practice of self-abnegation. But to shrink into a state of "fetal existence," to lose everything one has and is in order to be reborn, is not something that's going to be understood by many.

Despite the warnings of Istanbul's Jews, Rabbi Nachman boarded the last ship permitted to leave, ignoring every danger. He and Rabbi Simeon arrived in the port of Haifa on the eve of Rosh Hashanah, September 10, 1798. The Hasidim there received him with full honors, fitting his dignity as a direct descendant of the Baal Shem Tov. He visited his grandfather Nachman's grave in Tiberias. Rabbi Abraham Kalisker received him there with great respect. He also visited the tomb in Meron of Rabbi Simeon Bar Yohai, the man the Hasidim believe is the author of the Zohar. There are some cryptic stories about what happened there: since he himself was reputed to be a reincarnation of Simeon bar Yohai, Rabbi Nachman may have indicated the relationship.

But for all the distance he'd come, he never actually made his way to Jerusalem. This seems to have been deliberate. The time was not yet right for him to enter that city. Likewise "The Loss of the Princess" ends abruptly with the viceroy poised to enter the city of Jerusalem to retrieve the lost princess. To recover her would be to bring on redemption. That is not yet to be.

Rabbi Nachman left the land of Israel in spring of 1799. Napoleon's navy had taken Haifa, and Acre was under siege. Rabbi Nachman and Rabbi Simeon mistakenly boarded a Turkish warship and found themselves in the middle of a naval battle with French forces.

There were days of storm in a leaking vessel, with a murderous crew and a captain who previously had sold Jews into slavery. Rabbi Nachman and Reb Simeon huddled in their cabin in fear and devout prayer. It's said in one of Rabbi Nathan's accounts that during this perilous trip Rabbi Nachman attained the level of performing mitzvahs purely spiritually, of no longer needing a body at all. At the Greek port of Rhodes the Jewish community ransomed the pair, and they returned to Ukraine in summer 1799.

According to Rabbi Nathan, "Before the Rebbe reached the Holy Land he suffered terribly and encountered the most overwhelming obstacles." Yet the purpose of the whole journey was achieved the moment he arrived. "As soon as he walked four paces in the Holy Land he was worthy of attaining everything he had wanted in going to the Holy Land." In the Holy Land he achieved the higher wisdom, and it is from the higher wisdom he believed that he drew down his tales of the ancient of days.

38

The Big Joker

Most of Rabbi Nachman's tales are journeys. Their common template is his journey to the land of Israel. That is evident in "The Humble King." For when the wise man enters the land of the humble king, we learn it is really the land of Israel.

> Among all countries there is one country which includes all countries (in that it serves as the rule for all countries). In that country there is one city which includes all cities of the whole country which includes all countries. In that city there is a house which includes all the houses of the city which includes all the cities of the country which includes all countries. And there is a man who includes everybody from that house, etc. And there is someone there who performs all the jests and jokes of the country.[1]

The country that includes all countries is Israel, the city that includes all cities is Jerusalem, the House that includes all the houses is the Temple (known in Hebrew as "the house" or "Ha-Bayit"). The man who includes everyone in the house is the High Priest.

The High Priest enters the Holy of Holies on the holiest

hour of the holiest day of the year. "And there is someone there"—in the Holy of Holies—"who performs all the jests and jokes of the country."

This is the ultimate joker, the comedian in chief. The origin of humor is a mysterious thing, and to Rabbi Nachman, it is a holy thing, for joking originates in the Holy of Holies.

Rabbi Nachman's ideas about joking are quite profound. The simple Jew, the *tam*, avoids all irony with a simpleton's request, "Only no joking." But what about the spiritual sophisticate like Rabbi Nachman? What is joking ultimately about? Who is the big Joker? The ultimate source of the joking in the land is even higher than the High Priest. He seems to be the king himself. For as Rabbi Aryeh Kaplan explains in his commentary, "The Talmud says that God laughs with the wicked in this world and with the righteous in the World to Come (*Shabbat* 30b)."[2]

God laughs with the wicked in this world, because God and the wicked know the same truth: that evil has no substance. It is nothing. Evil has no ultimate reality. It only appears real, but at core, it is nothing. No one knows this better than the evil person who deliberately deceives another and then laughs in his face the way the merchant in "The Rabbi's Son" laughs in the father's face after revealing his deceit. For that sort of cynical laughter, we are told mournfully by Rabbi Nathan, is the way of the wicked in this world.

Rabbi Nachman once related a parable of a man who runs through a village holding his fist in the air. Everyone believes he's holding a gold coin and follows him until they've gone astray, and then he opens his fist and there's nothing in it. Our delusions lead us astray, we spend our whole lives chasing them, and in the end they are nothing. So God laughs with the wicked in this world, for both know this same truth about the vacauity of evil.

But in the world to come it's different. God laughs with the righteous in the world to come. Even though the righteous may suffer in this world, when they receive their reward they finally appreciate why things are the way they are. They understand what is almost impossible to understand, the profundity of the overall plan, and how even those events that appear most destructive and evil somehow are part of the purpose. From this lofty perspective, the righteous laugh with God in the world to come.

In a certain way Rabbi Nachman did not believe in the ultimate reality of evil—as a monotheist he really couldn't. Evil, too, has its divine purpose, and the jokes played on mankind are part of the overall system, even if Joseph K. probably speaks for most of us when he is so indignant with the priest about "lies [that] are built into a universal system."

We can appreciate the daring of Rabbi Nachman's tale in identifying the land of the humble king with the land of Israel, and saying that even the Holy Land is full of lies and corruption and deceit. That raises the stakes.

There is another way in which the journey of the wise man in the tale reflects moments of Rabbi Nachman's journey to Israel. If we look closely at the strategy of the wise man, we can find an analogue for Rabbi Nachman's "smallness" in Istanbul. Just as Rabbi Nachman deliberately courted mockery and insult, so, too, having learned from the jokes of the land, that the country was full of lies from beginning to end . . . he went and traded in the country and he let himself be cheated in commerce. He went to trial in a court, and he saw that they were all full of lies and bribery. On this day he bribed them, and on the next they did not recognize him. He went to the higher court, and there, too, everything was a lie, until he reached the senate and they, too, were full of lies and bribery. Finally he came to the king himself.

The wise man, acting the part of a dupe, gets himself humiliated every step of the way. In that sense he, too, practices "smallness." Yet this smallness leads him to greatness. He comes to the highest place, which is the court of the humble king.

What happens there, at the end of the story, comes as a complete surprise.

Here he gets an answer, as Joseph K. did not. He attains the higher wisdom, that is, he obtains a "portrait of the humble king."

He has, that is, a new perception of the divine. But to acquire it, he must work through his own gravest doubts, which he expresses to the king with some chutzpah.

"When he came to the king he stated: Over whom are you king? For the country is full of lies, all of it, from beginning to end, and there is no truth in it!"

It sounds like he is about to accuse the king of being a liar. But just at this moment, he does a *teshuvah*, he turns himself around.

The wise man concluded: "And one could say that the king, too, is like them, that he loves deceit like the country.

But from this I see how you are 'a man of truth.' You are far from them, since you cannot stand the lies of the country."

He started praising the king very much.

"From this I see." What happens here? What did he see? Rabbi Nachman does not say what "this" is. But it is a pivot of the story, the moment of *teshuvah*. He willingly abandons the logic of the world, which judges the king. He opens his mouth to praise.

Here we see an enactment of Rabbi Nachman's struggle with doubt. The sophisticate asks the most challenging questions about the lies and contradictions of the world; the simpleton feels only awe. But suppose you are a sophisticate who wants again to be simple? Suppose you are a wise man who wants to be foolish for God. How do you shift from one consciousness to the other? That's a huge paradox: to see the world clearly as the joke it is—and then nevertheless praise the king. To know the world is royally messed up, but not to blame the king. But "from this I see" that the king by his very nature can have nothing to do with such a world. Because he is a "man of truth."

The wise man who is truly wise and knows the joke of the world becomes at this moment utterly simple, humble, and small. And in response to his "smallness" comes a paradoxical revelation: "the humble king" himself becomes small.

"The king was very humble, and his greatness lay in his humility. And this is the way of the humble person: the more one praises and exalts him, the smaller and humbler he becomes."

"Because of the greatness of the praise with which the wise man praised and exalted the king, the king became very humble and small, till he became nothing at all."

Nothing at all. In the Yiddish *"ayin mamash,"* for "real nothing."

"And the king could not restrain himself, but cast away the curtain to see the wise man: 'Who is it who knows and understands all this?' And his face was revealed. The wise man saw him and painted his portrait and he brought it to the king."

His face was revealed, but what face exactly? What face does the wise man see in this moment of revelation? Here is the punch line.

After all this journey, here is a paradox more extreme than anything in Kafka, for here nihilism rides close to the highest perception of God, and the atheist has to steal a glance at the kabbalist and wonder. With all the portraits of God that we carry, good, bad, cracked, and distorted, God's ultimate face is *ayin mamash*. Nothing.

And if this was also the knowledge Rabbi Nachman brought back with him from the land of Israel, it must have been terrifying.

Because it sounds like the biggest joke of all.

39

Uman Uman

Sunday, September 28–Monday, September 29

We took a Saturday night train from Kamenetz and arrived in Kyiv early Sunday morning. I spent Sunday touring Kyiv with kind Wawa. Cossacks on statues and on friezes, lunch of birch beer and pirogies, and a newly renovated synagogue.

Monday morning, Yohanan and I met again in Maidan station to catch the 7:30 a.m. AUTOLUX bus to Uman, which is about halfway between Kyiv and Odessa. Lots of small neat farms—a goat ate from an apple tree on the side of the road. This is the land of black earth, rich for agriculture. Yohanan explained the system of "arenda." Jews held leases from Polish overlords that entitled them to collect rents from Ukrainian peasants, run mills and taverns. In times of upheaval, such as the Chmielnicki uprisings, hatred was directed at the Jewish middlemen. The road was easy traveling and I saw no signs of crazy driving that the Lonely Planet guidebook had cheerfully promised. The bus played a video to entertain the kids, a Soviet movie from the sixties about a cheerful healthy singing blond woman who pumps gas with gusto for long-haul trucks.

At the bus station in Uman there's no indication of a huge pilgrimage going on. Per my e-mail from Rabbi Ozer Bergman, I am looking for Parouska Street and a house with a green gate. Yohanan inquires but no one has ever heard of Parouska Street. The name sounds fishy to him. Someone points us in the general direction of the Rebbe's *kever*, his grave.

The pilgrimage to Uman had its origins in Rabbi Nachman's lifetime, for every year his followers made a special effort to be with him at Rosh Hashanah. "Rabbi Nathan arranged the first pilgrimage to the Rebbe's Tziune* [that is, the rebbe's tomb]—in the winter of 1811. . . . But out of the hundreds that had come for the Rebbe's last Rosh Hashanah, only about sixty traveled to Uman the following year." Then Rabbi Nathan built a synagogue, the Kloyz—made ready by the summer of 1834. But he was denounced by his religious opponents to the czar and placed under house arrest in Nemirov.

The pilgrimage Rabbi Nathan established continued after his death in 1844, and by the early twentieth century, people came to Uman from Poland and Israel. But the border was closed after the Russian revolution and all through the Soviet period official pilgrimages were banned. There was a slight thaw in 1988—a few hundred Hasidim were allowed to visit. Then a thousand the next year, and two thousand the next. These days nearly twenty thousand pilgrims swarm into the small town of Uman.[1]

Uman is a very poor town whose residents, some one hundred thousand, only have fresh water on a limited basis. It's

---

*Tziune is a monument.

hard for the town to supply the needs of these visiting Jews, but the annual pilgrimage is big business. Millions of dollars are spent. The locals collect rents, they supply food. Some move out of their housing near the Tziune just for the week and collect enough rent to live on for months. It's important to keep any untoward incidents out of the papers and off the record. The Ukrainian police are everywhere, and according to Yohanan's investigations, the Israeli police are also around.

Breslovers from Israel have bought up about a third of the local real estate near the grave.[2] They've built impressive tall buildings. I saw a large Moshav Breslov apartment complex and a nine-story Shaare Tzion Kosher Hotel with a kosher restaurant and supermarket on the first floor. There's also an Uman emergency clinic about two minutes from the Kloyz. Yohanan and I were searching for the modest apartment owned by the Breslov Research Institute. But we were having a hard time finding it.

I was wheeling my suitcase. Inside was my Kafka coffee mug, too many books, and a supply of tuna fish. Yohanan seemed concerned that the name I had from Rabbi Ozer, Parouska Street, made no sense. My mood was light; after all I was the personal guest of Rabbi Nachman.

At a checkpoint where local policemen directed traffic, I asked a guy with a cell phone who looked quasi-official which way to the Jews—and he pointed. Now on either side of a grass-lined street was an improvised *shuk*, where in the early afternoon hours before *yuntiv*,* people sold kosher cookies and bottled water, bright oil paintings, Israeli

*The holiday.

falafel, and tufted yarmulkes. The white yarmulkes were the traditional Rabbi Nachman style, but some were also inscribed with black Hebrew letters, spelling out magical words revealed to a Breslover Hasid in Tiberias, Rabbi Israel Dov Odesser.

In 1922, Reb Israel was a thirty-four-year-old Breslover living in a yeshiva in Tiberias. He was heartbroken because he ate food on the morning of the fast of Tammuz. In his despair he prayed alone, until he heard a voice that directed him to look at his bookshelf.

Open any book, the voice said. He opened a book, and a piece of paper fell out that seemed to be a letter addressed to him:

VERY HARD IT WAS FOR ME TO DESCEND TO YOU, MY PRECIOUS STUDENT TO TELL YOU THAT I BENEFITED GREATLY FROM YOUR SERVICE AND UPON YOU I SAID MY FIRE WILL BURN UNTIL MESSIAH WILL COME BE STRONG AND COURAGEOUS IN YOUR SERVICE

The letter ended with cryptic words, that seemed to be a signature:

NA NACH NACHMA NACHMAN ME'UMAN

Only the last two words make any sense, they were the words I wrote on the slip of paper before entering the Borispol airport, "Nachman of Uman."

Suppose in Kafka's parable the message from the emperor finally did arrive and all it said was "*Na Nach Nachma*

Nachman Me'Uman." I wonder how that would feel after such a long wait.

But Reb Israel was so thrilled and joyous, he began dancing and wouldn't stop. Others in the yeshiva came in to see him, until they got worn out just watching him. He danced all night[3] and his followers are still dancing today.

The miraculous letter created a movement. Reb Yisrael taught that *"na nach nachma Nachman me'uman"* is a song to bring on redemption. He himself lived to 106 and made his last pilgrimage to Uman in 1994. The year I visited, the Na Nachs raised up a controversy because they wanted to remove Rabbi Nachman's remains from Uman and bring them to the land of Israel, a move that would also have Messianic implications. Some important religious figures in Israel also support the move probably because they'd prefer to keep Israelis closer to home during Rosh Hashanah. But most of Rabbi Nachman's Hasidim want him to stay in Uman.

The Na Nachs wear white shirts and white yarmulkes. White is the Messianic color Rabbi Nachman wore that fateful spring of 1806 when the burnt book was read from town to town. Now these new Hasidim travel from town to town in Israel in white vans. Some call themselves Na Nachs, some have changed their last names to NaNach. Steven NaNach. Micah NaNach. In Jerusalem and Tel Aviv and Hebron, they pull up at an intersection, blaring techno-music Rebbe Nachman songs. They dance in the streets chanting the mysterious words. On banners hanging over apartment buildings in Jerusalem, on cars and trucks, the words are repeated. I saw a YouTube of a Na Nach skydiving, holding a yellow Na Nach bumper sticker and screaming his head off as he fell. This was a descent for the sake of an ascent.

Young Sephardim have come back to religious observance through this movement's emphasis on ecstatic dancing and music, which fits, they believe, with the main message of Rabbi Nachman: *simchah*, joy.

Other Hasidim, including the folks in dark hats and coats, are less enthusiastic about the Na Nachs. The black they wear is the color of mourning and exile, the white the Na Nachs wear is of redemption. Both black and white are phases of the great Lurianic scheme, of exile and redemption, of the shattering of the vessels and *tikkun olam*.

Next to the enthusiastic out-there Na Nachs selling their yarmulkes and CDs, some local Ukrainians sat looking somewhat disconsolate, with their wares on blankets. Their items looked like rejects from a garage sale. One woman sold fox skins for twenty-five dollars.

Yohanan asked them about Parouska Street, but no one had heard of it. No one knew about the house with the green gate. After the *shuk*, we walked dusty streets and turned up an unmarked road. With hope we knocked on a door with a green fence. Wrong house. Then a teenager led us. We had the name wrong, as Yohanan suspected. Not Parouska but Perovskaia, after the revolutionary Sofia Perovskaia.

We passed a small store selling vodka and beer . . . closed—and a garbage dump. On a dusty littered street we came to a green gate marked with a handwritten sign:

UMAN RITZ CARLTON

We opened the gate and walked into an outdoor area covered by a plastic roof, where we would have most of our meals. There was a kitchen and our own private ritual bath, a *mikveh*—and at the back two stories of small apartments. Hasidim regularly use the *mikveh* before prayer.

Ephraim, a carpenter from Massachusetts, was peeling potatoes for dinner. His crutches leaned against the wall. He'd sprained his ankle the day before leaving. Was that a sign? Ephraim told me Nachman teaches that God is with us and that whatever happens to us is for the good.

Did I believe that? I heard Kafka from his mug: "Sheer superstition!"

But we have our own superstitions, we neurotic jokers: the train we miss, the plane we can't catch, the accident on the road, the lost luggage. We see them as signs or portents of futility. We see them like the father in "The Rabbi's Son." "A journey that does not proceed without mishap . . . is not from heaven." That is a recipe for non-folly.

In the tale, the father misconstrues every obstacle. Only after his son dies does he learn that his opposition gave an opening to the Evil One, Samael.

Rabbi Nachman has a beautiful teaching about obstacles. He explained that when someone wishes to return—do *teshuvah*—obstacles would necessarily arise. "When a person who has spent all his days on the path of materialism wants to walk in the ways of God, the attribute of judgment denounces him and prevents him from going in God's ways—and arranges obstacles for him."

Out of love of justice, God must allow these obstacles, for justice is a divine attribute. But here is the amazing thing. God "hides in the obstacle. Thus someone who is wise will look at the obstacle and discover the Creator there." "For the truth is that there are no obstacles whatsoever in the whole world. . . . Specifically through the obstacles themselves one is able to draw closer to the Holy One, for God is hidden there. . . ."

Kafka's stories return us to an obstacle that cannot be overcome; *The Castle* that refuses the land surveyor, the higher authorities that Joseph K. can never meet. And that gate the man from the country stands before. In Kafka, the gate becomes the obstacle.

But for Rabbi Nachman, the obstacle becomes the gate.

40

Smallness

*Monday Afternoon, September 29,
Just Before Erev Rosh Hashanah*

Inside the green gate of the "Uman Ritz Carlton," Rabbi Ozer Bergman materialized, after years of our virtual friendship. It was a contemporary *gilgul*, from electronic reality to the flesh. He was exceedingly tall, and even more so with a handsome Russian-style black cloth hat. He explained that once Rosh Hashanah began that evening, he would be maintaining silence for the next day, a custom among the Breslover Hasidim. I'd miss his jokes—Ozer is a very funny guy.

But he's also a rabbi, a writer—scholar and researcher and translator, part of the editorial team associated with the Breslov Research Institute, which has brought out volume after volume of Rabbi Nachman's teachings translated into English. And he's written about the practice of *hitbodedut*, the practice of calling out loud to God, which I'd be hearing about again and again in Uman.

To prepare to see Rabbi Nachman, he directed me to the private *mikveh*, a luxury feature of the "Ritz." I undressed and came into a small tiled room, with a small pool, where floated a yellow rubber ducky. That had to be Ozer's touch. The water was gray. That was a bit of an obstacle. I thought, "For Rebbe Nachman then," got in the water, and plunged several times. I dressed and Ozer led me to the building around Rabbi Nachman's tomb, called the Tziune. The original cemetery where the Rebbe was buried was actually ten feet below us. It had been completely destroyed in a pitched battle between Russians and Nazis during World War II. In the postwar era, it was paved over for a housing complex. But Rabbi Nachman's Hasidim had protected his gravesite through various wiles, and now they had built a large platform over the former cemetery site. The structure has a temporary feel, the walls like a garden shed.

I was coming to the destination. I was going to fetch my portrait of the Rebbe. My fantasy was a personal quiet meditative event. Me and the Rebbe, the Rebbe and me. But it was a seething hive of Jews. Near the entrance is a washstand, as it's customary to wash hands on returning from a grave. But any sense of actually being at a grave is overwhelmed by the crowd. I'd come at the peak hour, just before Rosh Hashanah. Last chance to have a special conversation with Rebbe Nachman. For me, it would have to be a sort of shouting conversation and at a distance.

The place was packed with men of all colors, shapes, and sizes. No feminine energy here. No effort has been made by the various *havurot* to welcome or accommodate women during Rosh Hashanah in Uman. And that was always the complaint, back in the time of the Hasidim: that the men would leave their families and children behind on the Jewish holidays and journey to be in the court of the rebbes. The complaint then and now, too.

So it was all men then. All around me they prayed with great fervor, intent, eyes shut, urgently as if straining, crying, rocking, heaving, holding cell phones, shaking plastic buckets or holding out handfuls of change: long-haired Jews, dark Jews, black Jews, tall Jews, Moroccan Jews, Ethiopian Jews, Jews with towels from the *mikveh* over their heads, Jews perched high, Jews in the rafters, Jews outside pressing against the glass, white-bearded Jews, Hasidim in silk robes, and Jews asleep in the crowd ruckus, blurred loudspeaker prayers, a Tiny Tim Jew with long blond hair and no beard, Jews in U Penn sweats, little boys on shoulders, aggressive boys with long *peyot* pushing hard through the crowd, Jews in tallis and tefillin left over from *Shacharit* shaking the charity bucket. *Tzedekah* boxes, *pushkes* tied and chained to a column, blue strings from the ceiling, posters for "*Tzedekah* for the publication of the *sefers* of Rabbi Nachman." Giving *tzedekah* is also an important step before the old year ends and the new one begins. I had dollar bills and hryvnia and stuffed as many buckets and boxes as I could.

The room was packed. I saw Jews shaking hands and Jews with eyes to heaven, fingering *peyot* and rocking, palms out and arguing in deep eye-to-eye discussion, Jews in blue pin-striped robes, huge shouting Jews, Ozer in his black *shtreiml*, and his nearly identical brother Simcha, also in a *shtreiml*, two brothers named "Help" and "Joy," Jews changing twenty hryvnia for four dollars, *Adonai*-shouting-and-rocking Jews, pounding-on-the-walls Jew, hands clenched rocking against the wall . . . some wore Rebbe Nachman white yarmulkes with a tuft on top. The security wore yellow vests like traffic safeties and stood on benches holding megaphones.

I wanted to see the tomb, and as I edged closer, I got

sucked right into the crowd—white shirts and arms—I was pushed and squeezed hard around a bend. Above me standing on benches a man in a yellow vest with a bullhorn was shouting for us to hurry and waving his arms. I was now in an assembly line of men who puckered and bent to kiss the stone tomb. As they were pushed past, they ran their lips along the gray granite. I scarcely had time to touch it before I was pushed into a corridor. Oblivious to the swarm parting around him, a very short old man was bent over, in a large black velour hat. I could not see his face but his shoulders shook and I heard the sound of sobbing.

Now I was completely outside the Tziune in the sunlight. I made my way back inside and looked for Ozer at the prayer benches. He gave me a copy of *Tikkun Ha-Klali*, the complete remedy or perfect cure. These are ten psalms selected by Rabbi Nachman for purification.* Reciting the *tikkun* is another prerequisite before asking for Rabbi Nachman's help.

I opened the booklet. The psalms were in Hebrew, and I could read every word and understand about a quarter of them. I sat on a bench and recited the syllables of the opening psalm: "*Miktav david shamrani el. Ki hasiti vach.*" What is this . . . *Miktav david*—I know a *miktav* is a kind of psalm—of David. *El* is a name of God. *Shomer* . . . to protect . . . *shamrani el* protect me God . . . *Ki* . . . because. . . . My halting Hebrew halted.

Without the familiar pony of an English translation I struggled to piece together words into phrases. I focused on each word, each line, to make sense, but it was too much.

*Psalms 16, 32, 41, 42, 59, 77, 90, 105, 137, 150.

There were pages and pages of psalms to read. So I gave up making sense. I was determined to finish. I kept saying the syllables I could give no meaning to. As each syllable came, and I turned the pages, word by word, line by line, a feeling of sadness grew. A grown man who could not read a psalm. Something broke. My eyes filled with tears.

I'd studied Hebrew on and off again ever since college, taken private lessons like Kafka, and worked my way through textbooks. But I never mastered it. I looked up all around me and saw Jews with the *tikkun*, some chanting devoutly and rapidly, others slowly, meditatively. Kafka sat near the back of the class and I was sitting behind him. I felt broken and humbled. Who was I to come here among these Jews, any one of whom knew more Hebrew as a child than I did now?

Over at the washstand, a little boy played with a yellow balloon. Someone had twisted it into the shape of a dog and now he was washing it in the trough.

The psalms had broken me. I had given my penny to charity and recited the ten psalms, even if most of them came out in my head as gibberish. Now I came as close as I could to the tomb and just isolated myself from the surroundings. I was going to meet Rabbi Nachman.

I closed my eyes, but I still couldn't picture him in my mind. It wasn't just a matter of his face. What was I doing there? Who or what was I talking to or through? Kafka was no help, He was laughing about the whole thing. All these men swarming and sweating, wearing towels from the *mikveh*s around their shoulders. "Dirty and pure" he said, gray water in the *mikveh*. Then he went to sleep in his mug.

It was just me and this crush of Jews—and something in that granite tomb. A bone? Dust? Nothing?

Rabbi Nachman saw the mass grave of Jewish martyrs in Uman as a garden of souls. And he spoke of a Master of the Garden who knew how to rectify them. In his last days in Uman, he'd told Rabbi Nathan about this mission. Thousands of naked souls swarmed around him, begging for him to clothe them, that is, to give them spiritual garments to make up for the mitzvahs they had not had a chance to complete while they were alive.

So all around me, the live souls were swarming above, and the dead souls below. The Rebbe had confided in Rabbi Nathan near the end that he had a great decision to make and only he could make it. Should he continue to work with the living or the dead? It was much easier to work with the dead, he told Rabbi Nathan. The living offered far too much resistance. I knew what he meant. I was far from home and I missed my wife and my daughters, missed New Orleans. The idea of spending Rosh Hashanah so far from them seemed crazy just then. I couldn't see anything for the crowd, not even the tomb, but I prayed for my family, paused and felt them, named them in prayers. Then I tried again to feel a connection to Rabbi Nachman there in that granite tomb, or where? Where, really? How?

If I closed my eyes I had no image of him. I could not see his face. All that came to mind was that famous chair, which long ago a Hasid had presented to Rebbe Nachman. After his death, during czarist pogroms, there was a fear that the grandly carved chair would be destroyed. So his Hasidim had chopped it up into little pieces and smuggled it out of Breslov. Now that same chair sits in a yeshiva in Meah Shearim, so beautifully assembled you cannot tell it was ever broken. "If you believe you can damage," Rebbe Nachman once said, "believe you can repair."

Things got quiet in me. And I saw.

I saw a man with a scraggly beard and dark intense eyes. He wore a black raincoat. The boy beside him could have been no more than five, with dark eyes and short hair and curly *peyot*. A black *kippah* with a silver band. The father told the boy something and the boy listened intently. I came as close as I could, to eavesdrop. The father opened a copy of *The Complete Tikkun, Tikkun Ha-Klali*—there were copies on racks and scattered all over the place. He chanted a single syllable. *Mik*, the father chanted. *Mik*, the son repeated. *Tav*, the father chanted; *Tav*, the son repeated. *Da*, the father chanted. *Da*, the son repeated, *Vid . . . vid . . .* each time chanting with the same melody: high note, then low.

Sham . . . sham . . . Ra . . . ra . . . Ni . . . ni . . . El . . El. Shamrani El. Protect me, God.

The father's hair was not red. He was not thin, but maybe that didn't matter. I couldn't say that his eyes were beautiful. His forehead was creased, a scowl. Yet he was patient and beautiful with his son.

He had brought this boy from God knows where, brought him all the way to Uman. Maybe he believed the promise, that if a young boy came to Rabbi Nachman's Rosh Hashanah, someday he would also marry under the chuppah in a kosher Jewish wedding. Or maybe he just wanted to share this *tikkun* with his son. He was focused on his son, as his son was focused only on him. The transmission was never broken, the love that goes with the transmission, the intimacy of the learning. At least in that moment.

Father and son. The face of the father and the face of the son. The face of the teacher and the face of the student. Given all the ruptures in Jewish history, this transmission was still going on.

I'd felt broken by my failure to read the Hebrew. But now I thought: these broken syllables the father recited, what could they have meant to his boy? The *tikkun* was not in the meanings, it was not intellectual at all. The *tikkun* was in the feeling passing between them, in the melody the father used to carry it, high note, low note, high note, low note.

Sham . . . sham . . . Ra . . . ra . . . Ni . . . ni . . . El . . . El. Keep me, God.

That's when I saw Rabbi Nachman's face.

41

Self-Isolation

Monday Afternoon, September 29,
Just Before Erev Rosh Hashanah

When I came back from my first visit to the tomb of Rabbi Nachman, I met one of my roommates, Lee Weissman. During two full days of synagogue prayers in the Kloyz we would sit beside each other, and we would share a cramped space in the "Ritz Carlton" with Ozer and another roommate—two double bunk beds. Clothes and shoes and garbage bags were strewn all around. Yet these accommodations were luxurious compared to what most pilgrims would find. Lee reminded me that we'd met in India years before when I was on my way to the dialogue with the Dalai Lama I wrote about in *The Jew in the Lotus.* He was a student of Buddhism then; a Hasid of Rabbi Nachman now.

I told him about the wild scene at the *kever* and he shook his head. I said I wondered if this is really what Rabbi Nachman wanted. He said he wondered that himself sometimes. He said the Tziune has been taken over by the Sephardim who treat the pilgrimage as a celebration at the grave of a tzaddik, a festival known as *hillula.* There is a very large annual *hillula* on Lag b'Omer in Meron near Tsfat, where

Sephardim gather, dance, barbecue, and cut the hair of their three-year-old boys. At a *hillulah*, they feast, they sing, they celebrate. The Ashkenazim want to commune quietly, confess their sins, speak to God and recite *Tikkun Ha-Klali*.

Why are Sephardim attracted to a Hasidic master?

"They are attracted to his message: in a word *simchah*, joy. At one level Rabbi Nachman teaches Jews to be happy. To be a Jew is to be happy and especially among the Ashkenazim, many are grumpy, sour turnips."

In the streets when the second day of Rosh Hashanah ended, the energy was with the Na Nachs . . . dancing, chanting . . . loud music blaring, Rabbi Nachman teachings set to a rock beat. A beautiful bearded Elijah in a royal blue velvet coat blew an enormous twisted ram's horn, maybe six feet long—with a bumper sticker pasted on it: NA NACH NACHMA NACHMAN ME'UMAN. It was the big blast of the shofar; it was happiness in a new year. *Simchah*.

The Sephardim banged pots against the walls of their apartments and set off fireworks. They boogied in the streets. I ran into Yaakov of Savannah in his black hat and long black coat and he told me, "We're crying and they're dancing. But the Jewish people come in many different shades and colors. To God it's all one: we're crying and they're dancing."

Some say this wild energy is more akin to the early days of Hasidism at the time of the Baal Shem Tov, before the movement became more pious, *frummer*. For some Hasidim, Uman is a *frum* Woodstock, or a *frum* Burning Man, a way out of stricter Hasidic environments, like the Satmar kid I met at the "Ritz Carlton." He was still wearing the Satmar outfit, side curls, long black coat, knee socks. In his community just playing a DVD at home is a secret vice. He couldn't wait to go to college and study science and shed all the restrictions. He was curious about all the Jews from secular backgrounds looking for God with Rabbi Nachman. I heard him say to one, "You are going in and I'm going out. I'm interested in the people coming into what I'm leaving."

Coming in was Gershon of Scranton, a young man with his arm in a sling. I asked him what drew him to Breslov and he told me it was the practice of *hitbodedut*, of shouting out to God.

"It's so simple and yet it's meant everything to bring all my problems to God."

Years before I'd tried it in a desert east of Los Angeles, Joshua Tree National Park, the calling out to God, the screaming full of tears, full of everything you could put into it, a kind of primal scream therapy. Or an *amhoretz* banging at the gate of the law, forcing it open.

Because that sense of urgency is needed to get through the gate, that passion.

It's the urgency of prayer from the heart, not the prayers written down in books, not the Hebrew either, but the personal language of the heart, the language you use when you can't sleep at night and your mind is chasing itself around in circles, like Kafka's dog chasing its tail.

How can we learn to talk to God? This is what Rabbi Nachman learned as a boy: you go out into the woods, alone, and you pray your heart out. You scream, you cry, you beg and plead. You leave behind all your sophisticated vocabulary and your immense learning that you have worked so hard for, and you find your heart.

Rabbi Nachman was born just as the romantic movement, with its call for a return to nature, began sweeping Germany. Though he lived in a backwater, in nowhere

Ukraine, as a boy he was out there in the fields and among the flowers, the streams in the dark forest, on a boat, on horseback, talking talking talking with his great open heart. Talking to God in his own everyday language. That, too, was romantic, the shift to "a language really used by men,"* and here is Rabbi Nachman talking to God in the everyday Yiddish of his speaking heart.

He shared this practice with his followers. He taught them to do this "self-isolation," as he called it, *hitbodedut*, and like all Jewish innovators he claimed this practice was nothing new: prophet Elijah practiced *hitbodedut* praying alone in a cave; the tzaddikim knew this secret as well. You secluded yourself in nature and prayed.

Again and again when I spoke with Hasidim of Breslov, this is the practice they brought up because this is the practice of the broken heart, to go below the surface, to break through our irony, our distance, our darkness, and our numbness. And sometimes it is very difficult, almost impossible, to do.†

"Smallness" is an esoteric practice that involves deliberately being insulted and humiliated in the world. But for the Breslover Hasid *hitbodedut* is also a way to simplicity, of shaking off intellectuality and the burden of the sophisticate, of deepening, of becoming more childlike, more simple, and more accepting.

How had he come to it as a child, learned to seek this sort of spiritual intimacy apart from ordinary prayer practice? He was a lonely boy—that seems clear—and perhaps his

*Wordsworth's phrase from the Preface to *Lyrical Ballads*.
†For a down-to-earth guide, read Rabbi Ozer Bergman, *Where Earth and Heaven Kiss: A Guide to Rebbe Nachman's Path of Meditation* (Jerusalem: Breslov Research Institute, 2006).

father, Rabbi Simcha, was aloof or pursuing his own solitary meditations. For there's the ache of wanting a father in this heartfelt prayer. Rabbi Nachman explicitly compared the practice to "a child pleading before his father . . . a child complaining and pestering his father."

Because it is childlike, it is hard for adults to do. *Hitbodedut* requires method acting to break through our crust of aloofness and reserve. Rabbi Nachman explained that even if you are consumed with guilt or pain, it's important to speak like a child, because only as a child can you become reconciled to God as a parent.

"How very good it is," Rabbi Nachman wrote, "when you can awaken your heart and plead until tears stream from your eyes, and you stand like a little child crying before its Father."[1]

You have to become a child again to get through the gate. Once in Prague a little boy cried to his father, but his father didn't answer. He told his father about it years later in a letter that was never delivered:

> There is only one episode in the early years of which I have a direct memory. You may remember it too. One night I kept on whimpering for water, not, I am certain, because I was thirsty, but probably partly to be annoying, partly to amuse myself. After several vigorous threats had failed to have any effect, you took me out of bed, carried me out onto the *pavlatche*,* and left me there alone for a while in my nightshirt, outside the shut door.

*Czech for the long balcony in the inner courtyard of old houses in Prague.

I dare say I was quite obedient afterwards . . . but it did me inner harm. . . . That senseless asking for water, and the extraordinary terror of being carried outside were two things that I . . . could never properly connect with each other. Even years afterwards I suffered from the tormenting fancy that the huge man, my father, ultimate authority, would come almost for no reason at all and take me out of bed in the night and carry me out onto the *pavlatche*, and that meant I was a mere nothing for him.

That was only a small beginning, but this sense of nothingness that often dominates me (a feeling that is in another respect, admittedly, also a noble and fruitful one) comes largely from your influence. What I would have needed was a little encouragement, a little friendliness, a little keeping open of my road, instead of which you blocked it for me.[2]

The crying boy, the terrifying father, the locked door can be reconfigured into the *mashal* of the "man from the country," the gatekeeper, and the shut gate. It is the *mashal* Kafka lived to the end.

The anecdote could be read as the source of his uncertainty—his fretfulness. He calls it by its real name here: nothingness. The feeling of being nothing in relation to the father who is everything, and the hurt, the anger that continually arises from that sense of inadequacy. Yet he also acknowledges the experience as "noble and fruitful."

Perhaps if Kafka had been more direct in approaching his father, this rift between them could have been healed. But this never happened. The letter to his father was never received.

Kafka once dreamed of climbing a wall behind his father. Rabbi Nathan, long before he met Rabbi Nachman, dreamed of climbing a ladder "stretched from earth to heaven." He kept slipping down, climbing up, slipping down again. As he reached close to the top, he fell again and nearly despaired. At that moment a face appeared at the top of the ladder and said, "Fall but hold yourself firm!"

When Rabbi Nathan met Rabbi Nachman for the first time the following year, he recognized that the face in the dream was the Rebbe's.[3]

But what did the Rebbe look like? What face did he see? We can "fetch" no portrait of Rabbi Nachman. But one place to look would be the faces of his Hasidim. For the Rebbe taught that you can recognize the teacher in his Hasid's face. "When a student receives his teacher's wisdom, he receives the features of his face."[4] And Uman was full of Rabbi Nachman's Hasidim.

42

The Thin Thread of Metal, the Ball of Wax

Hitbodedut had brought Gershon of Scranton to wander alone in the beautiful park of Sofiyivka. But while deep in his conversation with God, two Ukrainian teenagers shouted at him. They ran at him with a stick. Gershon clenched a fist as if to strike them, feinted, and ran downhill as fast as he could, past the fake waterfalls of Elysium. He fell and rolled, hurting his shoulder badly, and ended up in the hospital where they fixed him up with a sling. On the way to the Kloyz, I heard Rabbi Chaim Kramer, who heads the Breslov Research Institute, giving him some words of comfort. Rabbi Kramer taught him: You hurt your shoulder because God wants to put something important on your shoulders.

To the Breslover the obstacle does not mean you should turn back. The obstacle is itself a divine message.

I think what scares me most about that idea is not that it's superstitious. What scares me is that it might be true.

"Nothing in the world is without significance," Rabbi Nachman told Rabbi Nathan just after Passover in Breslov, eleven days before he left for Uman. "All the events which take place in this world contain allusions to things of the highest order."[1]

According to Rabbi Nathan, "The Rebbe then said that everything that happens is merely 'working a thin thread of metal' in relation to the Infinite." Rabbi Nathan did not understand the metaphor of the thin thread of metal, and neither do I—though I think it is beautiful. Nathan confessed it was "impossible to explain it in writing because we are dealing with very exalted matters concerning the mysteries of God's dealing with the world." But "those who heard those things from the Rebbe directly could perhaps have a glimpse of understanding of the import of these words even if they could not really grasp them fully."

And for those of us who did not hear those words from the Rebbe's mouth and never saw his face? I know nothing certain about "the mysteries of God's dealing with the world." Isn't this the knowledge the wise man seeks in "The Humble King"? Is it also, in some way, the Law that the man from the country wants to reach while waiting outside the gate?

I do know that this conversation about the thin thread of metal came on a Sunday in the spring after Passover in 1810. Five days later came the fire that broke out while Rabbi Nachman was sitting at his Sabbath table. I know he said, just before the fire broke out, "Already, already," so perhaps he did know something in advance about this particular mystery of "God's dealing with the world." That was the night he waded across the Bug River with his Hasidim, who rescued the Torah scrolls from the flames, the night they all sat together on the opposite bank watching the smoke rise from his burnt house.

By the time he came to Uman, Rabbi Nachman seemed to be at peace with matters of life and death. With his books burnt, and his tales told, his body burning with fever, he told his dearest daughter, Udil, that "death is like going from one room to another." But he also promised her that "anyone who came to his grave would surely find him there."

They spoke in August when every day, sick as he was, the Rebbe would ride out of the city of Uman for fresh air. One day he could not find a coach so he rode on horseback. He was very ill and told a Hasid who saw him that there was nothing to be done, even through prayer. "I am so sick that I have lost my voice and when one loses one's voice, the merit of one's fathers doesn't help." Like Kafka, then, he also lost his voice at the end.

Two months later, on his very last day, he was coughing up blood. Rabbi Nathan gave him egg yolk mixed with hot water to soothe his throat. His attendants washed his beard and dressed him in his best robe. Rabbi Nachman got very quiet in contemplation, all the while working a little ball of wax with his fingers, "with the utmost delicacy."

I think of God working out our fate like "the thin thread of metal."

What happens the day a rebbe dies is in fact bound for legend, distilled in the love of the Hasid who tells it. To separate them again would be cruel. So Rabbi Nathan reports that while Rabbi Nachman was lying there, working the little ball of wax, a huge wind came through Uman and tore rocks out of the hills. Then a fire broke out, as if the mystery of God's dealings with the world required a flaming punctuation mark. Everyone ran out of the room to see about the fire, and Rabbi Nachman was alone. Even Rabbi Nathan left. When the Hasidim came back, they thought the Rebbe had died. Nathan cried and shouted, 'Rebbe! Rebbe! To whom have you left us?" But the Rebbe was not quite dead: he lifted his head one last time.

The gale, the fire, working the ball of wax, the "working of thin metal." Are there meaningless events? Or does a hidden law work from behind the curtain where the humble king hides his face? The boy with his father reciting the psalms, and the *mashal* that this touched on in me: my own pain about separation from my father. And deeper, what the soul knows about its separation from God, and the longing for a repair. Are these coincidences or meanings? Facts or stories? *Halakhah* or *aggadah*? We try to make one from the other.

All over his work, Rabbi Nachman describes this longing for connection, which Kafka felt so deeply, too: the longing for a message from a messenger. It's a belief that, were we to read every moment with enough sensitivity and depth, we could read all the way down below the surface, to our deepest feelings and images, and down below to that place Kafka called the indestructible. The place where our hurts live, and our pain, but also our love. The place our dreams show us.

It is from this place that Rabbi Nachman told his tales, from the place where he knew and wept in his own pain, because of losing his son. Later, with the very last tales, especially "Seven Beggars," he spoke again and again of this longing. He said in that tale that the whole heart of the world was calling out every hour with its longing, and he told this last tale, knowing he was losing his own life. From this place of the broken heart he spoke to the broken hearts around him.

43

Return of the Coffee Mug

Wednesday Evening, October 1

B ear witness to my words," I read in one of the pamphlets stuffed on a wall rack in the Tziune, the place of Rabbi Nachman's tomb. "If someone were to come to my graveside after my death, give a penny to charity in my memory and recite the Ten Psalms I prescribed I would span the length and breadth of the universe to save him." It was late at night after the second day of Rosh Hashanah had ended. The dancing and shouting were over. The shofars had stopped blasting. The streets were littered with trash, and groups of men headed to the edge of the *shuk* where taxis were lining up. Deals were being made for travel, haggling was going on in several languages on the trash-strewn streets of Uman, and I would be joining a group, including my friend Yohanan, leaving around midnight for the road to Borispol airport.

Rabbi Nachman swore very solemnly before two witnesses that even if you were on the road to hell, "I will pull you up by your side curls." I have no side curls, but I felt a little tug and took a copy of the *Tikkun* from the rack to take home with me. Maybe I would complete my Hebrew lessons, if not for Rabbi Nachman, then for Kafka. I replaced the *Tikkun* on the rack with Kafka's *Meditation*. I thought it was a good exchange: I know they both believed deeply in the imagination, in the power of stories to waken the soul.

The coffee mug I didn't know what to do with. I cupped it in my palms and thought of Franz Kafka and thought of Rabbi Nachman. I thought about the great fire each one knew within. I thought about all the words they wrote and burned. I thought about the burnt books of Kamenetz and of Berlin. Still after so much burning, Uman in the New Year of 5769 was packed with Rebbe Nachman's Hasidim. There are Jews in the world who believe, and Jews who can't believe. And Jews who want to believe, who come in hope or despair, and I came to Uman for them.

Rabbi Nachman even said at the end, there's no such thing as despair. And how does Kafka answer? I heard their voices contending and knew at last where these two meet. They meet in all of us who stand at the gate, looking for a glimpse of the light.

NOTES

Introduction

1. Etymologically *pre-* "before," *post-* "after," "preposterous" means that which comes after pretending to come before.

1. The Joke

1. Nathan of Breslov, *Tzaddik (Chayey Moharan)*, trans. Avraham Greenbaum (Jerusalem/New York: Breslov Research Institute, 1987), p. 46.

2. See Arthur Green, *Tormented Master* (Woodstock, Vt.: Jewish Lights, 1992), p. 186.

3. The chief biographical works that are available in English are Nathan of Breslov, *Tzaddik*, and Nathan of Nemirov, *Rabbi Nachman's Wisdom*, trans. Aryeh Kaplan (Jerusalem: Breslov Research Institute, 1973). Aryeh Kaplan, *Until the Mashiach: Rabbi Nachman's Biography: An Annotated Chronology* (Jerusalem/Brooklyn: Breslov Research Institute, 1985), has a detailed chronology. Chaim Kramer, *Through Fire and Water: The Life of Reb Noson of Breslov* (Jerusalem/New York: Breslov Research Institute, 1992), drawn from Rabbi Nathan's autobiography, also has important material.

4. Red hair is an oral tradition. Nathan of Nemirov, *Rabbi Nachman's Wisdom, Sichos haRan* (Wisdom #268) has that he had a *"kol av,"* a "thick," beautiful voice. From *Tzaddik* #13 (p. 31; *Chayey Moharan* #116): Anyone who never saw him dance never saw good in his life. Ibid. #263: The grace and beauty of his dancing was well known.

5. Quoting Pirke Avot 2:14. See Nathan of Breslov, *Tzaddik*, p. 353.

6. Franz Kafka, *The Trial*, trans. Breon Mitchell (New York: Schocken Books, 1998), p. 215.

7. Ibid., pp. 216–17.

2. The Coffee Mug

1. Franz Kafka, *Diaries*, trans. J. Kresh and M. Greenberg (New York: Schocken Books, 1976), p. 269.

2. Franz Kafka, *The Zürau Aphorisms*, trans. Michael Hoffman (New York: Schocken Books, 2006), #17, p. 17.

3. Franz Kafka, *Stories: 1904–1924*, trans. J. A. Underwood (London: Abacus, 2006), p. 252.

4. Franz Kafka, *Letters to Friends, Family, and Editors*, trans. Richard and Clara Winston (New York: Schocken Books, 1977), p. 144.

5. Maria Luise Caputo-Mayr and Julius Michael Herz, *Franz Kafka: internationale Bibliographie der Primär—und Sekundärliteratur, eine Einführung [International bibliography of primary and secondary literature, an introduction]* (Munich: K. G. Saur, 2000).

6. The bibliography, published in 2000, lists 221 pages of articles and 112 pages of books over the seventeen-year period of 1980 to 1997. There are approximately thirteen articles listed per page, and six books per page. That indicates one article published every other day for seventeen years and thirty-nine books published a year, or one book every ten days over a seventeen-year period.

7. Nathan of Breslov, *Tzaddik (Chayey Moharan)*, trans. Avraham Greenbaum (Jerusalem/New York: Breslov Research Institute, 1987), p. 336, #405.

8. Nathan of Nemirov, *Rabbi Nachman's Wisdom (Shevachay haRan, Sichos haRan)*, trans. Aryeh Kaplan (Jerusalem: Breslov Research Institute, 1973), p. 245, *Sichos haRan* #117. Arthur Green, *Tormented Master* (Woodstock, Vt.: Jewish Lights, 1992), p. 34.

3. The Waiting Room

1. http://www.sofiyivka.org.ua/index_en.html.
2. http://www.breslov.com/bri/umarrh.html#chapter4.

4. Kafka the Kabbalist

1. Gershom Scholem, "My Way to Kabbalah," in *On the Possibility of Jewish Mysticism in Our Time*, trans. Jonathan Chipman (Philadelphia: Jewish Publication Society, 1997), p. 23.

2. Gershom Scholem, "Revelation and Tradition as Religious Categories," in *The Messianic Idea in Judaism*, trans. Michael Meyer (New York: Schocken Books, 1971), pp. 295–96.

3. Gershom Scholem, "On Kafka's *The Trial*," in *On the Possibility of Jewish Mysticism in Our Time*, trans. Jonathan Chipman (Philadelphia: Jewish Publication Society, 1997), p. 193

4. Karl Erich Grözinger, *Kafka and Kabbalah*, trans. Susan Hecker Ray (New York: Continuum, 1994). He attempts to detail what kabbalah literature Kafka might have had access to.

5. Mark Zborowski and Elizabeth Herzog, *Life Is with People: A Culture of the Shtetl* (New York: Shcocken Eooks, 1952), p. 411.

6. Gershom Scholem, "A Candid Letter About My True Intentions in Studying Kabbalah (1937)," in *On the Possibility of Jewish Mysticism*, pp. 3–4.

7. Grözinger, *Kafka and Kabbalah*, p 2.

5. Last Request

1. Franz Kafka, *The Trial*, trans. Willa and Edwin Muir (New York: Modern Library, 1964), p. 328.

2. Ibid., pp. 329–30.

3. Reiner Stach, *Kafka: The Decisive Years*, trans. Shelley Frisch (New York: Harcourt, 2005), p. 114.

4. J. P. Hodin, "Memories of Franz Kafka," *Horizon* 17 (1948): 39.

5. Ibid., pp. 38–39.

6. Franz Kafka, *Diaries*, trans. J. Kresh and M. Greenberg (New York: Schocken Books, 1976), pp. 212–13 (September 23, 1912).

7. Ibid., p. 320 (December 8, 1914).

8. Stach, *Kafka: The Decisive Years*, pp. 116–17.

6. Miraculous Event

1. Franz Kafka, *Diaries*, trans. J. Kresh and M. Greenberg (New York: Schocken Books, 1976), p. 134 (December 8, 1911).

2. Nathan of Nemirov, *Rabbi Nachman's Wisdom*, trans. Aryeh Kaplan (Jerusalem: Breslov Research Institute, 1973), p. 178, *Sichos haRan* #73.

7. Wavering at the Heights

1. Reiner Stach, *Kafka: The Decisive Years*, trans. Shelley Frisch (New York: Harcourt, 2005), p. 128.

2. Ronald Hayman, *Kafka: A Biography* (New York: Oxford University Press, 1981), p. 88.

3. Franz Kafka, *Diaries*, trans. J. Kresh and M. Greenberg (New York: Schocken Books, 1976), p. 233 (October 15, 1913).

4. Ibid., p. 321 (December 13, 1914).

5. Franz Kafka, *The Trial: The Definitive Edition*, trans. Willa and Edwin Muir (New York: Schocken Books, 1992), p. 229.

6. Kafka, *Diaries*, p. 302 (August 6, 1914).

7. Franz Kafka, *Letters to Friends, Family, and Editors*, trans. Richard and Clara Winston (New York: Schocken Books, 1977), pp. 332–33 (July 5, 1922).

8. Burnt Books

1. Nathan of Breslov, *Tzaddik (Chayey Moharan)*, trans. Avraham Greenbaum (Jerusalem/New York: Breslov Research Institute, 1987), p. 35.

2. Ibid., p. 77.

3. Aryeh Kaplan, *Until the Mashiach: Rabbi Nachman's Biography: An Annotated Chronology* (Jerusalem/Brooklyn: Breslov Research Institute, 1985), p. 204.

4. Chaim Kramer, *Through Fire and Water: The Life of Reb Noson of Breslov* (Jerusalem/New York: Breslov Research Institute, 1992), p. 210. The original source is Reb Noson's autobiography, *Temei Moharnat*, I #65.

9. The Burning Bush and the Thorns

1. Gustav Janouch, *Conversations with Kafka*, trans. Richard and Clara Winston (London: Quartet Books, 1985), pp. 149–50. There are questions about how much of this is remembered, and how much imagined. Scholem called them a "work of highly dubious authenticity" but Brod felt they "unmistakably bore the stamp of Kafka's genius." Kafka makes several mentions of Janouch in his letters to Milena and to Klopstock.

2. Nathan of Breslov, *Tzaddik (Chayey Moharan)*, trans. Avraham Greenbaum (Jerusalem/New York: Breslov Research Institute, 1987), p. 282, #291.

3. Ibid., p. 457.

4. Ibid.

10. Fire from the Rebbe's Mouth

1. Nathan of Breslov, *Tzaddik (Chayey Moharan)*, trans. Avraham Greenbaum (Jerusalem/New York: Breslov Research Institute, 1987), p. 324, #389.

2. Ronald Hayman, *Kafka: A Biography* (New York: Oxford University Press, 1981), pp. 86–87. The quotes are from Brod's novel *The Magic Kingdom* in which one of the characters, Garta, is a stand-in for Kafka.

3. *Likutey Moharan* II, Lesson #32. The BRI translation has not yet been published. For the paragraphs that follow I've relied on a rough translation of the Hebrew supplied by Rabbi Ozer Bergman and on a second translation found in Marc-Alain Ouakhnine, *the burnt book: Reading the Talmud*, trans. Llewellyn Brown (Princeton, N.J.: Princeton University Press, 1995), pp. 267–68.

4. Nachman of Breslov, *Likutey Moharan [The Collected Teachings of Morenu HaRav Nachman]*, trans. Moshe Mykoff, vol. X (Jerusalem/New York: Breslov Research Institute, 1999), LM I, Lesson #192, p. 437.

5. Ouakhnine, *the burnt book*, pp. 267–68.

6. This is permitted. See *Shulchan Arukh, Orach Chaim* 334:12.

7. R. Ishmael said: "[One can reason] a minori: If in order to make peace between man and wife the Torah decreed, Let my Name, written in sanctity, be blotted out in water, these, who stir up jealousy, enmity, and wrath between Israel and their Father in Heaven, how much more so; and of them David said, Do not I hate them, O Lord, that hate thee? And am I not grieved with those that rise up against thee? I hate them with perfect hatred: I count them mine enemies. And just as we may not rescue them from a fire, so may we not rescue them from a collapse [of debris] or from water or from anything that may destroy them" (BT *Shabbat* 116a, Soncino edition).

8. Arthur Green, *Tormented Master* (Woodstock, Vt.: Jewish Lights, 1992). See Chapter 5, "Messianic Strivings," pp. 182ff.

9. Nathan of Nemirov, *Rabbi Nachman's Wisdom*, trans. Aryeh Kaplan (Jerusalem: Breslov Research Institute, 1973), p. 333, *Sichos haRan* #189, per Aryeh Kaplan, *Until the Mashiach: Rabbi Nachman's Biography: An Annotated Chronology* (Jerusalem/Brooklyn: Breslov Research Institute, 1985), pp. 115, 122.

10. Kaplan, *Until the Mashiach*, p. 329.

11. Tales of the Seventy Faces

1. This chapter relies greatly on Arthur Green's research and his discussion of the tales in *Tormented Master* (Woodstock, Vt.: Jewish Lights, 1992), pp. 337–67.

2. Jiri Langer, *Nine Gates to the Chassidic Mysteries*, trans. Stephen Jolly (New York: Behrman House, 1976), p. 22.

3. Nachman of Breslov, *Likutey Moharan [The Collected Teachings of Morenu HaRav Nachman]*, trans. Moshe Mykoff, vol. XI (Jerusalem/New York: Breslov Research Institute, 2000), LM I, Lesson #234, p. 165.

4. Ibid., LM I, Lesson #248, p. 229.

5. Langer, *Nine Gates*, p. 23.

6. Letter to Oskar Pollak (January 27, 1904).

7. See Nachman of Breslov, *Likutey Moharan [The Collected Teachings of Morenu HaRav Nachman]*, trans. Moshe Mykoff, vol. VII (Jerusalem/New York: Breslov Research Institute, 2003), LM I, Lesson #60, part 6, p. 137.

8. Life, Psalm 90:10; nations: *Sukkah* 55b, languages: *Sanhedrin* 17a.

9. Green, *Tormented Master*, p. 344.

12. Kafka's Last Parable

1. Robert Alter, *Necessary Angels: Tradition and Modernity in Kafka, Benjamin, and Scholem* (Cambridge, Mass.: Harvard University Press, 1991), p. 3.

2. Walter Benjamin, "Franz Kafka," in *Illuminations*, trans. Harry Zohn (New York: Schocken Books, 2007), p. 134.

3. Franz Kafka, *Letters to Milena*, trans. Philip Boehm (New York: Schocken Books, 1990), p. 249.

4. Max Brod, *Franz Kafka: A Biography* (New York: Schocken Books, 1947), p. 213.

5. Ibid., pp. 176–77.

6. http://www.nytimes.com/2008/08/18/world/africa/18iht-kafka.4.15396459.html?_r=1.

13. Sealed in Flame

1. Franz Kafka, *Diaries*, trans. J. Kresh and M. Greenberg (New York: Schocken Books, 1976), pp. 398–99.

2. Martin Buber, *Tales of the Hasidim: Early Masters*, trans. Olga Marx (New York: Schocken Books, 1961), p. 49.

3. Ronald Hayman, *Kafka: A Biography* (New York: Oxford University Press, 1981), pp. 86–87. The quotes are from Brod's novel *The Magic Kingdom* in which one of the characters, Garta, is a stand-in for Kafka.

4. Chaim Kramer, *Through Fire and Water: The Life of Reb Noson of Breslov* (Jerusalem/New York: Breslov Research Institute, 1992), p. 42.

14. To Feel at Home

1. Franz Kafka, *Letters to Friends, Family, and Editors*, trans. Richard and Clara Winston (New York: Schocken Books, 1977), p. 147.

2. Franz Kafka, *Diaries*, trans. J. Kresh and M. Greenberg (New York: Schocken Books, 1976), p. 147.

3. Egon Kisch, *Sensation Fair* (New York: Modern Age Books, 1941) as cited in Maria Foi, "Prague as a Literary City," in *The City of K: Franz Kafka and Prague* (Barcelona: COPA, 2002), pp. 138–44.

4. Franz Kafka, *Letter to His Father*, trans. Ernst Kaiser and Eithne Wilkins (New York: Schocken Books, 1966), p. 21.

16. Who by Water, Who by Fire

1. Franz Kafka, *Diaries*, trans. J. Kresh and M. Greenberg (New York: Schocken Books, 1976), p. 59.

2. Franz Kafka, *The Complete Stories*, trans. Willa and Edwin Muir (New York: Schocken Books, 1971), p. 85.

3. Franz Kafka, *Letters to Friends, Family, and Editors*, trans. Richard and Clara Winston (New York: Schocken Books, 1977), pp. 284–86.

17. The Rabbi's Son

1. Dan Ben-Amos and Jerome Mintz, trans. and eds., *In Praise of the Baal Shem Tov* (Northvale, N.J.: Jason Aronson, 1993).

2. *Rabbi Nachman's Stories (Sippurey Ma'asioth)*, trans. and annotated by Aryeh Kaplan (Jerusalem/New York: Breslov Research Institute, 1983), p. 155.

3. Nathan of Breslov, *Tzaddik (Chayey Moharan)*, trans. Avraham Greenbaum (Jerusalem/New York: Breslov Research Institute, 1987), p. 17, #108.

4. Chaim Kramer, *Through Fire and Water: The Life of Reb Noson of Breslov* (Jerusalem/New York: Breslov Research Institute, 1992), p. 25.

5. Cf. *Brakhot* 58a, Zohar 157a and III, 176b. Karl Erich Grözinger in *Kafka and Kabbalah* (trans. Susan Hecker Ray [New York: Continuum, 1994]) has shown in detail where Kafka may have learned certain kabbalistic ideas, see in particular pp. 61–69 and 83–94.

6. Nathan of Breslov, *Tzaddik*, p. 95, #195.

7. From Rabbi Kaplan's commentary on "The Rabbi's Son" in *Rabbi Nachman's Stories*, p. 158.

18. In His Father's House

1. Ronald Hayman, *Kafka: A Biography* (New York: Oxford University Press, 1981), p. 28.

2. Frederick Karl, *Franz Kafka: Representative Man* (New York: Ticknor and Fields, 1991), pp. 2–3.

3. Hayman, *Kafka: A Biography*, p. 27.

4. Franz Kafka, *Letter to His Father*, trans. Ernst Kaiser and Eithne Wilkins (New York: Schocken Books, 1966), p. 85.

5. Franz Kafka, *Diaries*, trans. J. Kresh and M. Greenberg (New York: Schocken Books, 1976), p. 104 (November 5, 1911).

6. Ibid., p. 98 (October 31, 1911).

7. Ibid., p. 103 (November 3, 1911).

8. Ibid., p. 138 (December 14, 1911).

9. Ibid., p. 173 (January 24, 1912).

10. Gershom Scholem, *From Berlin to Jerusalem*, trans. Harry Zohn (New York: Schocken Books, 1988), p. 44.

11. "Martin Buber's Conception of Judaism" in Gershom Scholem, *On Jews and Judaism in Crisis: Selected Essays*, ed. Werner J. Dennhauser (New York: Schocken Books, 1976), p. 138.

12. Martin Buber, *On Judaism*, trans. Eva Jospe (New York: Schocken Books, 1995), p. 39.

19. Annihilation of the Self

1. Franz Kafka, *Letter to His Father*, trans. Ernst Kaiser and Eithne Wilkins (New York: Schocken Books, 1966), p. 21.

2. Franz Kafka, *Diaries*, trans. J. Kresh and M. Greenberg (New York: Schocken Books, 1976), p. 260 (February 15, 1914).

3. Ibid., p. 101 (November 2, 1911).

4. Ibid., p. 224 (July 21, 1913).

5. Ibid., p. 201 (May 6, 1912).

6. Gershom Scholem, *From Berlin to Jerusalem*, trans. Harry Zohn (New York: Schocken Books, 1988), p. 55. See also "Martin Buber's Conception of Judaism," in Gershom Scholem, *On Jews and Judaism in Crisis: Selected Essays*, ed. Werner Dannhauser (New York: Schocken Books, 1976), pp. 126–71.

7. Franz Kafka, *Letters to Felice*, trans. James Stern and Elizabeth Duckworth (New York: Schocken Books, 1973), pp. 185–86 (February 10, 1913).

8. Kafka, *Diaries*, p. 245 (December 9, 1913).

21. Hasidic Parables

1. For Rashi's exact words, please see M. Rosenbaum and A. M. Silbermann, eds., *Pentateuch with Targum Onkelos, Haphtaroth and Rashi's Commentary, Genesis* (Jerusalem: The Silbermann Family, 5733), p. 2.

2. Abraham Joshua Heschel, *Between God and Man* (New York: Free Press, 1959), pp. 175–78.

3. See Haim Nahman Bialik, *Revealment and Concealment: Five Essays*, trans. Leon Simon (Jerusalem: Ibis Editions, 2000), p. 46.

4. See Aryeh Wineman, *The Hasidic Parable* (Philadelphia: Jewish Publication Society, 2001), pp. xx–xxii, for a fascinating discussion of Dov Ber's view of the parable.

5. Martin Buber, *Ten Rungs*, trans. Olga Marx (New York: Schocken Books, 1970), p. 17. See also Buber, "The Axe," in *Tales of the Hasidim: Early Masters*, trans. Olga Marx (New York: Schocken Books, 1961), p. 64.

6. Wineman, *Hasidic Parable*, p. xxii.

7. *A Midsummer Night's Dream*, Act V, Scene 1.

22. King and Messenger

1. "The King's Two Messengers" in Aryeh Wineman, *The Hasidic Parable* (Philadelphia: Jewish Publication Society, 2001), pp. 82–84.

2. Ian Johnson, translator. http://www.kafka.org/index.php?id=162,165,0,0,1,0.

3. David Stern, *Parables in Midrash* (Cambridge, Mass.: Harvard University Press, 1991), p. 223.

4. Kafka inserted the parable "An Imperial Message" in a story, "The Great Wall of China," as a scripture explaining how instructions from even a dying emperor could still hold force in the provinces. Kafka uses "Chinese" as a stand-in for the Jews, who likewise live in obedience to ever-awaited, building instructions for the Third Temple. In the same story, Kafka introduces a midrash that asserts that the Great Wall is intended as a foundation for the Tower of Babel. The implication is that all three projects—Temple, Wall, Tower—are exercises in futility. "The Great Wall of China" itself remained an unfinished project.

23. Uncertainty Principle

1. Kafka signaled in his diary a possible Greek influence on this parable, too. "Zeno, pressed as to whether anything is at rest, replied: Yes

the flying arrow rests" (December 1910). Kafka was a human "flying arrow." Zeno's paradoxes prove the impossibility of motion, and Kafka's messenger resembles Achilles chasing the tortoise. Again and again the messenger advances, but always "nothing will have been achieved."

2. Franz Kafka, *Diaries*, trans. J. Kresh and M. Greenberg (New York: Schocken Books, 1976), p. 271 (May 27, 1914).

3. Aryeh Kaplan, *Until the Mashiach: Rabbi Nachman's Biography: An Annotated Chronology* (Jerusalem/Brooklyn: Breslov Research Institute, 1985), p. 165.

4. Isaac Bashevis Singer's Yiddish story *"Gimpl Tam"* is translated by Saul Bellow as "Gimpel the Fool."

5. Nahman of Bratslav, *The Tales*, trans. Arnold Band (New York: Paulist Press, 1978), p. 15.

6. Ibid., pp. 154–55.

7. David Roskies writes:

This is a clue. As charming and precise as is Reb Nahman's portrayal of religious simplicity, his counterportrait is surprisingly accurate. It is clear that Reb Nahman has visited the seat of reason himself. Elsewhere he taught that only the zaddik can risk studying the "seven wisdoms" for any lesser mortal would surely stumble and fall. In proscribing those "seven wisdoms" from his disciples, he did not differentiate between works of medieval Jewish philosophy [such as Maimonides] and the newfangled heretical tracts [of the *maskilim*]. But where did that leave him? Like the clever man in the story,

the zaddik too must "suffer greatly on the road, since he has no one to talk to because of his wisdom." Alone in his ivory tower of absolute perfection, tortured by knowledge and wisdom that he cannot share with anyone, constantly plagued by the fear of pollution, he desperately needs to be redeemed by the simple and the pure. "Only no mockery," says the simpleton, whose innocence saves him from doing evil.

David Roskies, "The Master of Prayer," in *God's Voice from the Void*, ed. Shaul Magid (Albany: SUNY Press, 2002), p. 89.

24. Talmudic Style

1. Franz Kafka, *Diaries*, trans. J. Kresh and M. Greenberg (New York: Schocken Books, 1976), pp. 158–59 (December 30, 1911).

2. http://en.wikipedia.org/wiki/Prague_Astronomical_Clock#Animated_figures.

3. Kafka notes in his diary (see Iris Bruce, *Kafka and Cultural Zionism* [Madison: University of Wisconsin Press, 2007], p. 92, and Franz Kafka, The *Diaries of Franz Kafka, 1914–1923*, ed. Max Brod, trans. Martin Greenberg, vol. 2 [New York: Schocken Books, 1949], p. 101):

> Instead of working—I have written only one page (exegesis of the "Legend")—looked through the finished chapters and found parts of them good. Always conscious that every feeling of satisfaction and happiness that I have, such, for example, as the "Legend" in particular inspires in me, must be paid for, and must be paid for moreover at some future time, in order to deny me all possibility of recovery in the present" (December 11, 1914).

4. Heinz Politzer, *Franz Kafka: Parable and Paradox* (Ithaca, N.Y.: Cornell University Press, 1962) focuses on the paradoxical parable as a form in Kafka.

5. Kafka, *Diaries*, p. 129 (November 29, 1911).

6. Julian Preece, ed., *The Cambridge Companion to Kafka* (Cambridge: Cambridge University Press), p. 154.

7. Ed Greenstein, "Wisdom Undermined," unpublished lecture delivered at Bar Ilan University Conference on Bible and Literature, December 9, 2009. Per Greenstein, cf: Job 9:4–10; cf. 23:9; Isa. 13:14, 14:16, 44:24; Job 38:31–32; Ps. 136:4; et al.

8. Kafka, *Diaries*, p. 244 (December 4, 1913).

25. Dirty and Pure

1. Franz Kafka, *Diaries*, trans. J. Kresh and M. Greenberg (New York: Schocken Books, 1976), p. 341 (September 14, 1915).

2. Frantisek Langer, "Introduction," in *Nine Gates to the Chassidic Mysteries*, trans. Stephen Jolly (New York: Behrman House, 1976), p. xv.

3. Jiri Langer, *Nine Gates to the Chassidic Mysteries*, trans. Stephen Jolly (New York: Behrman House, 1976).

4. Ibid., p. 20.

5. Franz Kafka, *Letters to Friends, Family, and Editors*, trans. Richard and Clara Winston (New York: Schocken Books, 1977), p. 122.

6. Ibid., p. 122. Cf. Iris Bruce, *Kafka and Cultural Zionism* (Madison: University of Wisconsin Press, 2007), pp. 90ff.

26. Blue Light of Dawn

1. Franz Kafka, *The Trial*, trans. Breon Mitchell (New York: Schocken Books, 1998), p. 216.

2. Nachman of Breslov, *Likutey Moharan [The Collected Teachings of Morenu HaRav Nachman]*, trans. Moshe Mykoff, vol. XI (Jerusalem/New York: Breslov Research Institute, 2000), LM I, Lesson #234, part 1, pp. 165–67.

3. Kafka, *The Trial*, trans. Mitchell, pp. 230–31.

27. Kafka, Buber, Nachman

1. Franz Kafka, *Letters to Felice*, trans. James Stern and Elizabeth Duckworth (New York: Schocken Books, 1973), p. 161 (January 19, 1913).

2. Ibid., p. 164 (January 20–21, 1913).

3. The parable is not one of the canonical thirteen tales, but is appended in some editions.

4. Howard Schwartz, *Reimagining the Bible* (New York: Oxford University Press, 1998), p. 16.

28. Sleeping and Awakening

1. See Nachman of Breslov, *Likutey Moharan [The Collectea Teachings of Morenu HaRav Nachman]*, trans. Moshe Mykoff, vol. VII (Jerusalem/ New York: Breslov Research Institute, 2003), LMI, Lesson #60, part 6, p. 135, and p. 19 of the second introduction in *Rabbi Nachman's Stories (Sippurey Ma'asioth)*, trans. and annotated by Aryeh Kaplan (Jerusalem/New York: Breslov Research Institute, 1983).

2. Franz Kafka, *Diaries*, trans. J. Kresh and M. Greenberg (New York: Schocken Books, 1976), p. 342 (September 16, 1915).

3. Nachman of Breslov, *Likutey Moharan [The Collected Teachings of Morenu HaRav Nachman]*, trans. Moshe Mykoff, vol. VII (Jerusalem/ New York: Breslov Research Institute, 2003), LM I, Lesson #60, part 6, p. 135.

29. A New Kabbalah

1. Franz Kafka, *Diaries*, trans. J. Kresh and M. Greenberg (New York: Schocken Books, 1976), p. 404 (January 23, 1922).

2. Ibid., pp. 398–99.

30. Circus Acts

1. "The Animal in the Synagogue," an unpublished story from 1920–1922, is the one exception.

2. Franz Kafka, *Letters to Felice*, trans. James Stern and Elizabeth Duckworth (New York: Schocken Books, 1973), p. 517 [postcard] (October 7, 1915).

3. Franz Kafka, *Letters to Friends, Family, and Editors*, trans. Richard and Clara Winston (New York: Schocken Books, 1977), pp. 288–89 (June 1921).

4. Franz Kafka, *Stories: 1904–1924*, trans. J. A. Underwood (London: Abacus, 2006), p. 95.

5. Franz Kafka, *Diaries*, trans. J. Kresh and M. Greenberg (New York: Schocken Books, 1976), p. 405 (January 24, 1922).

6. Kafka, *Stories: 1904–1924*, p. 120.

7. Ibid., p. 121.

31. The Turkey Prince

1. Nathan of Breslov, *Tzaddik (Chayey Moharan)*, trans. Avraham Greenbaum (Jerusalem/New York: Breslov Research Institute, 1987), p. 19.

2. Dan Ben-Amos and Jerome Mintz, trans. and eds., *In Praise of the Baal Shem Tov* (Northvale, N.J.: Jason Aronson, 1993), pp. 86–87.

32. Movements of the Soul

1. *Rabbi Nachman's Stories (Sippurey Ma'asioth)*, trans. and annotated by Aryeh Kaplan (Jerusalem/New York: Breslov Research Institute, 1983), p. 167.

2. See Nathan of Breslov, *Tzaddik (Chayey Moharan)*, trans. Avraham Greenbaum (Jerusalem/New York: Breslov Research Institute, 1987), pp. 56–57.

3. Nathan of Breslov, *Rabbi Nachman: Advice (Likutey Etzot)*, trans. Avraham Greenbaum (Jerusalem/New York: Breslov Research Institute, 1983), p. 321.

4. Nathan of Nemirov, *Rabbi Nachman's Wisdom*, trans. Aryeh Kaplan (Jerusalem: Breslov Research Institute, 1973), p. 8. See *Sichos haRan* #48.

5. Nathan of Breslov, *Tzaddik*, pp. 219–21.

6. Nathan of Nemirov, *Rabbi Nachman's Wisdom*, p. 99.

7. John Zilcosky, *Kafka's Travels: Exoticism, Colonialism, and the Traffic of Writing* (New York: Palgrave Macmillan, 2003), p. 172.

8. Franz Kafka, *Diaries*, trans. J. Kresh and M. Greenberg (New York: Schocken Books, 1976), p. 405 (January 24, 1922).

9. Nathan of Breslov, *Tzaddik*, p. 100.

33. Aliyah

1. The cultural and "synthetic" Zionists emphasized more than the purely "political" Zionists the activity called in Zionist debates *Gegenwartsarbeit*, i.e., "work in the present." See "Diaspora," *Encyclopaedia Judaica*, vol. 21, p. 548.

2. Franz Kafka, *Letters to Friends, Family, and Editors*, trans. Richard and Clara Winston (New York: Schocken Books, 1977), p. 505 (September 22, 1916).

3. Iris Bruce, *Kafka and Cultural Zionism* (Madison: University of Wisconsin Press, 2007), pp. 165–67, 179ff.

4. Franz Kafka, *Letters to Friends, Family, and Editors*, trans. Richard and Clara Winston (New York: Schocken Books, 1977), pp. 372–73.

5. Ronald Hayman, *Kafka: A Biography* (New York: Oxford University Press, 1981), p. 291.

6. Franz Kafka, *Letters to Ottla and the Family*, trans. Richard and Clara Winston (New York: Schocken Books, 1982), p. 84 (fourth week of October 1923).

7. Kathi Diamant, *Kafka's Last Love: The Mystery of Dora Diamant* (New York: Basic Books, 2003), p. 49, as cited in Bruce, *Kafka and Cultural Zionism*, p. 184.

8. Franz Kafka, *Diaries*, trans. J. Kresh and M. Greenberg (New York: Schocken Books, 1976), p. 394 (October 19, 1921).

9. Diamant, *Kafka's Last Love*, p. 119, as cited in Bruce, *Kafka and Cultural Zionism*, p. 185.

34. Rabbi Nachman's Journey to Kamenetz

1. See Aryeh Kaplan, *Until the Mashiach: Rabbi Nachman's Biography: An Annotated Chronology* (Jerusalem/Brooklyn: Breslov Research Institute, 1985), pp. 139, 152. On page 152 the rebbe's journey of 110 miles is described as "a little over two days' journey."

2. Nathan of Breslov, *Tzaddik (Chayey Moharan)*, trans. Avraham Greenbaum (Jerusalem/New York: Breslov Research Institute, 1987), p. 104.

3. Ibid., p. 102.

4. Parable 26, "The Tainted Grain," in *Rabbi Nachman's Stories (Sippurey Ma'asioth)*, trans. and annotated by Aryeh Kaplan (Jerusalem/New York: Breslov Research Institute, 1983), p. 481.

5. Aryeh Kaplan, *Until the Mashiach: Rabbi Nachman's Biography: An Annotated Chronolgy* (Jerusalem/Brooklyn: Breslov Research Institute, 1985), p. 134.

6. Account follows closely Hillel Zeitlin's version of Rabbi Nathan's telling in Nathan of Breslov, *Tzaddik*. For Zeitlin, see http://www.shemayisrael.co.il/parsha/review/archives/vaeschanan.htm. Translations and original material copyright © 1998 by Yaacov Dovid Shulman.

7. Yohanan Petrovsky-Shtern, "Russian Legislation and Jewish Self Governing Institutions: The Case of Kamenets-Podolskii," *Jews in Russia and Eastern Europe* 1, no. 56 (2006): 114–15.

8. Nathan of Breslov, *Tzaddik*, p. 46.

9. See Gershom Scholem, "Devekut, or Communion with God," in *The Messianic Idea in Judaism*, trans. Michael Meyer (New York: Schocken Books, 1971), pp. 221ff.

10. See Zvi Mark, *Mysticism and Madness: The Religious Thought of Rabbi Nachman of Bratslav* (New York: Continuum, 2009), pp. 173–217, for a clear but far more learned discussion of these matters.

35. The Narrow Bridge

1. *Rabbi Nachman's Stories (Sippurey Ma'asioth)*, trans. and annotated by Aryeh Kaplan (Jerusalem/New York: Breslov Research Institute, 1983), p. 129.

36. Two Kings

1. *Likutey Moharan*, vol. II, Lesson #212 (Jerusalem/New York: Breslov Research Institute, 2000), p. 77.

2. His prooftext is Hosea 12:11: "by the hands of the prophets I am

depicted." "And with this the verse 'he peers at God's portrait' is fulfilled" (Numbers 12:8).

3. *Rabbi Nachman's Stories (Sippurey Ma'asioth)*, trans. and annotated by Aryeh Kaplan (Jerusalem/New York: Breslov Research Institute, 1983), p. 129.

4. *Likutey Moharan*, vol. II, Lesson #212, p. 77, n. 3. According to this footnote, "the features of God's portrait are the Divine qualities described by the prophets in their attempts to depict the unknowable Holy One. The Zohar teaches that these descriptions stem from the level of *Malkhut*, for only through the *sefirah* representative of this world are we able to imagine and gain some degree of understanding of that whch is on High.

5. Nathan of Breslov, *Tzaddik (Chayey Moharan)*, trans. Avraham Greenbaum (Jerusalem/New York: Breslov Research Institute, 1987), p. 141.

6. Ibid., p. 44.

37. Rabbi Nachman's Journey to the Land of Israel

1. Nathan of Breslov, *Tzaddik (Chayey Moharan)*, trans. Avraham Greenbaum (Jerusalem/New York: Breslov Research Institute, 1987), p. 48, #30 (133), *Chayey* 5:5.

2. May 4, 1798.

3. Nathan of Breslov, *Tzaddik*, p. 52.

4. Zvi Mark, pp. 173–217.

38. The Big Joker

1. Nachman of Bratslav, *The Tales*, trans. Arnold Band (New York: Paulist Press, 1978), p. 118.

2. *Rabbi Nachman's Stories (Sippury Ma'asioth)*, trans. and annotated by Aryeh Kaplan (Jerusalem/New York: Breslov Research Institute, 1983), p. 133.

39. Uman Uman

1. "Uman! Uman! Rebbe Nachman!" Publication of Breslov Research Institute, http://www.breslov.com/bri/umanrh.html# chapter5.

2. http://www.forward.com/articles/4791/. Nathaniel Popper, "Unrest Brews at Rebbe's Resting Place," *Forward*, September 29, 2006.

3. http://www.moharan.com/pages_angl/page_rabbi_israel_angl .htm#18.

41. Self-Isolation

1. Nathan of Nemirov, *Rabbi Nachman's Wisdom*, trans. Aryeh Kaplan (Jerusalem: Breslov Research Institute, 1973), pp. 112–13.

2. Franz Kafka, *Letter to His Father*, trans. Ernst Kaiser and Eithne Wilkins (New York: Schocken Books, 1966), p. 17.

3. *Aveneha Brazel*, p. 7, cited in Nathan of Breslov, *Tzaddik (Chayey Moharan)*, trans. Avraham Greenbaum (Jerusalem/New York: Breslov Research Institute, 1987), p. 296.

4. Nachman of Breslov, *Likutey Moharan [The Collected Teachings of Morenu HaRav Nachman]*, trans. Moshe Mykoff, vol. XI (Jerusalem/ New York: Breslov Research Institute, 2000), LM I, Lesson #230, p. 155.

42. The Thin Thread of Metal, the Ball of Wax

1. Nathan of Breslov, *Tzaddik (Chayey Moharan)*, trans. Avraham Greenbaum (Jerusalem/New York: Breslov Research Institute, 1987), p. 275 (Sunday, 25 Nisan 1810).

CHRONOLOGY

70 CE   Fall of the Temple in Jerusalem.

c. 100 By the end of the first century CE, the canon of the Hebrew Bible is largely established.

c. 135 Rabbi Simeon Bar Yohai is said to spend twelve years in a cave hiding from Roman rulers of the land of Israel and immersed in the study of Torah. Talmudic stories attribute miraculous powers to him, and Hasidim believe him to be the author of the Zohar. His grave in Meron is a Jewish pilgrimage site and his *yahrzeit* at Lag b'Omer is a *yom hillulla*, or day of celebration.

c. 220 Rabbi Oshaiah Rabbah, a scholar of the first generation of rabbis of the Palestinian Talmud, founds his own academy in Caesarea after the death of Rabbi Judah Ha-Nasi.

1040   Solomon ben Isaac, later known as Rashi, is born in Troyes, France. He will grow up to become the greatest Jewish biblical exegete and will write indispensable glosses on the Talmud as well as the Bible.

c. 1280–1286   The Zohar, the primary text of kabbalah, or Jewish mysticism, is composed in Guadalajara, Spain, by Moses de Leon.

Chronology

c. 1569–1570   Rabbi Isaac Luria moves from Egypt to Tsfat. A tremendously influential kabbalist, he developed from the Zohar mystical theories of three phases of Creation: *tzimtzum*, *shevirat ha-kelim*, and *tikkun olam*.

1609   Rabbi Judah Loew, also known as the Maharal, dies in Prague. An important and original Talmudist, philosopher, and commentator, he is later associated with the legend of the golem.

1648–1649   Peasant uprising in Ukraine led by Bogdan Chmielnicki destroys hundreds of Jewish communities. Many thousands of Jews are killed.

1652   Chmielnicki's followers once again attack the Jews of Kamenetz.

1665   Followers of Sabbatai Zevi anoint him Messiah in Gaza; he continues to gather supporters throughout the Jewish world.

1666   Sabbatai Zevi converts to Islam; many of his followers become apostates.

1672–1699   Jews in Podolia province enjoy full rights while under Ottoman rule. In 1699 Podolia returns to Polish rule with its restrictions on Jews.

c. 1735   Israel ben Eliezer, known as the Baal Shem Tov, founds the Hasidic movement, which stresses ecstatic prayer and mysticism over study. His influence soon spreads among the Jews of Eastern Europe.

1750   King Augustus III expels the Jews from Kamenetz-Podolsk.

1754   Moses Mendelssohn, an early proponent of the *haskalah* or Jewish Enlightenment, begins to publish his writings.

June 1757   Bishop Dembowski of Kamenetz forces rabbis to debate followers of the false Messiah Jacob Frank, who continued the practices of the Sabbatean heresies of the previous century.

October–November 1757   Bishop Dembowski declares the Frankists winners of the debate, and burns copies of the Talmud.

September 1759   Jacob Frank converts to Catholicism. Many of his believers follow him into apostasy, while secretly still affirming that he is the Messiah.

May 1760   The Baal Shem Tov dies.

1764   Rabbi Nachman of Horodenka, a disciple of the Baal Shem Tov, settles in Tiberias in the land of Israel.

1768   Thousands of Jews are massacred in Uman by rebel Cossacks.

1772 Death of Dov Ber, the Maggid of Mezritch, one of the most important
disciples of the Baal Shem Tov.

1772 Rabbi Nachman is born in
Medzhibozh, Ukraine. His mother,
Feiga, is a granddaughter of the Baal
Shem Tov, and his father, Simcha,
is a son of Rabbi Nachman of
Horodenka.

1777 Rabbi Elijah ben Solomon Zalman, a
great scholar and leader of Lithuanian
Jewry who was known as the Vilna
Gaon, leads a movement to
excommunicate the Hasidim.

1785 Rabbi Nachman marries his first wife,
Sashia.

Spring 1798 Rabbi Nachman travels to Kamenetz
from Bratslav.

Late spring 1798 Rabbi Nachman sets off for the land of
Israel, accompanied by his disciple
Rabbi Simeon.

September 10, 1798 Rabbi Nachman arrives in Haifa on the
eve of Rosh Hashanah.

Summer 1799 Rabbi Nachman returns to Ukraine
from the land of Israel. He settles in
Zlotopolye.

1802 Rabbi Nachman moves to Bratslav,
having been driven out of Zlotopolye

by the nearby rebbe, Rabbi Aryeh Lieb of Shpola.

September 1804   Rabbi Nachman begins writing the manuscript that will become the burnt book.

May 1805   Rabbi Nachman's son, Shlomo Ephraim, born.

May 1806   Yudel and Shmuel Issac, two Hasidim of Rabbi Nachman, ride from to town reading the manuscript of the burnt book.

June 1806   Sholomo Ephraim dies.

July 1806   Rabbi Nachman tells his first tale, "The Loss of the Princess."

September 1806   On Rosh Hashanah, Rabbi Nachman gives teaching on the power of tales to awaken those who are asleep. This lesson is said to be the key to the tale "The Loss of the Princess."

Late winter 1807   Rabbi Nachman becomes a voluntary wanderer, performing a Hasidic practice known as "undertaking exile."

Spring 1807   Rabbi Nachman's first wife, Sashia, dies. He is at her side.

1808   Rabbi Nachman is ill with tuberculosis in Lemberg. He asks Rabbi Simeon to burn the manuscript that is known as the burnt book.

Chronology

Summer 1808 *Likutey Moharan,* a collection of Rabbi Nachman's Torah teachings, is printed in Ostrog.

Late winter 1809 Rabbi Nachman tells the tales "The Rabbi's Son" and "The Sophisticate and the Simpleton."

March 30, 1810 Rabbi Nachman begins the ten-day telling of his most famous tale, "The Seven Beggars."

October 16, 1810 Rabbi Nachman dies in Uman on the second day of Sukkot.

1811 Rabbi Nachman's disciple Rabbi Nathan organizes the first pilgrimage of Rabbi Nachman's followers to his grave.

1815 Rabbi Nathan publishes Rabbi Nachman's tales in a Hebrew-Yiddish edition. *In Praise of the Baal Shem Tov* also appears this year.

1834 The Kloyz synagogue in Uman, built by Rabbi Nathan to house pilgrims to Rabbi Nachman's grave, is completed.

1841 In a relaxation of anti-Jewish restrictions, Bohemia allows Jews to own land.

1844 Rabbi Nathan dies.

1849 After the 1848 Revolution, which was accompanied by some anti-Jewish rioting, liberal legislation in Austro-Hungary grants Jews new freedoms.

1867   Full civil rights are granted to Jews in Austro-Hungary.

July 3, 1883   Franz Kafka is born to Hermann Kafka, a Prague businessman, and his wife, Julie Lowy Kafka.

1889   Ahad Ha'am, a leading Zionist thinker, begins publishing essays that shape modern Jewish identity and explore the spiritual and cultural aspects of return to the land of Israel.

1894   Captain Albert Dreyfus is convicted of treason in France. He is sentenced to life imprisonment amid a wave of anti-Semitic sentiment in France.

1897   Theodor Herzl holds the first Zionist Congress in Basel, Switzerland.

1897   Anti-Jewish riots in Prague lead to the founding of the Bar Kochba Society, a Zionist organization.

1906   Martin Buber publishes *The Tales of Rabbi Nachman* in German.

1909–1911   Buber gives several lectures at the Bar Kochba Society, in which he calls for a Jewish renewal in the form of spiritual intensity without the requirements of ritual.

Chronology

1910   Kafka begins his diaries in spring.

December 1910   Kafka's sister, Elli, marries and leaves home.

July 1911   Menachem Mendel Beilis is accused of the ritual murder of a twelve-year-old boy in Kiev, Ukraine; this blood libel inflamed public opinion throughout Europe. Beilis was acquitted at trial in 1913.

October 1911   Kafka becomes passionately involved with Yiddish theater, meets actor Yitzhak Lowy.

February 1912   Kafka arranges a one-man show for Lowy in Jewish Town Hall and gives speech in defense of Yiddish.

September 22, 1912   Kafka writes "The Judgment" in an all-night session, the beginning of a sustained burst of writing that will last through 1914 and produce "The Metamorphosis," "In the Penal Colony," "The Stoker," "Before the Law," and *The Trial*.

October 1912   Working at his father's asbestos factory makes Kafka suicidal. He writes to his friend Max Brod for help.

November 1912   Kafka writes "The Metamorphosis."

April 1914   Kafka becomes engaged to Felice Bauer, having first proposed to her in June 1913.

June 28, 1914   The assassination of Archduke Franz Ferdinand of Austria triggers the outbreak of World War I.

July 1914   After a confrontation with family members in a Berlin hotel, the engagement with Felice is broken off. Kafka starts writing *The Trial*.

August 2, 1914   Kafka writes in his diary, "Germany has declared war on Russia—Swimming in the afternoon."

November 1914   Kafka writes "In the Penal Colony."

December 1914   Kafka writes "Before the Law."

September 12, 1915   Kafka visits the wonder rebbe of Grodek in the Prague suburb of Ziskov with Jiri Langer and Max Brod.

July 1916   Kafka spends evening at Marienbad with the Belzer Rebbe, accompanied by Jiri Langer.

1916   Hebrew poet Haim Nahman Bialik publishes his essay "*Halakhah* and *Aggadah*" in which he argues that law and lore must exist side by side in Judaism.

Chronology

1916–1918   Kafka writes stories that are collected in *A Country Doctor*.

May 1917   Kafka begins to study Hebrew using Moses Rath's textbook.

July 1917   Kafka is engaged to Felice for a second time.

August 1917   Kafka suffers his first hemorrhage, followed by a diagnosis of tuberculosis on September 4, 1917.

Fall 1917   Kafka studies Hebrew while convalescing in the Bohemian rural village of Zürau. He also composes aphorisms some scholars call the "Zürau Aphorisms."

December 1917   Kafka breaks off his second engagement with Felice.

November 1918   Armistice ends World War I. The Czech republic is declared.

Summer 1919   Kafka becomes engaged to Julie Wohryzek over objections of his parents, then breaks off the engagement.

November 1919   Stung by this failed engagement, Kafka writes *Letter to His Father* in Schelesen.

January 1920   Kafka is introduced to Gustav Janouch.

April 1920   Kafka begins an intense romantic correspondence with Milena Jesenská, his Czech translator, who was married to Ernst Polak.

November 1920 Anti-Semitic riots occur in Prague, and
Kafka's letter to Milena references
"cockroaches."

February 1922 Kafka writes "A Hunger Artist" and
begins *The Castle*.

July 9, 1922 Rabbi Israel Dov Odesser, a Bratslaver
Hasid in Tiberias, finds a note signed
"Na Nach Nachma Nachman
Me'Uman"; the phrase becomes a
mystical chant for certain of
Nachman's modern-day
followers.

July 20, 1922 The first nine chapters of *The Castle* are
completed.

October 1922 Kafka asks Brod to destroy his work
after his death.

Winter–spring 1923 Kafka studies Hebrew with Puah
Bentovim, a physics student who had
come to Vienna from Jerusalem.

Summer 1923 Kafka meets Dora Diamant at Müritz
on the Baltic Sea.

August 1923 Gershom Scholem leaves Berlin to
make aliyah to Palestine.

September 1923 Kafka and Dora Diamant take an
aparment together in Berlin.

March 1924 Kafka writes "Josephine the Mouse
Singer," his last story.

Chronology

May 1924   After consulting the Gerer Rebbe, Dora's father refuses Kafka's request to marry his daughter.

June 3, 1924   Tended by Robert Klopstock, Franz Kafka dies in a sanitarium in Kierling.

1925   Max Brod, Kafka's friend and literary executor, publishes Kafka's unfinished novels *The Trial* and *The Castle*.

1927   Max Brod publishes Kafka's *Amerika*.

1937   Kafka's friend Jiri Langer publishes *Nine Gates to the Chassidic Mysteries*, a remembrance of his life with the Belzer Rebbe.

March 15, 1939   Nazis occupy Czechoslovakia; Max Brod flees to Palestine with Kafka's remaining unpublished manuscripts.

August 1941   A total of 23,600 Ukranian and Hungarian Jews are massacred in Kamenetz-Podolsk.

July 1974   Gershom Scholem receives German literary prize from Bavarian Academy of Arts.

September 1988   In the first thaw since the Russian Revolution, a few hundred Hasidim are allowed to make the pilgrimmage to Uman for Rosh Hashanah. By 2008 tens of thousands of Jews are making pilgrimage there.

December 2009–April 2010   Israel demands return of Kafka's original manuscript of *The Trial* from Germany. The court fight over other Kafka papers and manuscripts left by Brod to the Hoffe family continues in Israel.

September 24, 2010   The two hundredth anniversary of the death of Rabbi Nachman, according to the Hebrew calendar, is observed on his *yahrzeit* on the second day of Sukkot.

ACKNOWLEDGMENTS

Every book needs a strong circle of friends. Jonathan Rosen, my editor, said yes and keeps saying yes. To my editors at Schocken, Dan Frank and Altie Karper, thanks, and to my agent, Katinka Matson, thanks as well. Rabbi Ozer Bergman, my friend and help, first invited me to Uman years ago and patiently taught me in phone and in person. Professor Yohanan Petrovsky-Shtern accompanied me to Kamenetz and Uman and was a lifesaver. Maria Baczynskyj helped ease me into Ukraine. Thank you so much Wawa. I thank the faculty at the Kamianets-Podilsky National University for their hospitality and friendship. Years ago my friend Richard Katrovas first brought me to the Prague Summer Program to teach Kafka and the golem. Arthur Samuelson, Howard Schwartz, Moira Crone, Yohanan Petrovsky-Shtern, and Rabbi Ozer Bergman all read and commented on the manuscript in various stages. Professor Brian Horowitz at Tulane Jewish Studies gave me the opportunity to teach this material in spring 2009 with the help of a Posen Foundation Lectureship. My own university, LSU, supported me with a Regent's Research grant, a sabbatical grant, and a travel grant. I first came to some of this material while teaching a course at LSU on "Kabbalah and Literature." I want to thank the students of Tulane and LSU for their questions and their answers. I owe a huge debt

Acknowledgments

to the Breslov Research Institute for publishing their editions of the Tales, the "Teachings of Rabbi Nachman," and important biographical works by Rabbi Nathan. Also I thank BRI and Rabbi Chaim Kramer for putting me up and putting up with me at the Uman Ritz Carton. My debt to Arthur Green, author of the most important Nachman biography in English, *Tormented Master*, can be found in every page. His scholarship and sensitivity set a very high mark. Marc Ouakhnine's the burnt book gave me an idea and a title. Like Rabbi Green, Rabbi Jack Riemer, Howard Schwartz, and others, Rabbi Ouakhnine noted similarities between Kafka and Rabbi Nachman. A very recent work by Professor Zvi Mark, *Mysticism and Madness*, was extremely helpful. Also important were works about the parable by Aryeh Wineman and David Stern.

All of the Kafka scholars and biographers mentioned in this book were important, but I particularly acknowledge my debt to Reiner Stach, Iris Bruce, Ronald Hayman, Frederick Karl, and John Zilcoski. As in almost everything I write, there's something of Rabbi Zalman Schachter here. For the work on Kafka's dreams I owe a debt to Marc Bregman of North of Eden. For my wife, Moira, my beloved, I owe everything, her patience and her faith.

BIBLIOGRAPHY

Rabbi Nachman's stories fascinate Jewish thinkers of all persuasions. The tales have been retold and popularized by Meyer Levin, Elie Wiesel, Rabbi Adin Steinsaltz, Rabbi Zalman Schachter, and Howard Schwartz. In 1979, Rabbi and Professor Arthur Green, a chavurah leader in the '60s, wrote a landmark biography and close study of Rabbi Nachman and his tales. His *Tormented Master* is a contemporary classic. A compendium of essays, *God's Voices from the Void* (2002), anthologizes eighty years of scholarship, and serious readers of Rabbi Nachman will feel indebted to book-length studies by Ora Wiskind-Elper and Zvi Mark. I owe a special debt to Marc Ouakhnine's study, the burnt book, which puts Rabbi Nachman's work in a Talmudic context.

The tales have also reached a more popular Jewish audience. The Breslov Research Institute has published an English translation of the thirteen tales with a detailed commentary by Rabbi Aryeh Kaplan. They have also published popular spiritual guides based on individual tales. Arnold Band's translation of the tales is excellent and has a scholarly orientation.

Rabbi Nachman of Bratslav: Primary Source Works

Kramer, Chaim. *Through Fire and Water: The Life of Reb Noson of Breslov*. Jerusalem/New York: Breslov Research Institute, 1992. The original source is Reb Noson's autobiography, *Yemei Moharanat*.

Bibliography

Nathan of Breslov. *Tzaddik (Chayey Moharan)*. Translated by Avraham Greenbaum. Jerusalem/New York: Breslov Research Institute, 1987.

Nathan of Nemirov. *Rabbi Nachman's Wisdom (Shevachay haRan, Sichos haRan)*. Translated by Rabbi Aryeh Kaplan. Jerusalem: Breslov Research Institute, 1973.

Rabbi Nachman of Bratslav: Secondary Biographical Works

Green, Arthur. *Tormented Master*. Woodstock, Vt.: Jewish Lights, 1992.

Kaplan, Aryeh. *Until the Mashiach: Rabbi Nachman's Biography: An Annotated Chronology*. Jerusalem/Brooklyn: Breslov Research Institute, 1985.

Editions of *The Tales of Rabbi Nachman*

Buber, Martin. *The Tales of Rabbi Nachman*. Translated by Maurice Friedmann. New York: Horizon Press, 1956.

Nahman of Bratslav. *The Tales*. Translated by Arnold Band. New York: Paulist Press, 1978.

Rabbi Nachman's Stories (Sippurey Ma'asioth). Translated and annotated by Aryeh Kaplan. Jerusalem/New York: Breslov Research Institute, 1983.

Teachings of Rabbi Nachman

Nachman of Breslov. *Likutey Moharan*, Volumes I– Edited and translated by Moshe Mykoff. Jerusalem/New York: Breslov Research Institute, 1993–2008.

Nathan of Breslov. *Rabbi Nachman: Advice (Likutey Etzot)*. Translated by Avraham Greenbaum. Jerusalem/New York: Breslov Research Institute, 1983.

Rabbi Nachman's Tikkun: The Comprehensive Remedy (Tikkun HaKlali) with Shemot HaTzaddikim (Names of the Tzaddikim). Compiled and translated by Avraham Greenbaum. Jerusalem/New York: Breslov Research Institute, 1984.

Popular Works About the Teachings and Tales of Rabbi Nachman

Bergman, Ozer. *Where Earth and Heaven Kiss: A Guide to Rebbe Nachman's Path of Meditation*. Jerusalem/New York: Breslov Research Institute, 2006.

Doron, Erez Moshe. *The Exchanged Children*. Jerusalem/New York: Breslov Research Institute, 2007.

Elbaum, Dov. *Masa Bahalal Hapanui* (Journey into the Void). Jerusalem: Am Oved, 2009.

Greenbaum, Avraham. *Garden of the Souls: Rebbe Nachman on Suffering*. Jerusalem/New York: Breslov Research Institute, 1990.

———. *Under the Table and How to Get Up: Jewish Pathways of Spiritual Growth*. Jerusalem/New York: Tsohar Publishing, 1991.

Schachter-Shalomi, Zalman. *Fragments of a Future Scroll*. Germantown, Pa.: Leaves of Grass Press, 1975.

Scholarly Works About Rabbi Nachman

Magid, Shaul, ed. *God's Voice from the Void: Old and New Studies of Bratslav Hasidism*. Albany: State University of New York Press, 2002.

Mark, Zvi. *Mysticism and Madness: The Religious Thought of Rabbi Nachman of Bratslav*. London: Continuum, 2009.

Ouakhnine, Marc-Alain. the burnt book: *Reading the Talmud*. Translated by Llewellyn Brown. Princeton, N.J.: Princeton University Press, 1995.

Wiskind-Elper, Ora. *Tradition and Fantasy in the Tales of Reb Nahman of Bratslav*. Albany: State University of New York Press, 1998.

Bibliography

Hasidic and Historical Contexts for Rabbi Nachman

Dynner, Glenn. *Men of Silk: The Hasidic Conquest of Polish Jewish Society*. New York: Oxford University Press, 2006.

Hundert, Gershon David. *Essential Papers on Hasidism: Origins to Present*. New York: New York University Press, 1991.

The Memoirs of Ber of Bolechow (1723–1805). Translated by M. Vishnitzer. London: Oxford University Press, 1922. Reprint edition Ayer Publishers, 2000.

Rosman, M. J. (Moshe Rosman). *The Lords' Jews: Magnate-Jewish Relations in the Polish-Lithuanian Commonwealth During the 19th Century*. Cambridge, Mass.: Harvard Ukrainian Research Institute and the Center for Jewish Studies, Harvard University, 1990.

———. *Founder of Hasidism: A Quest for the Historical Ba'al Shem Tov*. Berkeley: University of California Press, 1996.

Hasidic Storytelling

Ben-Amos, Dan, and Jerome Mintz, trans. and eds. *In Praise of the Baal Shem Tov*. Northvale, N.J.: Jason Aronson, 1993.

Buber, Martin. *Tales of the Hasidim: Early Masters*. Translated by Olga Marx. New York: Schocken Books, 1961.

———. *Ten Rungs*. Translated by Olga Marx. New York: Schocken Books, 1970.

Schachter-Shalomi, Zalman, and Netanel Miles-Yepez. *A Heart Afire: Stories and Teachings of the Early Hasidic Masters*. Philadelphia: Jewish Publication Society, 2009.

Franz Kafka: Novels

Kafka, Franz. *Amerika*. Translated by Willa and Edwin Muir. New York: Doubleday, 1946.

————. *The Castle*. Translated by Mark Harman. New York: Schocken Books, 1998.

———— *The Trial*. Translated by Breon Mitchell. New York: Schocken Books, 1998.

————. *The Trial*. Translated by Willa and Edwin Muir. New York Modern Library, 1964.

————. *The Trial: The Definitive Edition*. Translated by Willa and Edwin Muir. New York: Schocken Books, 1992.

Franz Kafka: Stories, Parables, Aphorisms

Kafka, Franz. *The Complete Stories*. Translated by Willa and Edwin Muir. New York: Schocken Books, 1971.

————. "An Imperial Message." Translated by Ian Johnson. http://www.kafka.org/index.php?id=162,165,0,0,1,0.

————. *Meditation*. Translated by Siegfried Mortkowitz. Prague: Vitalis, 1998.

————. *Parables and Paradoxes*. New York: Schocken Books, 1966.

————. *Stories: 1904–1924*. Translated by J. A. Underwood. London: Abacus, 2006, p.252.

————. *The Zürau Aphorisms*. Translated by Michael Hoffman. New York: Schocken Books, 2006.

Franz Kafka: Letters, Diaries, Conversations, Dreams

Hall, Calvin, and Richard Lind. *Dreams, Life, and Literature: A Study of Franz Kafka*. Chapel Hill: University of North Carolina Press, 1970.

Janouch, Gustav. *Conversations with Kafka*. Translated by Goronwy Rees. London: Quartet Books, 1985.

Kafka, Franz. *Diaries*. Translated by J. Kresh and M. Greenberg. New York: Schocken Books, 1976.

————. *Letter to His Father*. Translated by Ernst Kaiser and Eithne Wilkins. New York: Schocken Books, 1966.

Bibliography

————. *Letters to Felice.* Translated by James Stern and Elizabeth Duckworth. New York: Schocken Books, 1973.

————. *Letters to Friends, Family, and Editors.* Translated by Richard and Clara Winston. New York: Schocken Books, 1977.

————. *Letters to Milena.* Translated by Philip Boehm. New York: Schocken Books, 1990.

————. *Letters to Ottla and The Family.* Translated by Richard and Clara Winston. New York: Schocken Books, 1982.

Franz Kafka: Bibliography

Caputo-Mayr, Maria Luise, and Julius Michael Herz. *Franz Kafka: Internationale Bibliographie der Primär- und Sekundärliteratur, eine Einführung* [International bibliography of primary and secondary literature, an introduction]. Munich: K. G. Saur, 2000.

Franz Kafka: Reference Works

Gray, Richard, Ruth Gross, Rolf Goebel, and Clayton Koelb, eds. *A Franz Kafka Encyclopedia.* Westport, Conn.: Greenwood Press, 2005.

Rolleston, James, ed. *A Companion to the Works of Franz Kafka.* Rochester, N.Y.: Camden House, 2002.

Franz Kafka: Biographical Works

Brod, Max. *Franz Kafka: A Biography.* New York: Schocken Books, 1947.

Hayman, Ronald. *Kafka: A Biography.* New York: Oxford University Press, 1981.

Hodin, J. P. "Memories of Franz Kafka." *Horizon* 17 (1948): 26–43.

Karl, Frederick. *Franz Kafka: Representative Man.* New York: Ticknor and Fields, 1991.

Mailloux, Peter. *A Hesitation Before Birth: The Life of Franz Kafka.* Newark: University of Delaware Press, 1989.

Pawel, Ernst. *The Nightmare of Reason: A Life of Franz Kafka*. New York: Farrar, Straus, Giroux, 1984.

Robert, Marthe. *As Lonely as Franz Kafka*. Translated by Ralph Mannheim. New York: Schocken Books, 1986.

Stach, Reiner. *Kafka: The Decisive Years*. Translated by Shelley Frisch. New York: Harcourt, 2005.

Franz Kafka and Gershom Scholem

Alter, Robert. *Necessary Angels: Tradition and Modernity in Kafka, Benjamin, and Scholem*. Cambridge, Mass.: Harvard University Press, 1991.

Bloom, Harold. *The Strong Light of the Canonical: Kafka, Freud and Scholem as Revisionists of Jewish Culture and Thought*. City College Papers #20, 1987.

Scholem, Gershom. "Devekut, or Communion with God." In *The Messianic Idea in Judaism*, trans. Michael Meyer, pp. 203–27. New York: Schocken Books, 1971.

———. *From Berlin to Jerusalem*. Translated by Harry Zohn. New York: Schocken Books, 1988.

———. "My Way to Kabbalah." In *On the Possibility of Jewish Mysticism in Our Time*, trans. Jonathan Chipman, pp. 20–24. Philadelphia: Jewish Publication Society, 1997.

———. "Revelation and Tradition as Religious Categories." In *The Messianic Idea in Judaism*, trans. Michael Meyer, pp. 282–304. New York: Schocken Books, 1971.

———, ed. *The Correspondence of Walter Benjamin and Gershom Scholem: 1932–1940*. Translated by Gary Smith and Andrei Lefevre. New York: Schocken Books, 1989.

Franz Kafka and Jewish Contexts

Benjamin, Walter. "Franz Kafka." In *Illuminations*, trans. Harry Zohn. New York: Schocken Books, 2007.

Bruce, Iris. *Kafka and Cultural Zionism*. Madison: University of Wisconsin Press, 2007.

Bibliography

Diamant, Kathi. *Kafka's Last Love*. New York: Basic Books, 2003.

Gilman, Sander. *Franz Kafka, The Jewish Patient*. New York: Routledge, 1995.

Grözinger, Karl Erich. *Kafka and Kabbalah*. Translated by Susan Hecker Ray. New York: Continuum, 1994.

Jofen, Jean. *The Jewish Mystic in Kafka*. New York: Peter Lang, 1987.

Langer, Jiri. *Nine Gates to the Chassidic Mysteries*. Translated by Stephen Jolly. New York: Behrman House, 1976.

Politzer, Heinz. *Franz Kafka: Parable and Paradox*. Ithaca, N.Y.: Cornell University Press, 1962.

Robertson, Ritchie. *Kafka: Judaism, Politics and Literature*. Oxford, UK: Clarendon Press, 1985.

Zilcoski, John. *Kafka's Travels: Exoticism, Colonialism, and the Traffic of Writing*. New York: Palgrave MacMillan, 2003.

Martin Buber

Buber, Martin. *On Judaism*. Translated by Eva Jospe. New York: Schocken Books, 1995.

"Martin Buber's Conception of Judaism" in Gershom Scholem, *On Jews and Judaism in Crisis: Selected Essays*, ed. Werner J. Dennhauser, pp. 126–72. New York: Schocken Books, 1976.

Parable, Midrash, Storytelling

Bialik, Haim Nahman. *Revealment and Concealment: Five Essays*. Translated by Leon Simon. Jerusalem: Ibis Editions, 2000.

Greenstein, Ed. "Wisdom Undermined." unpublished lecture delivered at Bar Ilan University Conference on Bible and Literature, December 9, 2009.

Schwartz, Howard. *Reimagining the Bible*. New York: Oxford University Press, 1998.

Stern, David. *Parables in Midrash*. Cambridge, Mass.: Harvard University Press, 1991.

Wineman, Aryeh. *The Hasidic Parable*. Philadelphia: Jewish Publication
 Society, 2001.

Prague

Kisch, Egon. *Sensation Fair*. New York: Modern Age Books, 1941.
Prague: Eyewitness Travel Guide. London: Dorling Kindersley, 2005.
Salfellner, Harald. *Franz Kafka and Prague* Prague: Vitalis, 1998.
Wagenbach, Klaus. *Franz Kafka: Pictures of a Life*. New York: Pantheon
 Books, 1984.

Ukraine

Johnstone, Sarah, and Greg Bloom. *Ukraine*. Melbourne: Lonely Planet,
 2008.
"Kamyanets in Podillya: Touristic Guide." Khmelnitsky: Oium, 2007.

ABOUT THE AUTHOR

Rodger Kamenetz is the author of *The Jew in the Lotus*, *The History of Last Night's Dream*, and seven other books of poetry and prose. A winner of the National Jewish Book Award, he is LSU Distinguished Professor Emeritus at Louisiana State University, where he was founding director of its Jewish Studies Program. He lives in New Orleans with his wife, the novelist Moira Crone, and works as a dream therapist. His Web site is kamenetz.com.